DIRTY BAGGS

Another Mike Romano Police Novel

By Joe DeCicco

Featured on American Heroes Talk Radio

Joe's other novels:

Worms in the Apple
Angel with a Gun

This book is a work of fiction. All names, characters, organizations and incidents are either a product of the author's imagination, or, if real, are used fictionally without any intent to describe their actual account.

Contact the author by E-mail at romanonovels@yahoo.com

Printed in the United State of America
Charleston, North Carolina
for

JNJ Associates Inc.
PO Box 237, Hampstead, N.C. 28443

First Published: September 7, 2011

ISBN 10: 0-9897227-2-4
ISBN 13: 978-0-9897227-2-8

Dedication

A Loving thank you is given to my wife Judy, who once again has graciously acted as my editor. She will always be my very special Alabaster Lady.....

"The Final Inspection"

The policeman stood and faced his God,
which must always come to pass.
He hoped his shoes were shining
just as brightly as his brass..

"Step forward now, policeman.
How shall I deal with you?
Have you always turned the other cheek?
To my church have you been true?"

The policeman squared his shoulders and said,
"No Lord I guess I ain't.
Because those who carry badges
can't always be a saint.

I've had to work most Sundays,
and at times my talk was rough...
And sometimes I've been violent
because the streets are awful tough.

But I never took a penny
that wasn't mine to keep...
Though I worked a lot of overtime
when the bills got just too steep.

And I never passed a cry for help,
though at times I shook with fear.
And sometimes, God forgive me,
I've wept unmanly tears.

I know I don't deserve a place
among the people here.
They never wanted me around
except to calm their fear.

If you've a place for me here,
Lord, it needn't be so grand.
I never expected or had too much,
but if you don't...I'll understand."

There was silence all around the throne
where the saints had often trod,
as the policeman waited quietly
for the judgment of his God.

"Step forward now, policeman.
You've borne your burdens well.
Come walk a beat on heaven's streets.
You've done your time in hell."

~ Author Unknown ~

Prologue

This is the third novel about the career of Michael Romano, a New York City Police Officer. When Officer Romano was still a child and a local parish priest told him that the stained glass picture of an angel killing a serpent was Saint Michael killing Satan, to keep God's world safe, Mike identified with the Archangel. Later, in his teens, young Romano learned that Saint Michael was the patron saint of police officers, he vowed to follow the example of his patron saint and protect society, but Saint Michael carried a sword, Michael Romano wears a gun.

Officer Romano always acted with understanding and a sense of justice, both in his professional and private life. Unable to bring his corrupt commanding officer to justice, Mike requested a transfer to his resident borough of Staten Island as a reward offered to him for making a bribery arrest while in plainclothes on "The Apple".

While working in his new command, Michael sometimes struggles to maintain his dignity, anger and moral code when an unforeseen incident changes the quality of his daily life.

As the story unfolds, the reader will see that sometimes the guardians of our daily lives are only just people.

CHAPTER ONE

Police Officer Michael Romano had just left his small furnished basement apartment in Westerleigh, an old area of Staten Island, ten minutes ago and it just started to rain. He was driving his '78 Chevy Caprice southwest on the West Shore Expressway, on his way to begin another set of tours at the 123 Precinct in Tottenville. It was a rather mild day for a Wednesday, March 28th, and Mike had been on Staten Island about eleven months after being transferred from Midtown South in Manhattan. The transfer was a reward for his last bribery arrest.

Driving at sixty miles an hour, the hum of the tires was almost hypnotic. Mike had been trying to push thoughts of his soon to be ex-wife out of his mind and to concentrate on the roadway. Mike Romano had never thought that he would be included in the national statistics of the police officer divorce rate of 60%-70%. In his almost trance like state, he absent mindedly reached to raise his window and didn't notice two men standing next to a black Ford Bronco that was stopped on the right shoulder of the roadway. As he drove past them, it happened, **POW, POW,** and **POW.** The cop in Michael Romano snapped back into the real world. Romano, with ten years on the job, heard the sound many times during his time in Harlem and in Midtown South. Those three gunshots brought a kaleidoscope of vivid memories beginning with a bullet that went thru his windshield as he drove home, the rooftop gun battle during the 1977 New York City Blackout and ended with another gun battle in the basements of Chinatown. Somewhere, close, probably behind him, a large caliber handgun had just been discharged three times in rapid succession.

Instantly, Mike's training took control of his body's auto responses. He defensively lowered his head, and cautiously peered into his right side view mirror to glance back as he swung toward the highway's shoulder and began slowing his vehicle. Again glancing in his side mirror, Mike saw the Bronco racing through the thick brush adjacent to the roadway. The truck had disappeared into a wooded area before he could bring his own vehicle to a final stop.

Once stopped, Romano put his hazard flashers on, and slowly backed up about twenty five yards before stopping again and turning off his engine. Leaving his flashers on, Mike drew his off duty revolver, swung his door open and slipped out of the driver's seat crouching low against his car. Silently, as the beat of angel wings thumped in his ears, he prayed, *Saint Michael, you have always been here for me, be here once again.* Before advancing any further, Mike froze, poised and ready to jump back into his vehicle while he scanned the area for any remaining shooters. His revolver followed his eyes as if they were physically attached to his gun hand, scanning right then left. Satisfied that he was safe, Mike stood up and cautiously moved forward to where he believed the truck had been. He had taken only a few paces when he saw a human form lying on the edge of the tall grass just off the pavement about twenty feet in front of him. Mike rushed forward, hoping the victim was still alive. The prone figure was a fully clothed white male, lying on his back with blood seeping from wounds in his neck and chest. He appeared to be between 30 and 40 years old with a full head of dark hair. His mouth was open, his eyes big as saucers, his face frozen in a look of apparent surprise and disbelief.

Mike kneeled down to check the victim for signs of life. Placing three fingers at the man's carotid artery and feeling no pulse, Mike knew the man was gone. The poor guy could not be helped now.

Remembering his training to always preserve a crime scene and await detectives, Mike sprinted back to his auto, cranked it up and turned it around, then drove back to the victim, stopping a few feet past the lifeless body. Mike was careful to remain on the roadway's paved shoulder as not to disturb any evidence or tire tracks that may have been created by the shooter's vehicle. To safeguard against on coming, gawking motorists, Mike shielded the victim's body with his car, parking precariously close to the traffic lane. Remaining in his vehicle, he turned on his bright headlights to alert oncoming traffic and began a long wait for a passing patrol car.

It was the 1980's and New York City's remote borough was still growing. Traffic was relatively light on week days except during rush hour. Mike looked at his watch. It was 2:30 p.m., 1430 hours in Department time. Reaching into the briefcase that he recently began carrying with the growing cache of material needed for his divorce attorney, Mike withdrew a sheet of paper and wrote, "Wednesday, March 28th, 1984. Time of shots, 1429 hours. Black Ford Bronco, possibly new or not too old. Very clean, looks to be in good shape."

Twenty minutes passed before a patrol car came into view. Anxiously, Mike leaned on his horn and feverishly flashed his headlights to attract the approaching cop's immediate attention. It was a Highway Patrol vehicle. As the car stopped, its emergency lights flashed to life. Mike exited his own car, pulled up his collar against the rain and held his police shield high above his head for identification and self-preservation, keeping his free hand in plain sight. He thought, *it's not smart to leave any chance that the highway officer would think I'm responsible for that poor guy on the ground.*

The uniformed driver quickly exited his vehicle, adjusted his equipment belt and rapidly advanced toward Mike who was, by that time, standing next to the downed man.

"Bill Awad, Staten Island Highway. What do we have here officer? An accident?" The highway cop looked down at the body, "Oh, Oh!" He then looked back at Mike. "Are you responsible for this? What's your name Officer?"

"No, I'm not responsible. Michael Romano here and I was on my way to the Two Three for a four by." Pointing at the dead man, Mike continued, "This is not an accident. I just witnessed a shooting. I think the poor guy is DOA. I may have seen the shooter drive off in a Black Ford Bronco at about 1430 hours. I just missed it. Hurry and call it in. Maybe we can get him."

Awad leaned into his auto and keyed his radio's microphone, "Staten Island Highway 2 here Central. I'm here on the south bound side of 440 about half mile south of Sharrot's Road, with an off duty member of the service at the scene of a shooting. We believe it's a homicide. We need squad assistance. Please notify the Detectives to respond. K" (K signifies the end of transmission).

The response was within seconds, "Detectives notified. Is the off duty hurt? K."

"Negative Central. The off duty stopped to help the victim. We're standing by, K."

Officer Awad didn't state that Romano was a witness, nor did he put the Bronco over the air. Awad, like any cop, was morally bound to protect any witness, especially, this one, a fellow police officer. Bill knew that if the shooter was a professional, he might have a police scanner.

Once it was established that assistance would soon arrive, Awad positioned his patrol vehicle to completely block the left lane and raised the roof light bars.

Mike could not wait to discuss what he had seen. "Awad, you should have seen the Bronco take off. It went like a bat out of hell into the brush and probably into Clay Pit Pond State Park. Hell, the guy could go in any direction from there and get away."

Awad responded with, "Did you get a plate number. Can we put it out over the air?"

"No, I didn't. It was gone before I really got my bearings and realized that someone had been shot. There is something you can do for me though. Please have the dispatcher notify the One Two Three, that I will probably be late for my tour of duty today. Thanks."

The dispatcher was notified and the 123rd precinct desk officer quickly acknowledged the notification. Romano was ordered to remain where he was and would be temporally assigned to assist the responding units, as necessary, for the entire four to twelve tour. He was to sign off duty by telephone if he was not returning to the Two Three by end of tour.

Romano and Awad each gave the area around the body a quick inspection, crossing each other's path to double check and found no shell casings. Both officers then went over to sit in the highway auto and wait for the detectives to arrive or for any further instructions. To pass the time, they exchanged small talk about the job, their careers and complained about the brass and working conditions as cops usually do when they sit and wait.

An Emergency Medical Services unit attached to Richmond Memorial Hospital, located only about five miles away, was the first responding vehicle to arrive at the scene. As the team of two medical technicians exited their ambulance, Mike immediately guided them to the victim. According to Police Department rules and procedures, Mike, being the first officer on the scene was in charge until Detectives and their supervisor arrived. He asked the medics to be extremely careful not to disturb any forensic evidence that may be in the area. Bill Awad followed closely behind.

One of the medical techs, Morales, confirmed that the victim was indeed dead. "There are three wounds, one near the collar bone, another piercing the chest cavity on the left side and another almost dead center on his chest." Gently placing a sheet over the victim, Morales continued, "That dead center one must have instantly stopped his heart. I'm sorry, I can't tell you which shot hit him first. The M.E. will probably tell you that after an autopsy."

Just as the techs stood upright, a marked patrol car containing a Patrol Sergeant and his driver and two plain looking Chevys roared to a stop alongside Mike's auto. The operator of the marked patrol car placed his vehicle behind the unmarked cars in a position directly in line with Awad's car. Crime scene tape was strung between the flashing patrol car and the Sergeant's vehicle to give the responding detectives an unimpeded work area.

"Sergeant Flynn, 120 Squad. You must be Michael Romano," as his right hand extended out to Mike.

Mike took the offered hand and responded, “Yes, Sir. I almost witnessed the shooting.”

Introductions began, “Officer Romano, meet detectives Joe Johnson and Bill Stattler,” Flynn waved his hand towards the two men closest to Mike. The men shook hands with Mike and exchanged pleasantries.

As the second team walked up to greet Romano, Flynn again made introductions. “Jim Pallack and Jim James.”

Again, handshakes. Mike was smiling, yet nervous; he tried to ease his own tension as he spoke, “Jim Jim, kind of catchy. Almost like stuttering. Your folks had a sense of humor, didn’t they? Bet they called you that when you were a kid.”

James answered coolly, “Yes, Officer Romano, now they just call me Detective.”

Mike retorted with, “Sorry. No harm meant, just trying to add some humor to the day.”

James didn’t answer.

Detective Sergeant Flynn ordered two of his men to examine the body and remove any personal property. He added that in addition to photographing the body and crime scene, they were not to pick up anything they found in the area without recording it and having him personally witness the recovery. Flynn then walked over to Mike leaving his driver to monitor the traffic.

Mike asked Flynn, “Hey Sarge, how did you know my name before I said it?”

“As we left the Two Oh (local cop jargon for 120 Pct.), the desk officer gave us your name. Seems you were on your way to the Two Three for a tour of duty on the ass end of the Island when this happened. Your desk officer called the Two Oh and gave your name as first officer on the scene.” Giving Mike a twisted grin, he asked, “A broad daylight shooting, not something you’d expect here on our quiet island. Is it? Actually we get our share of bodies, but they’re usually in the bad parts of the Two Oh, like Mariner’s Harbor and Park Hill. ”

“No Sarge, it sure wasn’t expected. I was deep in thought when I heard the shots; otherwise I may have seen it go down. But

I did get a good look at the perp's vehicle. It was a fairly new black Ford Bronco and fled into the brush towards Clay Pit Pond Park and was gone before I could react. I don't even know if there was more than one shooter, Sorry"

"Can't be helped Romano. At least you were here to secure the scene and see the truck. Maybe we can get lucky. Now tell us exactly what happened as you remember it."

When Mike's accounting was complete, Flynn stated, "You two guys did a great job safeguarding the scene. Were you informed that you are to remain here until someone, probably me, dismisses you?"

Mike answered, "I was, Sarge. It came over Awad's radio earlier. I'm all yours. What can I do? "

Flynn answered, "Nothing right now. Just hang loose until Crime Scene gets here. They're coming in from Manhattan. When they get here I want you to walk us thru the brush, taking the route of the Bronco as you best remember it. Thank you. Go sit in your car if you want."

Mike welcomed the chance and quickly retreated to his car. The rain, even though it began to taper off, had finally deposited enough water on him to begin to penetrate his clothing and make him uncomfortable. Once seated in his vehicle, he opened his briefcase. With a deep sigh he began pulling out a list of things his divorce lawyer stated he would need, and began to check them off as he removed each item and placed it face down next to him on the passenger seat. As Mike arranged the papers, he vividly remembered the Friday night back in July when he got home early and found a stranger's car in his driveway.

That chance occurrence dramatically effected Mike Romano's life.

CHAPTER TWO

Officer Michael Romano and his family had a piece of the American Dream, a home of their own on Staten Island, at that time it was almost like living in the suburbs of New York City. Shortly after his transfer to the Island, he and Betty realized that the loss of big city overtime hurt their family finances more than anticipated. His daughter, Annie was almost seventeen and his son, Donald was nine. The kids were capable of coming home from school and taking care of themselves for a few hours daily. He had rotating tours, allowing him to be home with his children often, freeing his wife to seek employment to supplement their income. Betty found work in the lower end of Manhattan and traveled there by taking a bus from the street adjacent to theirs to the ferry to Manhattan and returning home the same way. Married eighteen years, he thought they were happy.

***

For quite some time things went along quite well. Mike had become comfortable working in the Tottenville command, especially enjoying the old historic flavor of the area. Tottenville had history dating back to the Revolutionary War. The confines of precinct's boundaries were ripe with old homes, some of them, stately mansions dating back to that era. Mike had been there long enough to make some good friends, usually stopping at a local bar on Friday nights after a four by twelve shift, toss down a few beers and chat with fellow cops about their last set of tours before heading home. He would normally get home between two and three o'clock in the morning and quietly enter his house, careful not to awaken his family.

One fateful Friday night he was tired and not in the mood to hang out. Promptly signing out at midnight, Mike headed directly home to his twenty year old split level house near Clove Lakes Park, subsequently getting there much earlier than his customary beer night with the boys. That night, as he approached his house, Mike saw an unknown auto in front of his garage. Instantly, he went into police officer mode and accelerated slightly to gain momentum, and then after turning off his engine along with his headlights, he coasted silently into his driveway. When his vehicle rolled to a stop, Mike put the gearshift into park and hit the dashboard dimmer switch deactivating the door operated interior lights. He did not want any lights to go on as he exited his car and possibly alert the unknown driver of that strange vehicle. He anxiously slid out of the driver's seat, gently closed his car door, not allowing it to latch in an effort to prevent it from making any noise.

Mike then silently moved to the front of the unknown auto, staying in shadows as much as possible, and put the back of his hand in the center of the hood. It was cool to the touch, indicating that the car had been there for some time. Then he quickly moved forward and stood motionless against his house for several moments, just listening. Not hearing anything extraordinary, he moved on, staying low and hugging the building, as he slowly approached his living room windows. Inside, the lights were on and Mike was able to peer into the house thru a small space that was between the blinds and the window mullion. Romano could only see his wife, Betty, head thrown back in apparent laughter while sitting with her back wedged into the corner of their sofa. His viewing angle was bad, but it looked like she was still in her business attire, although her clothing was disheveled and she was obviously speaking to someone out of his line of sight.

His mind raced, *Holy crap is she cheating on me? After seventeen years together, I'll kill them both. No, I can't. I'll lose my job and that's all I'll have left now, but I gotta do something.* His head pounded as his blood pressure rose. This time he knew that the noise in his brain was not the beating of wings it was the pounding of his heart. With his gut in knots, Mike backed away from the window and hyperventilated. Regaining his composure, Romano went back to his car, reached in for something to write with and recorded the plate number of the suspect auto and then quietly proceeded to the rear of his house. Mike removed his house keys from his pocket, holding them tightly to avoid making any noise and slid the rear door key into the lock. Gently, as quietly as possible, he turned the key and opened the door, entering the mud room that was just off the kitchen.

Before going further into his home, Mike stopped to listen and heard his wife speaking, “John I haven’t had such a good time in years. I’m so happy I walked into your beauty shop. I think it’s really funny that all my friends think you’re gay. Some gay man you are. You make me squeal like a high school girl when we go at it.”

As Mike reached for his revolver, he heard, “Yeah, me too. I’ve never had a woman like you but I better leave now before your husband gets home. He’s liable to shoot me and claim that I was a burglar.”

Michael Romano balled his fists. He was a powerful man standing six feet tall and 200 pounds, with a muscular build from using the gym in every command he ever served in. He had thick black curly hair and bushy eyebrows, giving him a somewhat foreboding appearance. When adversaries looked at his hands, they got even more intimidated; actually, they were terrified, because his hands were as big as catcher’s mitts. His fingers resembled sausages and he wore a size 12 wedding band.

Again, instinctively, he reached for his off duty revolver. Feeling his inner rage, a sardonic smile twisted across his face as he closed the holster’s retaining strap. He decided that shooting an adulterer wasn’t worth losing his job over, there were other means. He thought *where the hell are the kids?*

Mike moved thru the kitchen in a heartbeat and bounded forward into the living room. Betty saw him before he was able to pounce on her obvious lover. She sprang up from the sofa shouting, “Mike, oh my God. No, no, it’s not what you think.”

Looking at Betty, Mike hesitated only a fraction of a second when an ample breast fell from Betty's unbuttoned tailored shirt. As long as he knew her she always, always wore a bra. "Whore," Mike shouted as he reached out to grab Betty's paramour.

John had raised his hands in a defensive manner as Mike went for him; his eyes were bulging out of his head with fear.

"You pig," Mike shouted as he smacked John's hands out of his way, grabbing John's shoulders and ripping him off the wing chair he was sitting in. In a continuous flow of movement, before John could even react, Mike quickly almost wrapped his left hand around the man's throat to prevent him from pulling away and thrust his right fist directly into John's nose. Mike's timing was exact, just as he bloodied the face of his wife's lover; Mike released the grip on his neck. The force of the blow catapulted John against the back of the chair causing the chair to topple backwards and John along with it.

Betty screamed and attempted to cover up. "Whore, don't even speak or move. Sit. I'll deal with you later," Romano shouted as he advanced toward the downed man.

John, somewhat recovered from the crushing blow, was trying to speak, "Butttt, you're nuts, hitting me like that. I haven't done anything. I'll have your badge for that." The man was shouting but his words were barely audible because his hands were cupping his bleeding nose.

Reaching down, Mike yanked John's left arm, raising him to his feet while twisting the arm behind his back. John yelled as Mike bent the arm far beyond its normal boundaries. "Get up you bastard. If you attempt to resist, I'll break your arm and your wrist too!"

Betty was curled on the sofa in a fetal position, whimpering and sobbing. She sounded like a wounded puppy.

As Mike forced John to the front door, he laid out some rules. "Listen you moronic pig, I don't think you should try to make any complaints against me. I know where you work and I'll find out where you live. I'm a cop and know all the tricks. I'll kill you and get away with it. If I ever see you near this house or my wife again, you'll regret it." Mike was on a roll as he began twisting John's wrist for more effect and continued, "Better still I'll cripple you so you can't ever work or be with another woman again." For emphasis, Mike applied additional force, causing John to howl. As John continued to beg for relief, Mike leaned into John's ear and menacingly whispered, "Remember I'll get away with it."

By the end of Mikes' ranting, he had moved John to the front door. "Now use your free hand to let yourself out," Romano shouted. As John opened the door, Mike struck the back of John's neck with the palm of his hand almost knocking the man to the floor as he flew past the portal and down the front steps.

John staggered to his car while he painfully rotated his injured arm and wrist. Opening the unlocked door he dropped into the driver's seat, quickly started the engine and lurched backward out of the driveway, knocking down the Romano's mailbox in his haste to get away. Mike had obviously terrified him.

Romano slammed the door shut and returned to his errant wife. "Betty," he shouted as he worked to control his rage, "Just what the hell is going on here? Where are the kids?" His hands twitched as he spoke. Betty thought that Mike was about to hit her and tried to back further away from her husband. Her movements instantly erased any doubts that Mike had figured out was going on. Betty, in her attempt to crawl away, caused her skirt to rise above mid-thigh, revealing the blonde fluff of her womanhood. Seeing the mother of his children exposed like that after just being with another man, Mike felt a need to hit her and actively resisted the compelling desire by hyperventilating once more.

Betty was terrified at the sound he made and didn't notice her exposure as she whined, "But Mike, he's my hairdresser. Sometimes when I leave work in the City and go to his shop, he does my hair. There's nothing between us. I swear. He drove me home so I didn't have to take the express bus. Sometimes he does that. "You're always working. We only see each other when you do day tours and only after I get home from work. Sometimes we don't even talk. He pays attention to me." Her statement was punctuated with sobs and sniffles.

"Liar! Where's your bra. You always wear one, why is your blouse unbuttoned and where the hell are your panties??"

Shocked as she realized that her skirt was too high, she quickly tugged it down and feebly answered, "In my purse. It was too tight so I took it off."

"You're lying. Were your drawers too tight too? I heard everything from the kitchen. How long has this been going on??"

"Mike, it's nothing. It's over. Believe me."

"You bet it's over! It's over between us! Get out of my sight before I lose my self-control and beat you bloody. Where are the kids? The bedroom is mine. Move your things to the guest room. You have one hour and do not speak to me unless I speak to you first." Mike backed away from her to avoid the impulse to strike her as she rose from the sofa. As Betty ran out of the room, Mike went to their liquor cabinet and grabbed a bottle of Dewar's White Label, retreated to his car and drank himself to sleep.

***

It was 9:00 a.m. when Mike opened his eyes with an awful headache and a lousy taste in his mouth. After going into the house and checking to see if Betty was still in the guest room, she was apparently asleep. He then returned to the master bedroom, showered and put on clean clothes. When he went into the kitchen to find something nonalcoholic to drink, he saw a note on the kitchen counter, next to the coffee maker. It was from his errant wife stating that the kids were staying with his sister- in- law Kelly back in Queens for the weekend. Mike never found out when the note was written. *Nice,* he thought, *she packs the kids off to her sister and goes out whoring and brings the guy home.* Luckily he was on a seventy two hour swing and had the next three days off. Mike knew that most attorneys didn't work on weekends, but he wanted to keep busy and was anxious to get a divorce action started. He was thankful that he could delay speaking to his children and went looking for a divorce attorney.

Just before noon he was lucky enough to find an attorney whose office was in Stapleton, near the old bandstand in what was commonly known as Stapleton Park. Mike found the door unlocked and the lawyer, an old timer named Arthur Slotnick, in his office catching up on some work. After meeting him and discussing a few formalities, Mike engaged his services on the spot, promising to bring a retainer in on Monday morning. Twenty minutes later, after relating a few more particulars to his new attorney, Mike left to begin hunting for a temporary place to stay for a few weeks while he sorted out his options. After checking locations, he found a moderately priced motel and paid for a week in advance. After looking at the room, he picked up some necessary items and went back to plan his next move. After mulling over some ideas, Mike decided that on Monday morning his first stop would be to his bank.

The Romano's had joint checking and savings accounts. After a very gut wrenching weekend, Mike went directly to his bank and almost emptied both accounts, leaving behind a total of five hundred dollars and then opened a new savings account, in his name only, depositing everything else keeping just enough money to give his new attorney a cash retainer. Mike felt that he could do without a checking account until he established a new residence and would look for an apartment to rent during off duty hours until he found one. Mike also decided that the next meeting he had with his lawyer, he would try to force the sale of their house.

At his next meeting with Slotnick, Mike handed him the promised retainer and asked what the next move was. Arthur suggested that the children should stay with their mother until the house was sold. It would ease the trauma of divorce for his children and she would be unable to have men remain overnight. Arthur further promised that he would put that requirement into the divorce agreement. That suggestion alone gave Mike confidence in his attorney, but Arthur Slotnick had other qualities too, he was affable, at least 65 years old and claimed that he was practicing law at least as many years as Mike was old. Arthur was a straight shooter just like Mike. All in all, they liked each other.

CHAPTER THREE

As Mike was returning all his papers to his briefcase, he noticed that it was no longer raining and was grateful because he would not get any wetter when he would have to leave his vehicle. Before opening his door, Mike looked at his watch and noted it was 1530 hours just as the Crime Scene Unit pulled alongside of him. Mike closed his briefcase, threw it onto the rear seat and got out of his car.

"Romano, get over here. I want you to meet the Crime Scene team," Flynn shouted.

"On the way Sarge," Mike responded as he closed his car door.

"Officer Michael Romano, meet the Crime Scene Team," Flynn said as he gestured with his hand for them to respond. Both men wore CSU windbreakers and caps. They looked sharp and professional.

In turn, the two men answered in turn, "Jim Black here. Pleased to know you"

"Steve Jones. Let's get to it. What do you have"? He held out his hand in greeting.

Sergeant Flynn asked Mike to lead the CSU detectives along the route taken by the driver of the Bronco. Before they began walking, Flynn gave the CSU people an update. "We have a white male, about thirty five to forty years old, shot to death, probably with a handgun. Not a .22 caliber, based on what EMS and Romano here say. Romano says he heard three shots as he drove past the scene. He stopped and saw a black Ford Bronco flee the scene. We believe a revolver was used because we couldn't find any shell casings. Did I cover it all Romano?"

"Yeah, Sarge. You want me to show these guys where the truck drove. Right?"

"Correct. But first let them look at the body and check the surrounding area so we can have the guy removed. Get to it guys." Flynn then ordered the radio dispatcher to notify the Medical Examiner's office to respond and remove the body.

Jones and Black got right down to business. They photographed the victim from several angles, and commenting on what appeared to be stippling on the front of the victim's shirt, indicating that the victim was shot from a distance of three feet or less. Crime Scene used their high tech 35 mm camera to take photos of the victim, and the surrounding terrain from several angles.

The CSU team also found what appeared to be gouges in the turf that appeared to have been formed as the shooter punched the gas pedal to flee. There were only two gouges from the trucks wheels, side by side, indicating that the getaway vehicle was probably not operating in four wheel drive at the time of the shooting. Jones and Black carefully photographed them and made plaster casts of both. The team used the latest stuff on the market, a plaster-acrylic compound, containing a catalyst that created heat when mixed with water, making a quick dry cast, even on moist ground. To facilitate the possibility of having to make castings at a scene where no water was available as they just did, the CSU team always carried ample water in two five gallon jerricans when going into an outdoor location in addition to all the other equipment that they carried in their van.

Romano, fascinated by their work, followed them back to their vehicle as they put some of their equipment away finishing with the pour. Mike tried to digest all that he saw inside, in addition to the casting material they just used. Included in the plethora within his view were; racks containing dental plaster, several other cameras, static-imprinting kits, several different lighting sources for the detection of body fluids and DNA evidence. Included in the array of items were several marking tools and various envelopes and bags used for gathering and storing evidence. The two detectives answered some questions asked by the inquisitive cop as to what some of items are used for.

Knowing that the castings would take some time to harden, Jones asked, "OK Mike, show us the route you think the truck took. By the way, where can he go from here? I only see woods across that field."

"Those trees are part of Clay Pit Pond State Park. There's alot of dirt roads in there. Hope you have enough plaster," Mike quipped.

Jim responded, "If the name of the place is any indication, we should get some good casts in there. Lots of clay areas in there?"

"Some, but it's mostly dirt roads." Casting his eyes in the distance Mike continued, "From my car, once I stopped, and tried to see the direction of his escape, I'd say that he was headed towards the two tallest trees on the other side of the field. By the time I took a second look and got my bearings, he was gone. Do they line up with your casting spot? I think he went straight, no turns, like he was shot out of a gun."

Jones walked back to the wheel gouges, eyeballed the trees indicated by Mike and responded, "I think you're right Mike."

Flynn took over and authoritatively spoke while pointing at the target trees, "Ok guys, everyone form a line. We're going to walk towards those two big trees and since we didn't find shell casings near the body, we have to assume we're looking for a revolver. We also want anything that doesn't belong here."

Jones, not wanting to be upstaged, pulled Mike close and added, loud enough for all to hear, "According to our witness here, the shooter didn't have time to retrieve any casings, so a revolver it is. The guy may have tossed his weapon away as he fled the scene. Let's do what the sergeant says."

Flynn continued waving his arms in a sweeping motion as he barked another order, "All cops, Highway, Detectives, Sergeants and all form a line. Spread out from here, to the right and left of me, about six feet apart. Let's go." Before he took a single step, Flynn turned to the two med techs and ordered, "You two are hereby ordered to remain here and guard the body until the ME arrives. Call the dispatcher and ask for him again if he's not here in twenty minutes and we're still not back, thanks." Then with a slight chuckle he added, "You're officially deputized."

Slowly the line of cops moved forward and began searching the ground. It took about fifteen minutes before they reached the tree line. No gun or any other evidence was found, only matted down vegetation where the truck had passed.

Flynn, as he approached the beginning of the wooded area, looked intently at a small bare patch of ground. He was looking at tire tracks leading directly into the wooded thick growth. Brush and small trees were trashed and broken indicating that something, probably the Bronco went charging into the woods. The damage to the foliage looked fresh.

"All right every one, stop searching and come over here. Careful of the tire tracks where I'm standing. Jones, Black, go get your plaster. I want more castings."

As the new casts were being made, Flynn, along with the remaining men, slowly walked deeper into the trees following the path cut by the Bronco. It wasn't long before they came upon a dirt road running parallel to the highway and the highway was no longer visible. Flynn split up the men and ordered that each group travel in opposite directions along the road. He had little hope of finding anything of value because he knew, along with most of the Island cops, that the park was used by kids on motor bikes and four wheelers and sometimes it also doubled as a lover's lane.

An army of men would be needed to remove the various bits of sundried bottles, paint cans wrappers and other assorted debris before they could find anything that resembled anything as good as the "point of entry casting" that was just made. Flynn had neither. The efforts of his men were futile as he expected, because the road and surrounding ground was crisscrossed with tracks of all shapes and sizes, it would also take a truckload of plaster.

After a cursory inspection of the wooded area for a weapon by all parties and finding none, Flynn was prompted to say, "Well, gentleman, looks like the shooter probably took his gun with him. Maybe it's his favorite."

The Sergeant then ordered all the men to return to the original crime scene adjacent to the highway, and then he supervised the photographing and lifting of all the plaster casts.

By the time everything was wrapped up, the ME arrived and officially pronounced and tagged the body. The Coroner's Office van showed up five minutes later and removed the body. With the body removed Flynn dismissed the med techs and Jones recorded their contact information before they left.

With the victim removed, typical homicide procedures began. The men of the Crime Scene Unit marked and tagged the castings for future reference. Any evidence gathered, along with any castings, would be secured at the Staten Island Property Office after bring properly protected and boxed. Crime scene photos produced by CSU would be developed by the Photo Unit in One Police Plaza and vouchered accordingly. The 120 Squad would handle the homicide investigation and would also receive copies of Crime Scene's photos as soon as they were processed, in addition, the Crime Scene Unit would retain a copy for their case file and study. CSU would also attempt to identify the tire manufacturer and size from the castings and detailed photos of them. Any Polaroid photos taken by Flynn's men would remain in control of the assigned detective. Detective Stattler was next up in the catching order and officially assigned to the case by Sergeant. Flynn.

"Romano, you follow us into the Two Oh. Our office is upstairs. You can spend the remainder of your tour helping us to sort this out. Have any questions?"

"None at all, Boss. Gotta say though, this is one hell of a day."

***

Mike had driven past the One Two Oh many times without really noticing the building. All he ever noticed was that it was old and constructed of red brick. Now he had to park somewhere, if lucky and go inside. The area along Richmond Terrace near the

120 was lined bumper to bumper with parked cars. Mike found a space under a "Police Department Autos" sign, parked and placed his 123 Pct. parking tag on his dashboard before locking it and then took a few minutes to look at the building. The station house stood on a knoll across the street from the walled waterfront. The building's exterior appeared to be in good condition, actually better than the Two Three's, but then, it's possibly the second oldest working station house in the City. Next to the building, on the right side of it, was a white marble and granite building housing the Staten Island Family Court. On the left side of the police property was a small parking area. Mike counted spaces for only six autos, including a spot marked, "Commanding Officer". Romano then took a deep breath, climbed the broad granite steps and entered the building. Once in the station house, he went directly to the desk officer to report his presence. As Mike looked around for a few seconds, he thought, *nobody saves money on décor like New York City does; every building interior is painted the same institutional green with a lousy looking cream color halfway up the walls and on the wood trim.*

Mike presented himself , "Officer Michael Romano, Lieutenant," as he gave a less than snappy salute. Without waiting for an answer, Mike continued, "As I'm sure you know Lieutenant, I witnessed a shooting on the way to work today and Sergeant Flynn has requested me to finish my tour with his squad.

"Fine Romano, I'll make the appropriate entries into the Blotter. Just try to make it all the way into your own command on your next tour will you? We already have a full complement of men. By the way at end of tour, sign out here at the desk and we will notify your command. Ok?"

"Yes. I'll be sure to do that Lieutenant. Thank you". Mike turned, found the stairway to the second floor and went up to look for the squad's office.

The second floor of the building contained most of the offices within the command. Directly opposite the landing, down a short corridor, was an office that housed the Staten Island Latent Print Unit. Mike quickly looked inside to see four desks, three men in plainclothes, two long tables containing some equipment and a row of file cabinets.

To the left of the landing, down another corridor, were two offices designated as Clerical and Crime Prevention respectively. Mike returned to the stairway area and found, to the right of the landing, the 120 Squad. Officer Romano stepped through the open doorway, stopped and slowly surveyed the place.

It was one very large room containing a cornucopia of work chairs and desks that didn't quite match. The place appeared to have been furnished from a rummage sale. The perimeter of the room was painted that same cream color that reminded Mike of manila folders. Over in one corner there was a finger print board hanging on the wall making that particular corner a mess with smudges and blotches surrounding the work area. To the right of the fingerprint work space, was a row of clip boards tacked neatly in a row at eye level. They were laden with reams of paper containing various sets of material, most of which were covered with a sheet of brownish heavy, semi-gloss paper, labeled as to what each clipboard contained. The only clipboards that were not covered were holding wanted fliers.

The commander's office, to the right of the entrance door, was fabricated within the larger room using floor to ceiling metal and glass partitions, they too were painted the usual institutional green, the color of weak pea soup. All in all, to Mike, the place looked like a Hollywood movie set. With his emotional state somewhere between apprehension and excitement, Mike continued on and entered the squad office.

Before he could even speak, Joe Johnson, who had been hunched over a desk, stood and walked over to Mike, greeting him with, "Happy to see you Romano. The Boss is waiting in his office."

"Thanks, Detective Johnson. Is it?"

"Call me Joe. We're all here for the same reason, to catch the bad guy. Right? Anything you need, come to me."

Detective Jim James got up, mumbling, "Now, I gotta get some fresh air," as he left the room.

Romano ignored the remark and noticed that the door to Flynn's office was open and walked in, "Hey Sarge. Got here as quick as I could. Not many open parking spaces near the station. Is it always that crowded?"

"Yes it is, but like anything else, you get used to it. Please sit down. I don't know if you can help us very much. Tell me officer, why do you think the victim was shot outside and next to the perp's vehicle? We all saw how the thick nearby woods were and know that he could have brought his victim into the trees. Why did the shooter risk being seen, right alongside the roadway, I might add?"

"Well, I'm not a detective, but maybe they knew each other. Maybe the victim was in the Bronco willingly, and later was ordered outside or tricked to leave the truck, then was shot. Maybe the shooter wanted to keep the Bronco clean. Maybe it's his car. My guess, looking at the expression on his face, is that the victim never expected to get shot, I thought he looked surprised. As to why he wasn't shot in the wooded area, I have no idea at all unless the shooter wanted to, as they say in the movies, 'leave a message'. Do you know who he was?"

"Got a wallet from the guy's rear pants pocket. There was a New Jersey driver's license with a picture on it that looks like our guy. Says here his name is Paul Capria and his address of record is in Bayonne. We're running that info and his prints now. The body was transported directly to the ME's office in Manhattan. We should have preliminary reports by tomorrow morning."

Mike had only served in the patrol force during his time on the job. Up to that time he had never been involved so closely with detectives and found it exciting but tried not to show it. To the men in the squad room, he wanted to convey an, *"it's just another work day"* attitude.

"What else can I do to help Sarge? You have me for the next five hours."

Handing Mike several photos taken with the squads Polaroid camera, he asked, "Look at these closely and tell me what you see."

Mike thumbed through the lot, putting a few to the side. After he was finished, he asked, "This may sound silly, but do you have a magnifying glass? I think I see something in those photos."

"Nothing is silly in a homicide investigation. Why do you need a glass?"

"Well, I think, that one or two of these photos show something that may be useful if that Bronco is ever found. I think the tire treads might give you something. It looks to me like a chunk is missing from one of them."

Smiling at Mike, Flynn gently ordered, "Go across the hall and ask the print guys for one. I have to compose an Unusual Occurrence Report on this shooting and fax it out to various commanders. There's already an alarm out on the truck." Flynn put some paper into his IBM Selectric typewriter, then pointed to the door and continued, "Tell them, I want it and say nothing else. They're a nosey group."

"Sure, right away." As Romano was leaving the office, he almost bumped into the returning Detective James. James looked at Mike with disdain. In his mind, Mike thought, *Now, I have another person to dislike, my ex, her lover and Jim Jim.*

Mike walked directly into the Latent Print office with his right hand extended and spoke, to no one in particular, "Michael Romano here. I'm next door with the squad and we need a magnifying glass if you have one please. Sergeant Flynn needs it for something."

The unit's commander, a tall lanky man with thinning blonde hair walked up to Romano and took his extended hand. "Paul Stonner, Lieutenant Paul Stonner. I'm the supervisor in charge of this crew. What does Andy need a glass for? Going over old family photos?"

Mike didn't know Flynn's first name and haltingly answered, taking some time to make the name association, "Loo, I, huh, don't know off hand. Yeah, he just asked me to get one if you have a spare or borrow yours."

"Sure thing Romano. Hang on a minute will you?" The Lieutenant walked to the far corner of the room, moved around a large desk that faced all the others and opened what was probably a drawer, and rooted around for a few seconds. Obviously finding what he was looking for, with a triumphant smile on his face, Stonner stood up holding a large square magnifying glass with a thick handle.

The lieutenant then motioned for Mike to come forward and take it, "Here you go Romano. It even lights up, he said, as he turned on a bright light near the handle that focused to an area just under the glass itself. Andy should be able to see the color of his baby's eyes."

As Mike walked over to the lieutenant, he looked around the room a bit. Two men were hunched over at their respective desks, one of them was peering thru a glass similar to what Stonner held except that it was mounted on a stand and powered by an electric cord. The man had both hands free and was moving several fingerprint cards around under the lens.

The second man was looking at something thru a short, round tubular device that he manipulated across his flat subject matter, other fingerprint cards. He sensed Mike's gaze and stopped moving his hands. Holding the device aloft, while never looking up, said, "Ten power fixed position glass. It makes the work easier. Want to try?"

"No thanks. Got to get back inside. The boss is in a hurry. Thanks anyway."

As he re-entered Flynn's office, the Sergeant was sitting at his desk. Mike held out the glass, "Here you go Sarge."

"You keep it Romano. Use it to find what you think you saw in the photos. Find it and show me what it is, so we can both know."

Mike put the glass down on Flynn's desk, picked up the stack of photos he just went thru and selected one. It was a picture of one of the tire castings. Mike then took the glass again and slowly examined the photo. "Sarge, I think I see a cut or nick in one of the tire treads. Here take a look", he stated as he handed the two items off to Flynn.

"Boy, kid, you sure have good eyes. How old are you anyway?"

To Mike, Flynn appeared to be about 55 years old. "Thirty Nine, sir", was Mike's response as Flynn examined the photo.

"Good looking out Romano. I think you're right, it sure looks like it may be something, and then again it just might be a piece of chipped plaster or dirt on the lens. We'll have to check the actual castings." Flynn stood up and smiling at Mike, walked to his office doorway, "Johnson, take Romano and go down to the Property Office at Edgewater Plaza and bring back all of the tire castings. I want a close look at them. Ask for the crime scene photos too, but I doubt if they've been delivered yet."

Johnson responded, "Ok Romano, you heard the man, let's get on it."

Climbing into the dark blue Chevy with Johnson at the wheel, Mike promised himself that one day he would rise to the rank of Detective. In his mind, Mike quietly listed some thoughts on the matter; *this is the way to work. No family disputes. No handing summonses to motorists while standing in the rain looking at them dry remaining inside their cars. No more abuse from irate citizens who you were trying to help. Solving crimes after the dirt and dust has settled is the way to go. Last, but not least, a raise in pay and enormous prestige. There's a certain mystique about the title Detective, that can't be disputed and I want it.*

***

The Department's offices at Edgewater Plaza were relatively new. In the late Seventies, much of the waterfront on The Island had been reclaimed and renovated. In the not too distant past, Staten Island had many bustling businesses, because of the Island's close proximity to the mouth of New York Harbor. It had become a busy commercial port with many loft buildings right on the waterfront. Most of those defunct businesses were engaged in manufacturing and shipping, with an occasional coffee warehouse thrown in. Edgewater Plaza, a former coffee warehouse that had fallen into disrepair after being abandoned for decades, was recently purchased by a private developer, renovated, and now served as an office complex. The City of New York was one of the tenants.

The Police Department, with the Island's residency growing, needed larger quarters for property storage, having out grown the basement of the Two Oh and took over an entire top floor of One Edgewater Plaza.

Johnson and Romano entered the building's elevator, and as Johnson punched the fifth floor button, he turned to Mike and said, "Romano, I know that during your career, you must have signed out property hundreds of times, but this is a squad case so let me do most of the talking. Ok?"

Joe's statement stung Mike a little, he knew his place, yet he felt like a rookie as he heard those words. He hoped that Detective Johnson wasn't showing his true colors and beginning to act like that arrogant buffoon, Jim James. Mike paused, smiled and responded friendly as possible, "Sure, Joe", to show his annoyance, Mike continued by seemingly correcting himself, "Detective Johnson, no problem. One can always learn something new by listening. No problem at all."

"Listen Romano, Mike, since you are involved in the case, between you and I, it should be Joe and Mike. Let's not be so formal. OK?"

Mike felt better and extended his hand saying, "Sure thing Joe. We're both cops trying to catch the bad guy. Right?"

"Yes, we are. I only spoke the way I did because this is a 120 case and if we get the shooter, I don't want any defense attorney to have anything that might work against us. They'll use anything, even statements by investigating officers. Some slick lawyer might even subpoena the property man and try to work us against each other."

"Yeah. I got it Joe. Less is more. We're good."

The elevators opened and the two men went directly to the sign in desk. The entire working area of the loft was behind a reinforced wire screen. It was like the big cat cages at the zoo, but without the vertical iron bars. The entire loft, as usual, was painted that ugly institutional green, like almost every building interior in the Department. Mike thought, *that must be the Department's motto "if it doesn't move, paint it green."* Surprisingly, the screen was some sort of non-offensive cream color.

Directly opposite the elevators there were two window sized openings in the cage. One of the openings was obviously the intake window because it had a log book that was not accessible to the visitors' side of the cage. The second window was outfitted with a sign out log, an inkless finger print pad and a camera mounted on a post about 18" above the counter with a white square painted directly under it on the counter top. Mike knew that the camera was used to photograph whoever was withdrawing property while simultaneously photographing the removing officer's identification card. The windows were attended by a uniformed police officer and like all uniformed cops; his name tag identified him only by his surname, Shiller.

The area behind the screen was vast. Mike had seen the property room in One Police Plaza many times and marveled at the size of it. From where he stood, this one looked just as large as the one downtown. Back in the recesses of that labyrinth of metal shelving, Mike was able to catch a brief glimpse of a second uniformed cop moving about.

"What can I do for you guys?" The cop behind the screen asked.

Johnson pulled out his shield and stated, Johnson, 120 Squad. We're here to pick up some property that came in earlier today. It was vouchered by Crime Scene. We have copies of the vouchers. Our boss wants to see 'em."

"Ok. Let me have what you got. If we got 'em, I'll find them for you."

Johnson pulled the copies from the inside pocket of his sport coat and unfolded them. "Here. They're tire track castings." Joe handed the property man green copies of vouchers V22345-SI and V22346-SI.

Shiller checked his intake log and after running his finger down the listings twice looked up and said, “The stuff is here and logged in but it hasn’t been shelved yet, too soon, I’ll have to find my partner. He’s shelving everything that came in today and he should know where they are.”

“Thanks, we’ll wait,” was Johnson’s response. Mike shuffled his feet in anticipation.

Shiller shouted, “Hey Neil, I need some castings for two Detectives up here. Come on up and shake your ass, they ain’t got all night.” He was as loud as a wounded bull elephant.

From somewhere within the labyrinth came a response, “Hold on to your pants. They can wait; I have stuff in my hands. I’ll be there soon. Take a valium! Will you?”

Joe and Mike engaged in idle chatter while they impatiently moved around the waiting area.

Within minutes, a very portly officer waddled up to the counter. He was wearing a uniform shirt, well-worn faded blue jeans and old black high top sneakers. His shirt was soiled with dark vertical smudges, as if he wiped his hands on his chest every time he handled property. His nametag was crooked, his shield was tarnished and his hair looked as if it was last combed when Teddy Roosevelt was the Police Commissioner, however, he did have a pleasant smile.

“Ok Shiller, give me the voucher numbers and I’ll locate the stuff. You called me, so I know it hasn’t been put away yet and there’s no location numbers on the sheet.” He scratched the voucher numbers down on a small pad he snatched from somewhere under his side of the counter and disappeared into the maze of shelves. Joe sat in a straight backed bench, and judging by the patina on it, obviously well used, to wait while Mike kept busy by walking around and reading anything that he found hanging on the walls. There were at least half a dozen clipboards containing Department bulletins and notices. Mike shook his head to the fact that, pasted to the walls, were also several warnings regarding the returning of property in a timely and procedurally correct manner. “Infractions would result in charges and specs”, was boldly printed in red, a distinct reminder of the dreaded Trial Room. He found it a pity that New York's Finest needed to be reminded of that obvious fact.

About five minutes after he had disappeared, Neil returned pushing a steel cart and rolled it up to the service window. On the cart were six cardboard cartons, their sides inscribed with voucher numbers. Each carton also had a clear plastic pocket taped to it that contained a copy of the corresponding voucher.

Neil slapped one of the cartons with his palm as he spoke, "Here you go men. My esteemed associate will finish the transaction." His sneakers squealed on the tile floor as he turned and disappeared from view.

After Shiller recorded the vouchers and appropriate carton numbers into the receipt book, Detective Johnson put his thumb print and signature next to each corresponding transaction in the sign out log. He then placed his Department Identification Card on the small pad under the camera facing him and stood on the floor marker that was three feet in front of the mechanical Cyclops. Shiller hit a button on his side of the counter and the camera emitted a click and a buzz indicating that it had completed its task, automatically advancing for the next transaction.

"Ok, Mike let's get this stuff back to the office", Joe said as Shiller began passing the boxes out thru the opening towards them one at a time.

Turning to the attendant, Joe asked, "Hey friend, can we use your cart to bring this stuff down to the car?"

"Sure. Hold on and I'll bring it around," was the cheerful response.

Once they had the cart, Mike and Joe carefully loaded the six cartons on to it and waited for the elevator.

As they loaded the last of the castings into the trunk of their car, Joe asked Mike if he would return the cart to the property room. Mike cheerfully agreed.

With both men back in their vehicle, Joe asked, "Mike do you know why the boss wanted the castings?"

"We were looking at the squad's Polaroid photos of the castings and I thought that there was something in the tire treads that might help us. Sergeant Flynn agreed and sent us to pick up the castings. We'll soon find out if we were right."

The ride back to the office was filled with the usual small talk between cops, seniority, vacation picks and the usual lack of a working contract.

***

By 1930 hours, Johnson and Romano had made three trips to the car and back up to the Squad's office with their cartons. To lessen the chance of any mishap, each man carried only two boxes per trip, saving the last two, the heaviest, for the last trip, each man carrying only one box.

Flynn instructed the actual case officer, Bill Stattler, to open each carton, remove the contents and gently place each item on his desk. Stattler's actions were recorded by Flynn himself, should there any problem in court with the chain of evidence.

The photos taken by the squad back at the scene were matched against each casting to the best of the men's ability.

Flynn, Johnson, Stattler and Romano were examining their chosen photos against what they perceived were the appropriate castings as Detective Jim James walked in.

"Well, how nice. What does our favorite patrol officer have to say now? Did he solve the case yet?"

Before anyone could respond, Flynn, annoyed by Jim's less then complimentary remarks about Romano, snapped at him, "Jim, we have enough help right now. Don't you have cases to work on? Did you do any work on this case that's not documented on a DD-5 (Detective Follow up report) yet? Get out of here and go back to work. I'll call you if I need your input. Got it?"

Noting Flynn's displeasure with James, Mike looked up from what he was doing and asked, "Hey, Jim Jim how's it going?" James, embarrassed at being chastised by his boss, turned on his heel and beat a hasty exit while muttering to himself.

Mike looked at the fleeing James and mumbled, “Elitist A-hole.”

“Guys come over here will you? Look at this casting and tell me what you see,” Flynn commanded, as he waved a Polaroid photo, using it as a pointer to indicate a particular casting marked, ClayPit-No.4. The markings also included the date, 3/28/1984, the time of casting and the initials SJ for Steve Jones.

Each man in turn bent over the casting, first looking at it, and then slowly moving his hand over the tread marks. All three of them came to the same conclusion, that one of the castings represented a tire with an identifying mark on it, a piece of rubber appeared to be missing, creating a distinct notch and a deep lateral cut across two treads.

Without fanfare, Flynn complimented Romano, “Good looking out Mike, you were right. This will help us nail the shooter, if we ever find the truck. It will prove it’s the truck you saw fleeing the scene. I hope we can also get whoever was driving it. Good work.”

“Thank you Sarge. Just doing my job and I got lucky, that’s all, but thanks anyway.”

“Joe, take this photo, record that casting’s ID someplace on it and slap it on the copy machine. Make two copies and call Crime Scene. Oh yeah, first make two copies with the one to one camera too and then you can call Crime Scene and tell them what we found. Ask if they know anything about their photos being ready. Find out if they ordered us a set and ask if we can get our copies tonight. Go!” Flynn ordered as he held the photo up for Johnson to grab. “Oh, and do a five (DD-5) right away on this. Don’t forget to include Romano in it. It’s 8 o’clock now and if we can get those photos, I may extend the tour so we can work on ‘em.” Turning to Mike, Flynn asked, “Any problem if we go into overtime?”

“No Sarge, no problem at all.” Mike liked what he was doing and the working atmosphere and wished he could stay in the squad forever. Romano, in a strange way, even liked Detective James. Mike believed James felt threatened by his expertise and he considered it a compliment.

"Bill, take Mike here, and mark up the rest of our Polaroids matching them with their castings and then create a voucher for the photos and I'll sign off on it. We'll keep the voucher and the photos here in the command. Thank you."

To nobody in particular Flynn shouted, "Nobody leaves the squad for meal tonight. Somebody call that Lebanese pizza joint around the corner and get a couple of pies delivered. They're the best pies within ten miles of here and it's on me."

Jim Pallack shouted, "Pies here in twenty minutes Sarge. One cheese, one sausage, along with three large bottles of Coke."

Detective Johnson called out, "Sarge, Crime Scene reports that they put a priority rush on their film when they delivered it to the lab and the prints are ready. Jim Black says that he can pick them up from the Photo Unit and meet us with a set at the VZ (Verranzano Narrows) Bridge within an hour. He'll call us on city wide radio when he gets there. He also said that they're now working on identifying the tires, he thinks they might be BF Goodrich."

"Good. Everyone catch up on their DD5's while we're waiting for those pies. After we all grab a slice or two, Joe and Romano, go meet Crime Scene." The pies arrived on time and true to his word, Flynn picked up the tab.

Mike wandered around the office holding a paper plate with a slice of sausage pizza on it and a half filled paper cup of Coke-a-Cola, unable to find a place where he felt comfortable enough to sit and enjoy his dinner. Looking around at the men of the squad, he spotted Jim Jim smiling in his direction while spreading paperwork all over his desk. Mike knew the action was to prevent him from attempting to sit there. He wouldn't sit with James anyway and thought, *I've no intention to chance giving myself heartburn by being too close to that guy.*

Joe Johnson, seeing the uncertainty in Mike's face, called out, "Mike, sit here friend. You look like a little lost puppy," and cleared an area on his own desk for Mike to deposit his plate and drink. He then yanked a spare chair from the wall next to him and set it at the side of his desk, motioning for Mike to sit.

"Thank you Joe. Now maybe my pie won't get cold and my drink warm, before I eat."

"No problem at all Mike. You're welcome at my desk anytime. I always give courtesy to fellow cops, especially sharp ones like you."

Mike glanced over at Jim Jim who apparently heard Joe's remarks because he was again shaking his head and mumbling.

As Mike settled into his chair, Johnson spoke in a low tone, "Mike, you know that was pretty good looking out to spot those tire cuts on such small photos. Flynn obviously is pleased. Maybe some day we can work together in a more permanent nature."

Trying to play down Joe's comment in case James overheard their conversation, Mike responded, "Thanks. But it's no big deal." After biting off another mouthful of pizza, Mike continued, "I enjoy my job and that was just part of good police work. Being involved in this investigation does make it so much better though."

"Tell me Mike, what you think about the crime, do you think it looks like a contract hit? The mob usually dumps bodies in isolated areas to delay discovery. This body wasn't hidden. Was our shooting the result of an argument that went bad?"

Mike finished his pizza slice, washing it down with a long gulp of Coke before he answered. "Well, Joe, qualifying myself based on my limited experience, "I'd say the victim knew his murderer and never expected to be shot. At the scene, as soon as I saw the guy's face, I thought he looked surprised. I think that he and the shooter were standing alongside the Bronco engaged in some kind of conversation when the shots were fired and the guy never expected to be shot. Anyway, that's just a guess."

"Good theory, as good as any I've heard before. Let's go meet Crime Scene, get those photos and whatever else they might have for us. Flynn's anxious."

***

Detective Johnson again signed himself and Romano out in the squad's command log. Both men went down to the dark Chevy they had been using and climbed in. Johnson drove out to Wall Street, turning left down to Richmond Terrace, cut right along the Terrace, which became Bay Street after the ferry terminal, and on down to Fingerboard Road, turning right to loop around to the bridge toll plaza. He parked next to the administration building and switched the police radio to the city wide band. They waited only ten minutes before the radio crackled, "Crime Scene to One Two Oh Squad, your location? K."

Joe responded, "On the Island, on the south side of the toll plaza next to the administration building. We're in a dark blue Chevy right next to the TBTA tow truck. K"

"We're cresting the bridge now. See you in three minutes. K."

As a marked Department station wagon pulled into the plaza, Mike could see "Crime Scene Unit" emblazoned on the side. After it stopped parallel to them, the wagon's occupants, Jones and Black, the two men that Mike met earlier in the day on the expressway exited their car. Jones smiled and shook hands with the Staten Island cops. Black obviously remembered Mike and teased him by asking, "Romano why did you shoot the guy anyway? The story about the black Bronco was a good one", chuckling as he spoke.

Jones picked up the joke as he heard Mike's name. "Yeah, what did you do with the Bronco? Where did you stash it? Those tire tracks were a nice touch, and the look on the guy's face. Did he know you were a cop?"

Uniformed patrol Officer Michael Romano was happy to see that he was accepted by those detectives and treated as an equal and not like Jim James. He answered by pointing at Joe Johnson and saying, "I told you guys before, I didn't shoot him, he did." Everyone laughed.

Jones dipped back into the station wagon and returned with two large envelopes. "Here are our crime scene photos and blow ups of the tire marks. Since you called, Forensics and our office are in agreement that these tire depressions were made by BF Goodrich, 255/50/16's. When you look at them you'll notice, there are some identifying cuts on the treads of one of the tires. Judging by the spray of earth around the tracks, we believe it's on the inner edge of the left rear tire of the vehicle. That would indicate that the vehicle was traveling away from the highway and toward the trees, just like Mike had stated. If the truck is ever found, the treads can be matched proving it's presence at the scene. At least it's something. Forensic reports and DD-5's are in the envelope."

Johnson quickly said, "Thank you guys, that was pretty quick work. We would very much like to sit and chat, but our boss is in a hurry for this information. Thank you again." Joe handed the material off to Mike and extended his right hand for a parting handshake. Remembering that Crime Scene had printed the victim at the scene, Mike asked, "By the way, did you get his prints back?"

"Yeah. He's from New Jersey. Some place in Bayonne. He has a small sheet, some minor stuff. The results also are in the envelope."

After a quick exchange of pleasantries, the two guys from Crime Scene headed for the bridge while Jones and Romano headed back to the One Two Oh.

The ride back to command was uneventful. Once again Jones made Mike feel good by complimenting him again. With nothing special at the moment to talk about, the two men resorted to a typical cop pastime; they exchanged some dark humor, and ribald jokes.

***

Sergeant Flynn heard Johnson and Romano's footsteps as they approached the top of the stairway. He had been eagerly awaiting their return and bellowed, "All right boys get your asses in here. I want to see what kind of goodies you brought back. You're wasting time, bring it in."

Mike was surprised at the relaxed tone of Flynn's commands. Johnson laughingly answered, "We ran all the way Boss and we're tired. Keep your shirt on", as they entered the Squad Room. Mike hoped that someday he could enjoy the close working relationship the Squad shared.

"In my office and let's see what we have," Flynn ordered as he almost ripped the envelopes from Johnson's hand.

As he eagerly opened each envelope, Flynn separated its contents and placed them in different piles on his desk. Two piles of Crime scene photos 5 x 7 and 11 x 14. Photos of the tire treads were also stacked in two separated piles of the same sizes. There was an additional 11 x 14 enlargement of the cuts on one of the tires; an arrow was pasted on the photo to highlight those cuts. Included also was a copy of the results of the victim's fingerprint identification. Most importantly there were several DD-5's reporting the findings, and conclusions by the responding CSU detectives. Finally he stacked copies of the vouchers prepared by Crime Scene for the evidence they had gathered and catalogued.

Looking up at the two men standing before him, Flynn ordered, to no one in particular, "Someone get Stattler in here, he's the case officer."

Mike went to fetch Detective Stattler and returned with him. "Romano says there are some good results Sarge. I'm here and ready to do some real work. My DD-5's are up to date as of now. What have we got?"

"First we have the victim positively identified," Flynn said as he handed the victim's rap sheet to Stattler. "He took two hits for bookmaking when he was twenty two years old. He's been clean since. His listed occupation when he was last collared was as a butcher. His last recorded place of employment was Fucini Meat Packing Company, located somewhere on Duncan Ave. in Jersey City. That's something to work on. Somebody find out all you can about the place."

Pushing the blowup of the tire track in Stattler's direction, Flynn continued, "Looks like Romano here, was right on the mark. Crime scene says the left rear tire on the Bronco should be easy to recognize if we ever find the truck. The manufacturer and type of the tires are now confirmed and on paper."

Flynn was on a roll, he shouted towards the main room, "James, call the Medical Examiner's Office and try to get me a verbal on the caliber of the rounds that were used. Anything they will tell you, I want to know."

Mike heard Jim Jim talking to himself as he walked from the coffee area to his desk.

Flynn then turned his attention to Romano, "Officer Romano, Mike, we're about finished here and it's almost end of tour, you can hang out here or go back downstairs. You've done a terrific job. Joe or I will keep you informed as the case progresses. You've earned the right to know. Maybe someday, you can serve in the squad. You have enough time on the job. Don't you?"

"Yes Sarge, ten years in Manhattan, split in two commands before coming here. Thanks for including me in this. There's only twenty minutes before my tour ends, I'll sit here and sip some coffee if it's OK."

"Fine Mike, you can sit in my squad room anytime."

CHAPTER FOUR

It was 1:40 p.m. when the black Ford Bronco driven by a man known as "Baggs", a collector for an organized crime group, pulled up to the neatly appointed house at 250 Fifth Street in Bayonne New Jersey. Baggs worked for Johnnie "Eyes" Sanducci. The name Baggs, "With two g's", he proudly announced to every new person that he did business with, stuck because that's what he collected, bags of money from the various Sanducci Family enterprises. Baggs thought that his nickname being associated with his collection activity was fitting, his dark sense of humor showed when he said, "With two g's", adding to his mystique and of course as far as anyone knew, the nickname was never written down. Only the Sanducci's and their inner circle knew Baggs' real name and it was a closely guarded secret. Baggs was a valuable asset for the Sanducci's. Sometimes he was called upon to perform other necessary tasks and today was one of those days.

"Eyes" Sanducci was the Bayonne capo for the Sanducci crime family. He was Victor Sanducci's son and heir apparent. Johnnie earned his nickname because of his ability to use his steel gray eyes to drill into any adversary brought before him for any reason. The person would get completely unnerved and always bend to Johnnie's will. Once during the questioning of an errant member of his crew, one of his men commented that Johnnie's eyes could chill a man like those of a hungry timber wolf staring at cornered prey and gave Victor the moniker, Johnnie Eyes. The name stuck.

Baggs leisurely left his vehicle and walked up to the front door of the neat little house. To any passerby, Baggs appeared to be about thirty years old; average in height with dark neatly cropped hair, and would not stand out in a crowd. Today, he was wearing a dark waist length leather jacket and dark grey pants. Under his left arm, unnoticed by almost everyone, hung a .38

caliber Colt Diamondback revolver with a 2 ½" barrel and it was loaded with 158 grain jacketed hollow point rounds. Baggs was there on business; he glanced at his wristwatch and rang the doorbell.

Paul Capria smiled as he opened the door. "Hey, good to see you Baggs. You're a little early. You usually don't get here before six. What's up?"

"Nothing special, just picking up for Eyes as usual. You got everything ready? How's your lovely wife, Camille?"

"She's away at her sister's. I've been living the bachelor life the last few days; she's due back next Wednesday. Thanks for asking."

"That's good. It makes today's job a little easier."

"What do you mean? We got something to do? Nobody told me at the meat plant."

"Yeah we do. Rocco asked me to pick you up and bring you to his house on Staten Island. Some of the boys are there, maybe even Sam Costello, you know, 'Capo di tutti capi', from New York and he wants to talk over some business. With the wife away, you don't have to rush back. Maybe we can play a little poker later and then somebody can bring you home."

Rocco Lucelli was Sanducci's right hand man and ran most of his boss' enterprises. Baggs was Rocco's cousin, thus giving him a unique position in the organization, close to the men at the top.

"That sounds good Baggs. Let me get your package and we can go."

Paul retreated into a small room just off his kitchen. As he opened his safe, he wondered if anyone knew his visitor's real name. Baggs heard a metal door clang shut. For no particular reason Paul shouted, "By the way, there's over thirty grand here. It was a good week."

Baggs smiled and silently accepted the folded and banded brown paper bag that was handed to him and shuffled it from hand to hand as if testing the weight. After stuffing the bag into his jacket pocket, he walked toward the front door of the house with Paul following closely behind him.

Outside, after Paul locked his front door, Baggs motioned for him to lead the way to the Bronco. "The doors are unlocked." As they reached the truck, Baggs walked to the passenger side and while tossing the keys to Paul, saying, "You drive; I'm a little tired today. I had too much party last night. Take the Goethals Bridge and then swing onto 440 towards the golf course, get off at Bloomingdale Road. Thanks"

"Fine Baggs, you got it. Some poker is just what I need right now, especially with my wife out of town. She'll never know, my Camille frowns on my gambling you know."

As the two men climbed into the truck, Baggs causally threw the collection money package into the rear seat. When Paul pulled away from the curb, Baggs turned on the radio and searched the dial for an Italian station. Finding one, he turned down the volume, slouched down with his head back and appeared relaxed. He was not; he was planning Paul's demise.

Once on the Island, when the Bronco swung off the Staten Island Expressway and entered the West Shore Expressway, Baggs opened his eyes, looked around and waited about three minutes, then spoke for the first time since leaving Paul's house. "Paulie, do me a favor will you?"

"Sure Baggs. What's up?"

"Well, I'm sitting here with my head back and I think I hear a thump in the left rear tire. Soon as you get a chance, pull over on the shoulder, I want to get out and look at it. Maybe something's stuck in the tire or there's a bubble in it. I hope nothing's wrong because changing a tire on this thing is a big pain in the ass, but if I have to, I may need your help. Less chance of either of us getting greasy and dirty before we get to Rocco's, it's better to have two men handle the spare if needed. The last time I changed a flat on this thing, I had to hug the wheel to lift it because it's so heavy and got filthy. Thanks"

As they approached the area near Clay Pit Pond Park, Baggs said, “Paul, keep on the right side of the road, the shoulder is wider there. Thanks.”

When Paul changed lanes, Baggs announced, “You can stop here. I want to get out and look at the tire now.”

“Sure, but can’t it wait until we get to Rocco’s? We should be close now, right? And it’s starting to rain too.”

“Yeah it can, but Rocco won’t want to wait for us to look at my tires. Once we pull up, he’ll want to quickly get business over with so we can then sit down to play cards, probably Poker. You don’t know him like I do, so stop now.”

The slight change in the tone of Baggs response, made Paul nervous on two counts’, first, he knew that Baggs was related to the boss in some manner, and secondly, nobody seemed to know Baggs real name. He knew there had to be a heavy reason for that little fact. Paul quickly answered, “Sure thing”, as he stopped the vehicle.

Baggs got out of his truck and went directly to the left rear of the vehicle, away from the roadway and crouched down as if looking at the tire.

“Holy shit, I don’t believe this”, Baggs shouted as he reached under his jacket and released the lock on his shoulder holster while remaining near the rear of the truck. Baggs had a job to do and the faster he did it, the faster he could disappear from any possible prying eyes.

Paul had heard the expletive and began exiting the driver’s door as Baggs continued shouting, “Paulie, get out here and look at this thing. I don’t believe what’s in this tire.”

Hearing the excitement in Baggs’ voice relieved some of the stress that Paul had felt just seconds before when Baggs ordered him to stop. Paul jumped out of the truck and quickly moved around next to Baggs; Paul was beginning to relax again. “What the hell is it Baggs?”

Baggs, being a good actor, knew how to play people. It was a tool of his trade and he had developed it to a fine art. He responded, "Not much. I'm gonna take care of the problem now, but I wanted your opinion on it."

"What is it Baggs? Find out what the problem is?" Paul asked, getting nervous again.

In a flash, Baggs drew his Colt and he answered, "Just you, Paulie. You're a greedy little man who has been steeling his boss' money for months. Rocco tells me that you hit him for about twelve grand a month. You know the penalty. What do you think I should do?"

Paul's eyes went wide in disbelief. He thought, *how could they know?* Before he could say anything, Baggs leveled the gun and quickly fired three times. Paul died instantly, falling to the ground with his eyes and mouth wide opened.

Cold as ice on a frozen pond, Baggs, holstered his weapon and climbed back into his truck. In an instant, he had the Bronco in gear and rapidly drove from the scene through the adjacent open field, towards Clay Pit Pond State Park. Baggs only intent was to make a quick getaway and leave his handy work behind as a message to anyone thinking of stealing the Boss's money, he never noticed the Chevy backing up on the shoulder of the expressway.

***

Three hours had passed since Baggs had left Paul Capria lying dead on the shoulder of the expressway. With the black Bronco safely tucked away, Baggs was in his Blue Lincoln and he was on his way to deliver his collection "bags" to his boss, "Johnny Eyes", arriving at Eyes place about 5:30P.M..

Always careful in case he was being watched, Baggs parked about one hundred feet away from his destination. He walked to the house, leisurely smoking a cigarette as he approached, giving himself time to observe his surroundings before reaching Sanducci's home. The house was well constructed with a tan, glazed brick exterior. It was the center house on the end of a cul-de-sac with a high brick wall surrounding the entire home. On the right side of the entrance, reminiscent of an Italian villa and always present in the front of homes belonging to this group, was a statue of the Virgin Mary. Further to the right, were a wide driveway and a detached garage. Between the house and the garage was an ornate iron gate that was usually locked, today it wasn't. Baggs went thru the gate, closing it behind him. The rear yard had an in ground pool, a cabana, an outdoor grill and a very ornate stone patio. Stationed around the pool were several lounges. Near the grill was an enormous marble dining table surrounded by expensively ornate wrought iron chairs with flowered cushions. In the far two corners of the patio were enough tables and chairs to seat at least twenty people. The rear door to the house had a small entrance portico that any home owner would envy. Baggs walked up to the door and rang the bell. He was greeted by his cousin, Rocco Lucelli, Johnny's right hand man.

"Baggs, we are extremely pleased to see you. Did you see Paul today?"

"Yeah, Rocco, I collected your envelope and spoke to him too. He won't steal anymore. The results will probably be in the Staten Island Advance tomorrow."

"Good work Baggs. Nice and clean I hope? I'll let you deliver your collection directly to the boss. He's here you know."

"Who?"

"Banducci and the Don, Mr. Costello"

Baggs expressed surprise, "Wow, something big going on?"

"Not especially. They're in the game room. Come on, let's go." Baggs followed Rocco into the interior of the well-appointed home.

When Baggs entered the game room, he once again admired its size and décor. The walls were covered with warm maroon moiré wallpaper. One wall was lined with full bookshelves and contained a second entrance to the room that had two mahogany pocket doors. The rooms furnishings included two octagonal professional looking card tables, a full size slate topped pool table covered with the deepest green colored felt Baggs had ever seen, complete with heavy wooden legs and webbed pouches under each pocket. Hanging just 30 inches above the table was a long four shade lighting fixture, complete with, what were probably genuine Tiffinay shades. Behind the card tables were racks of cue sticks. On the far wall was a very well stocked wet bar behind which hung a very good hand painted copy of Francisco Goya's, The Naked Maja. There were also two leather covered sofas and four large matching leather smoking chairs. The chairs were occupied.

Rocco spoke first, "Baggs, this is Mr. Costello from New York City," as he pointed to the man. One by one Rocco continued pointing to the remaining men, "Of course, you know Johnny and his father, Victor."

Baggs nodded and said, "My pleasure Sir", to each man as he was introduced.

Eyes indicated the empty chair, "Please, have a seat Baggs. You can give your package to Rocco, thank you." Baggs did as he was told. Johnny Eyes continued, "We have come to value your services to our organization. You always do what is asked of you without hesitation which brings us to today. We hope today's assignment went off without any problems. Yes?"

"No problem at all sir. You should read about it in tomorrow's newspaper."

"I'm happy to hear that. You left nothing behind that can be used against you?"

Baggs smiled and responded, "Nothing. I'm always careful. My vehicle is safely stored and as usual I only carry a revolver, no shell casings, you know."

Victor was the next to speak, "Well now, that's finished, if you have some time, we would like you to join us for some drinks and a game of poker."

Baggs was not comfortable lingering in a home owned by someone of Victor's stature but he knew better than to refuse the invitation. "It would be my pleasure, thank you."

CHAPTER FIVE

Returning to his command the following day, just before roll call Mike ran into an old friend, Jerry Sullivan.

Jerry, usually called Sully, had been in Romano's Police Academy class. After graduation, both men were assigned to the 32nd Precinct in Harlem. They saw each other occasionally whenever their tours overlapped during their first three years on the job. Mike was transferred to the Midtown South during his sixth year in service. He had no idea what happened to Jerry after he left the Three Two, they had lost touch.

"Yeah, Jerry, I had no idea that you worked here in the Two-Three. It's such a small command, I thought I knew everybody. But, hey, I also had no idea that working on The Island would be as exciting as it was yesterday."

"Mike, I got transferred in yesterday from the Nine Oh (90) in Brooklyn. It looks like they put you and me in the same chart (charts were the work schedule of officers allowing overlapped tours as different working schedules ended and began). How about that? I got here a little early today and the place was buzzing about your little encounter yesterday. We have some time, tell me all about it."

Mike gave an account of the previous day's events to his old friend.

"Do you think they'll ever find the shooter?"

"I hope that they will, considering that Sergeant Flynn was happy with my input. It would give me some brownie points with the Borough Command for sure."

"Good luck Mike. Hope it works out for you. Let's get inside; roll call is in ten minutes, we'll have just enough time to suit up."

***

The two friends descended from the third floor locker room and joined the other cops loosely assembled in the small muster room that was opposite the desk. Jerry whispered to his old friend, "Where did they get this collection of chairs, at a rummage sale?"

Mike smiled and replied, "I have no idea, and they were here when I got here. Frankly, I think it gives the place flavor, especially that one in the corner. Maybe George Washington sat on it."

Sergeant Hogan entered the room and announced, "Roll call everyone. Listen up." After assigning teams to four sector cars, Hogan continued, "Romano, since you have no steady partner, team up with the new man, Sullivan. You guys have RMP (radio motor patrol) 1919, Sector Frank, Arden Heights. Special attention is required at PS 42 on Genesee Ave. The people are complaining about rowdy kids there. Handle it." Hogan began walking out of the room as he said, "Squad dismissed. Get out there."

Mike turned to Jerry and said, "You get a portable, I'll find the car and meet you outside."

"Only one? In the real world we each carried a portable. What gives?"

"Here, in this command, we're so small and there aren't too many heavy jobs, so when appropriate, we usually back up other teams. Teams are never separated on a job, so we need only one portable. Besides, the command doesn't have that many radios and they hold some back for a foot post once in a while and an occasional scooter man."

The previous day's adrenalin rush was wearing off and Mike was again thinking about his children and the pending divorce. He was only mildly happy about seeing an old friend and wished to be alone. Mike anticipated that Sully would probably spend the entire tour exchanging updates on how life has been since they last saw each other. He really was not in the mood for small talk and was preoccupied with a scheduled meeting with his attorney the following morning.

When Sully found car 1919, Mike was already sitting in the driver's seat with the engine running. As Jerry opened the passenger door Mike spoke, "You act as recorder for this half of the tour so you can look around as we drive and get to know the command. Besides, driving relaxes me and I've been a little tense lately."

"Sure thing Mike, it's no problem at all."

Mike put the car into gear and they drove off. Mike could have gone north by taking Amboy Road from the station house, but instead chose to take the long way to their sector by proceeding along Arthur Kill Road allowing him to drive past the entrance to Clay Pit Pond Park. Even though it was unlikely, he hoped to possibly get a glimpse of the black Bronco from the day before. Sully noticed the leisurely drive and asked, "I know that I'm not familiar with the precinct, but isn't Amboy Road a direct route to Sector Frank? Are you hoping to find that Bronco?"

"Yeah, you never know, anyway, Arden Avenue intersects with Arthur Kill; we can take it to our sector." As Mike drove, he gave thought to mentioning his divorce before Sully asked how he was doing. He decided to put it out there and caution his old friend not to mention it again. "Sully, before you ask or find out, I want to mention that I'm currently involved in divorcing my wife."

Sully was surprised and only said, "Oh, I didn't know. How could I, I just got here? Sorry to hear that. It must be hard."

"Yeah it is. I'm renting a garden apartment over in Westerleigh. My two kids are with their mother, the whore, until our house is sold. I don't know what's going to happen then. So if I get testy with you, don't take it personal. Oh, and please don't ask about, it ever. I caught her dirty and I'm kind of touchy about the whole thing."

"You got it my friend. Enough said. Now will you show me where the shooting happened?"

"Sure, I want to look around in the park anyway."

Mike drove at a leisurely pace along Arthur Kill road towards Clay Pit Pond Road. Even though it officially had a name, it was nothing more than a gravel road that ran into the park just north of Sharrot's Road. As they rode, Sully took in the scenery. On the left were scattered old dirt roads winding through thickets and old trees towards the waterfront of Arthur Kill. On the right side of the road were a few homes and small businesses.

Sully remarked, “Gee Romano, I never saw this part of The Island. It’s like being out in the country. From here a person could forget that he was in New York City.”

“Yeah, it’s not like Manhattan or the Bronx.” Mike slowed down, “Here we are, the gravel road up ahead,” as he turned into the park. “I don’t know if we can get to where the Bronco roared into this place yesterday or if I can even find the road I was on with Sergeant. Flynn and the Crime Scene guys, but I’m gonna try.”

Sully asked, “If we can’t find the road where you were yesterday, maybe we can access it from the West Shore. Will that help? What are you looking for anyway?”

Mike was in his hunting mode, “Anything I can find that doesn’t belong here.” Sully remained silent and just enjoyed the ride.

After using his blue and white Dodge patrol vehicle like a Jeep for twenty minutes, almost getting stuck twice and executing several broken u-turns, Mike drove back onto the pavement of Arthur Kill Road without satisfying his curiosity. When he straightened out their car, Mike stepped down on the gas pedal and said, “Let’s get to our sector; I wasted enough time here with nothing to show for it.”

***

Romano drove directly to Genesee Avenue and PS 42. Stopping at the intersection of Genesee and Wainwright Avenues, the team could see approximately eight to ten young people spread out on the wide sidewalk near the corner of Richmond Avenue. There was a car parked at the curb with its radio blasting and a boom box on the sidewalk playing the same station. The kids were shouting and singing. Mike now understood why the homeowners complained to the command. If he lived there, he would find it annoying too, yet it was only 4:20 p.m., Sully asked, “Guess that’s the disorderly group people are bitching about. We are gonna move them, right?"

"Yeah Sully, we are but it's early, first we ask them to tone it down. If they don't, we come back later, change tactics and move them if we have to."

Mike rolled down to the corner. One of the young people, a male who appeared to be no more than nineteen or twenty years old, was leaning against the booming car as Mike stopped next to it.

The kid walked to the front of his car and shouted, "What did we do officers?"

Sully being on the curb side answered, "You're playing your radios too loud. The neighbors are complaining. Would you guys please lower the volume?"

The young guy puffed up and answered, "No. We like it that way, you can't make us." The volume on the boom box sitting on the ground was lowered by a pretty blonde girl. The kid shouted to the girl, "Little pussy, just like a girl, afraid of the cops." Three of the other kids quietly began walking away.

Mike thought of his daughter, Anne, when he heard the girl berated by the young punk and thought, *if I hear of any kid talking to my daughter like that, I'm gonna bust his ass,* and immediately reacted. Mike exited the RMP and walked over to the boy, grabbed his shirt and told him, "Listen young man, first do not back talk to any police officer at any time, second, never speak to a young woman like that again, especially in front of me and third, we will be back and if you and your music is still annoying the neighborhood residents, we will issue summonses to those who have ID and lock up those who don't." As Mike released the grip on the boy's shirt, he asked," Do you understand?"

The kid's eyes were big as saucers, as he answered, "Yes Sir." Romano got the reaction he was going for and someone had picked up the boom box too. Mike turned without looking at any of the kids, and called, "Ok Sully, let's go. We'll come back later."

The kids had moved away from the corner when Sully said, "Mike, I didn't know that Island kids are so much like the kids from the Bronx. I never expected a smart mouth."

"Usually they're not, that young smart ass must think he's somebody. Maybe we'll find out later, if he's still here.

Mike put the car into gear, turned right onto Richmond Avenue and drove to Hylan Blvd. again turning right, continuing to the intersection of Arden Road, and made yet another right up to Annadale Road where he once more turned right to the train station of the Staten Island Rapid Transit.

Mike turned to his partner, "There's another smart mouth that hangs out in the train station and this little square, his name is Michael Guggalarie. He's younger then the guy on Genesee but as big a smart ass. Rumor has it that he runs up behind old ladies, bumps into them causing them to drop packages and sometimes their pocketbooks. He then dutifully helps them pick everything up, after looting their pocketbooks of valuables. I don't like him and want to put him away but he's under sixteen years old. Being young, he would go to kiddy court, so I watch him, waiting until he's sixteen, then he's mine. If we see him, I'll introduce you."

"What's he look like, maybe I can help you spot him?" answered Sully.

"Close cut blonde hair, about five feet nine with a decent build, and except for the smart ass grin when cops talk to him, he looks like an altar boy" responded Mike. The team circled the area twice before Romano announced, "It's not time for our meal break yet, but I'd like to stop at the luncheonette next to the garden shop for some coffee if you don't mind. Sometimes I get a line on Guggalarie from time to time, the owner; Leona is not a fan of the kid because sometimes he breaks her balls. Maybe she has an idea as to his whereabouts. Okay?"

""Sure Mike, coffee sounds good and if we find the kid, now I know what he looks like. Lead on."

Romano stopped in front of the luncheonette and went inside. Sully remained in the vehicle to monitor the radio. He observed Mike hold up two fingers and speak with a woman he thought to be Leona while a young girl filled two containers from a large coffee urn. The girl slid the two coffees and a small paper bag toward Mike. Romano thanked Leona, picked up the items and rejoined Sully in the car.

"Well Sully, she hasn't seen him today at all. It's just our luck. Here's a coffee for you." He put the bag on the seat between them saying, "Cream and sugar are inside if you use them, I take mine straight."

Sully gingerly balanced his container on the radio console, carefully removed the plastic lid then mixed in cream and sugar. He replaced the top, shook the container and took a taste, "It's real good. Thanks." Sully took a second drink from his cup then asked, "Know her well? Is she a special friend?"

"Yes, she is. She's been through a divorce too and we talk sometimes, it helps me cope. Please don't ask any more personal questions. OK?"

The team spent the next three hours driving around making small talk and handled only two calls for service, a past burglary and an ambulance call, known in the job as an aided case. Sully handled the paperwork for both calls. Their meal hour was scheduled for 2000 hours, 8 p.m., it was now 7:45 p.m. and almost dark when the radio crackled, "Two Three Frank, disorderly group at Genesee and Richmond, Please respond and acknowledge, K."

Sully answered, "Two Three Frank on the way Central, will check and advise, K"

Sully looked at Mike as he accelerated; he was smiling as he said; "Now we can have some fun with those kids if they're still there. It has to be them."

Mike approached Genesee from Wainwright Ave. stopping at the corner. Genesee dropped down an incline toward Richmond Ave. affording the team a clear view of the group in question. Mike turned to his partner, "It's them Sully, and smart mouth is there too, now it get's to be fun. When I tell you, open your car door and hit the lights and sirens. Just be careful not to let go of the door, we don't want to lose it."

“"What the hell are you going to do?'

"Drive down the sidewalk and clear the corner. Ready?" he asked as he first extinguished the headlights and drove the RMP onto the sidewalk, the kids never noticed them.

Romano headed down the sidewalk. Halfway down, the group noticed the car. Mike turned on the headlights and shouted, "Now Sully, hit it and open the door." The roof rack jumped to life and the electronic siren wailed while Sully held his door open as best he could without losing his grip on it.

The kids scattered like mice being chased by a cat, shouting, "What the hell?? It's cops! They're crazy!"

As the team reached the corner, Mike blocked the smart mouth's car. He was just getting ready to drive off. Sully stated, "Mike, you're right, this is fun but I still think you're nuts." Romano and Sully exited their car, first turning off the siren and leaving the flashing lights on and walked over to the kid.

"Sully, it's time to get your feet wet and write this young man a summons," stated Mike, not giving Sully a chance to back off. He turned his attention to the young man, "Young fella, will you please find your driver's license, car registration and insurance ID and hand it all to my partner. While you're doing that, explain to us why you think that you can smart ass the police."

The kid wasn't happy and moved rather slow as he dug out all the items requested by Mike. He asked," What are you guys doing, writing me a summons, for what?"

Romano ignored him and looked inside the guy's car. After a quick peek, he stated, "Well, you were in the driver's seat with the engine running and there are open beer cans in the back seat. That's one summons, disorderly conduct is another. Keep talking and not answering my question and we'll keep writing. Maybe we can even impound the car."

"Those cans are all empty, there's no beer in them officer, the kid stammered.

Mike was on a roll and having fun and forgetting his own problems. He continued, "Now be careful how you answer this question, when did you drink them, while you were driving or here on the corner?"

The guy was beginning to rock back and forth a little. Mike had him. Sully was taking it all in. "No, I didn't drink them while I was driving. They're mostly from yesterday, Sir."

"What about the others, the ones not mostly?" Mike asked.

He answered, "Maybe I drank one or two of them here. But nobody saw me though; I stayed near my car or sat inside it."

Mike was quick, "Partner, a public beer summons is in order and a disorderly conduct summons too for causing public alarm, after all we got a radio run on this little group." Officer Romano was not finished yet, he still wanted his first question answered and again asked, "Once again, why do you think you can badmouth cops and get away with it? What would your Dad say about it?"

Now it was this kid's turn to smile, "He would probably laugh and get me a good lawyer. My uncle is Carlo Banducci, know the name officer?"

In his head, Mike heard the beat of wings, he hadn't thought about his sister-in-laws boyfriend, Rocco Banducci since his divorce started. He thought, *careful how you answer that question Mike, your friend Rocco, is Carlo's nephew and the less people who are aware of your relationship, the better.* "Yeah, he's supposed to be a big tough guy in Manhattan. So what? Am I supposed to be nervous?"

"Maybe you should think about it."

Mike was now getting angry, "My name is Michael Romano and that's Jerry Sullivan, have your Daddy and uncle call me if they want to. I'll be happy to speak to them about your attitude." Sully was now quietly shaking his head and finishing the summonses.

Jerry Sullivan walked up to his partner, tapped him on the shoulder and said, "Mike, the kid here is John Pascal, he's nineteen years old and lives on Arbutus Avenue. The car's his father's, and his name is also John." Picking up some of Mike's attitude, Sully then handed the summonses and all his identification back to the kid with a warning, "We don't care who your family is, and don't come back here. Got it?"

The two cops waited until Pascal drove off and the corner was clear before they called the dispatcher. Sully called the job in, "Two Three sector Frank to central, K."

"Go Frank," was the quick response.

'The disorderly group on Genesee is ten-ninety six condition corrected, summonses issued. Frank requests ten-sixty two, meal, K"

Central responded as expected, "Ten-four, Two Three Frank, ten-sixty two."

The team took their meal at the Rock Dove Diner at the intersection of Arthur Kill and Richmond. During the meal, Sully asked, "Mike, aren't you worried about the kid's family? I know they're not gonna shoot us, but maybe they know a crooked politician and can give us trouble."

Mike gave a slight smile and answered, "Not really Sully. I've known wise guys my whole life and they don't like to bring attention to themselves over minor crap like their kids getting a summons. They have plenty of money to just pay the fine. The old man may even slap Mr. Smart Mouth for shooting off his face and bringing his family name into the fray, so, no I'm not worried."

***

Two Three sector Frank returned to their patrol duties by 9:00 p.m. with Sully taking the wheel. Romano and Sully spent most of the tour looking for Michael Guggalarie without any results. Mike wrote a red light summons, recorded two past burglaries and made a mental note to check those complaints the following day to see if Detectives responded to take finger prints.

By midnight, Sully parked their patrol car across from the station house. Without having police work to do, Mike began falling back into a funk over his pending divorce and his appointment with his attorney in the morning. He shook hands with his old friend, absent mindedly saying, "It was nice working with you Sully, maybe they'll hook us up together again. Sorry that

I wasn't better company." He wanted to be alone with his thoughts and rushed inside to change into civies.

***

Back in his apartment, Mike walked into the small kitchen, reached into the refrigerator and withdrew his daily tonic, a quart bottle of Dewars White Label. After pouring a healthy four fingers into a glass, he took a bracing mouthful of the amber liquid and retreated to the kitchen table to look over his divorce papers. He thought *how could this happen to me? I'm a caring, loving father and was always faithful to Betty. Cops have plenty of opportunity to stray with other women and I ignored every chance. I loved Betty and was always a good provider. Did this happen because she went to work in the city? Would she have cheated eventually? Did I cause this? What are the kids gonna do now without their father to guide them?* He took another drink and tried to concentrate on the seemingly endless pile of papers that lay before him, net worth statement, bank statements, joint charge accounts, copies of the children's birth certificates, copy of their marriage license, list of past residences, his monthly expenses, income tax filings, etc. Mike knew that he would have to have everything ready when he met with his attorney and forced himself to complete everything.

Mike's head felt like it was overstuffed with negative thoughts and he wished he was back on patrol or even better, back with Sergeant Flynn and his men working on yesterday's shooting, then he wouldn't have time to wallow in self-pity. He never remembered falling asleep.

Mike opened his eyes and found himself with his head on his arms and still sitting at the table. He shook the sleep out of his eyes and looked at his wristwatch, it was 9:00 a.m. and he was to meet with his attorney, Arthur Slotnick at 10:00 a.m. He quickly gathered all the papers into his briefcase and hurried into the bathroom to shave and shower.

***

Mike arrived at Arthur's office on time. Arthur spoke first, "Officer Romano, I'm pleased to see you. Would you like some coffee and piece of cake, you look tired?" Arthur always had coffee and cake in his office. The man loved to snack, it showed, he was almost as portly as William Howard Taft.

"Yes Mr. Slotnick, I would. I was up late going over all my paper work and didn't have a chance for breakfast. Thank you"

"Let me have your papers and you can help yourself from the server in the corner."

Romano opened his case, withdrew all his papers and handed then to Arthur, then he helped himself to a coffee and a piece of chocolate cake, saying, "Thank you again. I hope that they're in good order and I didn't make any mistakes."

"Don't worry Mike, that's why you pay me." Arthur took several minutes to look over the papers. He then slid a completed form towards Mike while saying, "Here is the net worth statement that your wife's attorney sent me, and I didn't know that she made more money than you did, but that's a good thing for you in court. I'm going to get you very low child support payments for your children."

Mike answered, "I knew that she made a good salary, bigger than my base pay without overtime, but how does that help me?"

"Well, my plan is that if we can get her to assume the mortgage payment, we'll give her the house and get her to waive any rights to your pension. By law, she's entitled to half because you're married over ten years. After reading her lawyer's demands, I think she's greedy and will go for it. Your salary will pay for your living expenses and hopefully low child support. What do you say?"

Mike was quiet for a moment and then asked, "The children get to stay in the house, right? But can you still put in the papers that no man can stay overnight?"

Slotnick smiled at his client and answered, “Sure I can Michael. We’re done for now. I’ll call you once all the details are worked out. OK?” Arthur rose to shake Mike’s hand and said, “Don’t worry, you’ll be fine.”

Mike felt a little better but still had to force a smile as he shook the attorney’s hand, “Thank you, and hope you’re right. Please hurry, I want to put this ugly stuff behind me as soon as possible. Thanks”

Wanting to be alone with his thoughts after leaving Slotnick’s office, Mike headed for the area of Clay Pit Pond Park and drove around the area for two hours in the hopes that he would spot the Black Bronco he saw two days before. Luck was not with him.

CHAPTER SIX

It was 3:00 p.m. when Mike parked down the block from his command. He would not go on duty until roll call at 3:45 p.m. and went to check on the burglary reports that he took the day before.

Department procedure on the Island decreed that Detectives notify the recording officer or the civilian assistant that's in charge of filing complaint reports if they responded to any past jobs in the command of record. There was no record of any detective visiting his two burglary locations. An idea began to form in his head and he went down to see his commanding officer, Captain Lars Anderson, a white haired, mustached, distinguished looking man.

The door to Larsen's office was open and he was sitting behind his desk. Mike stood in the doorway and knocked. Lars looked up and said, "Officer Romano, you want to see me? Come in."

Mike entered the room and nodded to acknowledge the invitation as he spoke, "Captain, it seems to me that we have more than our share of burglaries in this command. Yesterday, I responded to two residential burglary complaints and personally followed up those reports to see if detectives responded to check the locations for latent prints. Nobody showed up."

Before Romano could continue, Anderson asked, "What are you driving at? Is there something you're trying to tell me?"

"Yes Boss, I'd like you to start a latent print program in the command. Years ago, back when I was in the Three Two, I was a fill in man for the Latent Print Team in that command. It was monitored by my sergeant who was in charge of the Neighborhood Police Team. I don't even know if NPT is an ongoing program now. Anyway, you can look in my personnel folder and verify what I'm saying. I'd like to do it here, if you can arrange it."

The captain was interested. "Tell me how it worked Romano. Did the latent men work regular patrol too?"

Mike was encouraged and because he had no steady partner, he answered, "Yes Captain. Back in the Three Two, everyone patrolled in teams because it was a heavy house. Here, we have an occasional scooter man or a single man RMP carrying shotgun. I'm qualified both with the shotgun and scooter. As a matter of fact, I'm qualified on all Department vehicles. I have no steady partner, so whenever I work, I can work alone and respond to past burglaries. What do you think?"

Anderson asked, "What equipment do you need and where would you get it if I approved your idea?"

The equipment is available from the Latent Print Office in the Two Oh and thru normal Department Requisitions. To do recover latent prints you need, black and white dusting powder, two fine brushes, two feather brushes, wide clear tape to lift the prints and black and white cards to apply the contrasting colored recovered prints onto. The prints would be submitted to Lieutenant. Stonner's office in the Two Oh for identification."

"Ok Romano. Let me think about this for a few days and talk to the Borough Command and I'll let you know. Okay?"

Mike heard his heart thumping or was it the sound of wings in his head. No matter, he was happy that the Captain might make him the latent print man for the command and he thought, *it's a solution to me wanting to be alone with my divorce thoughts and I can catch the bad guys too. Almost like being a Detective. Maybe someday..............*

***

It was now three days, including the day of occurrence, since Mike had come within seconds of witnessing the homicide on the West Shore Expressway. Three days since he had a taste of working in a detective squad with Sergeant. Flynn, Det. Joe Johnson and the squads other members. He thought about that day as he climbed into his work uniform feeling that he found his future calling, working as a NYPD Detective. This was the last tour of his set of four by twelves' and he would stifle his excitement about the possibility of doing latent prints and finish the tour to the best of his ability. Mike went down to wait for roll call.

Sergeant Hogan entered the muster room and announced, “All right everyone, listen up”, and proceeded to assign posts. Mike was assigned to Sector Henry with Henry Capelli. The two men knew each other only in passing, being in different working squads and never exchanged more than a cursory, “Hello, how’s it going” or a nod of the head. Henry Capelli had been in the command for years and seemed well liked by the men. Mike spotted Capelli in the far corner of the muster room and walked over to him. Offering his hand, Mike said, “Mike Romano, we finally meet, I’ve seen you from time to time. You must work a different chart. Guess we overlap sometimes.”

Capelli took Mike’s extended hand in a friendly two handed grip and said, “Henry or Hank, pleased to meet you. Is this your last tour of your set?”

“Yeah Hank it is. You have to put up with me for only one night. Hope you don’t mind. I don’t have a steady partner.”

Capelli replied, “No problem. At least we’re both Italian, right? Maybe we can sit and have a good dinner when we go to meal at twenty hundred hours and I know a great place down on Arthur Kill.”

Mike thought *he seems like a good guy; at least my last tour should be pleasant enough and real food too. Not much of that since this divorce crap started.* He responded with, “I’ll grab a radio; you choose who’s first up and the meal sounds real good.”

After picking up a portable radio, Mike went into the street and found the car he and Hank were assigned to, Hank was already in the driver’s seat. Capelli chuckled and said, “I’m senior man here, and my steady partner, Vinnie, is on vacation, so I drive first. The first half of the tour is always the busiest; you’re my junior, so you do the work.”

Mike preferred to be kept occupied so he didn’t have time to wallow in the quagmire that began a few weeks ago with his cheating wife, so he answered, "You can drive all night if you want, I enjoy being busy."

The first hour of their tour was unremarkable with only one sick call that Sector Henry was required to respond to. Mike recorded all the pertinent information in his memo book and prepared an aided-sick and injured card that he would turn in at end of tour or sooner if they had reason to go in to the station house before that time.

Mike inquired how long Hank was assigned to the Two Three and found out that he was sent directly from the Police Academy just one month short of nine years ago. Hank, in turn, inquired about Mike's past commands and was interested in the fact that Mike had made multiple bribery arrests, both in Harlem and Midtown. He asked Mike for all the details and Mike, feeling a kinship with his new acquaintance, told him about each collar.

The two men chatted amiably for several hours about the usual, working without a contract, the un-appreciating and demanding public, with a cop story thrown in here and there. Michael Romano was enjoying his tour and not thinking about his personal problems.

At five minutes before 8 p.m., their assigned meal hour, Capelli headed for Arthur Kill Road and the vicinity of the Outer Bridge. He turned to Mike, "Romano, Mike, put us 10-62 meal. Give no location unless the dispatcher asks, will you?"

"Sure Hank, but, why the secrecy?"

"We, my friend are going to eat at the Lamplight Restaurant. I promised you a good meal, didn't I?"

"You know, I think I've seen it but never paid it any attention. Is it on the shit list with the job?"

"Yeah it is. The Borough claims they give discount meals to cops. I never asked for one, so who cares. Do you?"

"Not tonight," was Mike's reply, "I'm hungry."

After getting clearance for their meal hour, Capelli parked the RMP alongside the restaurant and led the way inside. Once inside, the men were guided by the hostess and seated off to the side in a small alcove that afforded a full view of the dining area.

Mike commented, “Very nice but it looks like a cheaters place being out of the way like this. Do you know anything about the place?”

“Yes Mike, I do. The food is terrific and this one is on me. Enjoy.”

“No, Hank. I can afford my own way.”

“I insist. The grapevine tells me that you are going thru a divorce. Allow me to make you feel better, at least tonight. OK?”

Mike was surprised that the man sitting across from him, a man he hardly knew, was up to date on his personal life. He wondered, what else did he know? “Then allow me to leave the tip at least”, was all Romano could say at the moment.

Capelli responded, “Fine, let’s order”, and picked up a menu from the table.

The two men shared a fried calamari appetizer, Mike had Mussels in red sauce and pasta, Hank dined on veal scaloppini and a side of pasta primavera. The two cops drank cokes with their meal.

After the meal Hank left the table to go to the cashier. As Mike stood up to place a generous tip on the table, he looked across the dining room and to his surprise saw the round red face, huge body, and bulbous red head of Dennis Bryan, The Great Pumpkin, his former commander while he was in Midtown South, with an attractive younger woman. His mind raced as he heard the beat of wings in his head, *I didn’t know he lived on the Island. That graft taking son of a bitch is up to his old tricks. I wonder if he’s still with his wife. I wonder if she knows and just tolerates his activities. I’ve got to get his address and watch him. Maybe I’ll still get a chance to burn his ass.* Mike spotted Capelli walking out and carefully, hoping not to be noticed by Bryan, the graft taking, immoral Pumpkin, followed Capelli out and to their car. Hank handed Mike the keys, “You’re up as the operator for the second half of the tour, have fun. By the way what did you think of the meal? You look a little dazed.”

Mike forced thoughts of Bryan out of his head and smiled, “I’m fine and the meal was terrific as promised. Too much food and we still have to work, but thanks for showing me the place. When I start dating again, I'll have to bring a girl there to impress her."

Capelli informed the dispatcher that, "Sector Henry in the Two Three is ten-ninety eight from meal." His transmission was acknowledged as Mike drove away from the restaurant.

Mike's last tour of his set ended without further incident. After signing off duty he again thanked Hank Capelli for the meal and headed home to his apartment. He planned to look for a telephone number to contact Rocco Banducci.

***

Mike walked into his apartment just twenty minutes after he signed out. He didn't even take his usual drink of scotch or remove his off duty weapon from his belt, but began his quest for his friend's contact number at once. After a few minutes of rummaging through every folder and scrap of paper he could find, Mike met with success and breathed a sigh of relief. *I'll keep trying to reach Rocco all day tomorrow until I get him. It's probably too late to call now. What the hell!* Mike thought as he dialed the number. After three rings, the line was picked up; "Hello, who the hell is calling at this hour?" was the less than courteous salutation.

Mike was not expecting that kind of reaction and gasped, "Rocco, I'm sorry to call so late but I saw Bryan today and need to meet with you. It's really important. Can you meet me somewhere, anywhere; I have the next two days off?"

The voice on the other end of the phone took on an immediate friendly tone, "Michael, sorry about your problems with your wife. It came as a surprise to me. Her family naturally is blaming you for the divorce. I'd like to hear your side and of course I'll meet with you. What sort of problem are you having with Bryan now?"

"I'm happy to hear that you can see me. I'm not having any problem with him but would like to discuss some things in person. When is it convenient for you?"

As usual, Rocco was quick, direct and cautious, with his answer, "Tomorrow night at our usual diner, about 7 p.m., OK?"

"It's fine with me and thank you."

"Just remember, you're still family and can always ask for help. Favor for favor. I haven't forgotten how you helped me in the past. See you." The line went dead.

Mike wrote Rocco's number on a small piece of paper and tucked it into his wallet. Naturally he didn't put a name next to it.

After some soul searching and feeling strong after his conversation with Rocco, even though it was late, he telephoned his old house. His daughter Anne must have been sitting next to the phone and picked it up after one ring, "Daddy" she screeched as she heard his voice, "Mom is out and Donnie is asleep. Wait, I'll get him to the phone." Before he could answer, all he heard was a thud of her dropping the receiver and a distant, "Donald, get up Daddy's on the phone and wants to say hello."

Mike heard the phone being grabbed by someone and a shout of, "Daddy, are you coming home?" and winced at the painful question.

"No Donnie, but you, Anne and I can all get together tomorrow. I have off and tomorrow it's a Saturday. What do you say Big Guy?"

"Yeah Dad, I love you and can't wait until tomorrow. What time?"

"Right now, I don't know what time. Please put your sister back on the phone and go back to bed. I love you too kid", Mike responded and wiped his hand across his moist eyes as his mind wandered aimlessly.

His daughter's voice brought Mike to reality. "Daddy, I was listening next to Donnie and heard everything you said. Can you come to the house to get us about 9 o'clock? Is that good?"

Michael Romano, father to two children mustered up a cheery voice and said, "It's a date Sweetie", he was about to lose it any second and added, "I gotta go now, it's late. Daddy loves you both. See you tomorrow."

As Anne responded, "Love you too," he hung up and felt bad about the whole situation.

Mike walked into the small kitchen, ripped his off duty revolver from its holster and almost dropped it on the counter. He took a tall glass, put some ice cubes into it and poured four fingers of golden elixir into it, then dropped onto his bed.

CHAPTER SEVEN

Mike was waiting for his children at exactly 9 o'clock the next morning as they came running out of the house. He could see a figure peering out thru the living room blinds. He knew it was probably Betty and asked the kids after hugs and kisses, "Is your mother home?"

Anne answered, "Yes, she told us to have fun and not come home too late. What are we going to do and where are we going?"

Mike needed time to plan something. "I'm starved, are you guys hungry. How about getting some breakfast first?"

The kids were happy to say yes as Mike started his car. By that time a thought jumped into his head and he asked, "Would you guys like to go to the zoo and then catch a movie?"

In unison they responded, "Yeaa"

Mike headed for the Hylan Diner on Hylan Boulevard and Clove Road. After breakfast it would be a short hop to the small Staten Island Zoo, then into Saint George to the movie house on Bay Street. During breakfast he explained to his kids, as gently as he could, that their parents were no longer in love with each other but still loved both of them. The kids expressed feeling sorry for both of their parents because loving someone made a person feel good. Mike was surprised at their mature attitude and never mentioned it the rest of the day. The visit to the zoo lasted only an hour and the double feature movie ended at 3:30 p.m. After the movie, Mike took his kids for a pizza to stretch out their time together.

It was just about 5 p.m., when Mike drove up to the front of his old residence. Betty was puttering in the yard. His emotions upon seeing her ran the gambit from longing for her soft touch of old to wanting to touch her with his fist and everything in between. He steeled himself against showing any emotion. After he stopped the car, he gave each of his children hugs and kisses, promising that he will always love them and would always be there for them, whenever they needed him. As they expressed their love for him and left the auto, his heart ached so much that he drove off without looking back. In two hours he would meet Rocco Banducci inside the Privateer Diner on Astoria Boulevard in Queens. He headed straight for the Staten Expressway and the VZ Bridge.

***

Mike arrived at the Privateer Diner with time to spare so he went directly into the rear dining area where he had always met with Rocco and ordered a BLT sandwich and a double Dewars on ice then tried to relax while he waited for his friend.

It had been some time since he first met with Rocco Banducci, his sister-in-law's boyfriend, a 'made man' as they say, in the "Mob", who Mike knew as running a toy distribution business. He also remembered when Rocco explained his family's background to him and the fact that he, Rocco, was actually born in Sicily, the birthplace of the Mafia. Mike recalled that it was on that day when Rocco first referred to him as family and explained that someday Mike would understand why.

Mike's mind was churning, *maybe after I explain that I want Bryan's address I'll ask him why he calls me family.* By the time Romano finished reviewing everything he liked about Rocco and disliked about Bryan; he had finished with his sandwich and was sipping his second double scotch. That's when he looked up to see Rocco Banducci standing next to him with his hand extended and a smile on his face. Mike rose up in his seat and shook Rocco's hand while babbling, "Rocco, I was deep in thought and didn't see you come in. Sorry, please sit down and order something, a drink or whatever."

Banducci took a seat opposite his friend and said, "Michael my friend, slow down, we have plenty of time to chat. We haven't seen each other in some time. Since all that divorce crap started, how have you been doing?" The waitress took Rocco's drink order and left.

"Physically, I'm fine, but emotionally, I run from just ok and good to depression and worrying about wasting all those years on a woman who turned against me and what the whole thing is doing to my kids."

Rocco was sympathetic towards his friend, "Mike, I thought you guys were the ideal couple. As far as I know even Kelly didn't know about Betty's extra-curricular activity. It sure put me into shock when I found out. Their family blames you for not giving Betty enough attention and never being around. I know that you are a caring guy, tell me your side."

"It hurts Rocco, but sure I'll tell you what happened. I got home early one night and caught her with a man, her hairdresser, from down where she works. I beat the crap out of him and wanted to beat her too but held back. The next day I found a lawyer and a place to live. He says the kids should stay with her for now until after the divorce is final. That's it in a nutshell."

"Well my boy, you and the children will survive and we will always be friends, no matter what. Now, to what do I owe the after midnight call? You sounded stressed, something about your old adversary, Bryan?"

Mike ordered his third drink and another for Rocco. "Yes, and I'm not too stressed out, I'm coping. But yesterday, I and another cop went into a restaurant and as we were leaving, I spotted Bryan in there. He was with an attractive younger woman. From what I remember, it was not his wife. Several years ago, he was caught cheating with another cop's wife and lost his command on Staten Island over it. Looks like he's doing it again and I still want his ass. You and I don't mix in each other's business, that's why we get along, but he's a hypocritical, graft taking bastard and that's why I dislike him so much."

"Mike, I offered my help to you years ago concerning Bryan and you refused, preferring to handle the man yourself. That's one of the reasons that I respect you so much, you never really cross the line and always maintain your personal moral code. Now, how can I help you?"

"I just want to know if you can raise his address for me and I didn't want to ask you on the phone. Now that I work on the Island, maybe I can watch him on and off duty, and give him more grief."

"Sure my friend, I should be able to get that information, but you can really get your ass in a ringer playing with him. You understand that, don't you?"

"Yeah, I know, but I only want to unnerve him from time to time. I'm not going to do battle with the guy. Will you do it?"

"For you, Mike, sure. Give me a few days and I'll call you with the info. Rocco paused, chuckled and added, "From a pay phone of course. Anything else?"

Mike had downed three double scotches during their conversation and while not intoxicated, had lost some inhibitions and answered, "How should I put this, why do you refer to me as family. We're not related, are we?"

Rocco paused before answering, then smiled and replied, "No Mike, we are not related but we almost were before your divorce thing came up. After all I've been dating Kelly for years and she's Betty's sister. If Kelly and I got married, then you would have been my brother-in-law and that's family."

Mike sensed that Rocco had put him off again and felt that he would not get anything else from him concerning the family thing and let it drop. After some small talk about nothing special, Mike waved for the waitress and the bill. Rocco snapped it from the girls' hand, folded some bills in it and returned the bundle to her before Mike could react. As Rocco stood up to leave, Mike said, "You did it to me again my friend, I wanted to pay the bill. Now I owe you another one."

Rocco patted Mike's arm and added, "You never owe me anything, never, I owe you. Remember the little incident in Midtown? Good night Mike, I'll call you", he said and walked toward the door leaving Mike still sitting at the table. Mike thought, *maybe someday he'll answer my question.*

Mike carefully drove back to his Staten Island apartment and went to bed. The following morning, he woke up late, almost noon and called his children to once again tell them that he loved them. He then settled in to remain at home until he had to go to work Monday for a set of Midnight Tours.

CHAPTER EIGHT

After a rather restful swing (days off between a set of tours), Mike rose early Monday morning, planning to take a nap if possible, before his twelve to eight tour began. After a quick shower and a bowl of Cheerios with milk he decided not to remain in his apartment and went to visit Sergeant Flynn and his men to ask if there was any progress regarding the homicide on the West Shore.

Mike walked through the squad's door at 10 a.m. and almost bumped into Detective James. He couldn't help himself, "Excuse me Jim Jim, sorry. I was lost in thought."

Detective James showed his annoyance and responded with, "Well, if it isn't our star patrol cop. Mike something, isn't it?"

Mike was quick with, "Yeah Jimmy, I have some free time and thought I'd lend a hand." James didn't respond but walked away from Mike as he usually did, mumbling.

Hearing the less than quiet exchange from his desk, Det. Bill Stattler, the case detective, rose from behind his desk, "Romano. Come on over here and we'll bring you up to speed on your case."

Mike hastened over and extended his hand saying, "Thanks, but aren't you the case officer? I just happened to be there when it happened. It's not my case or I would be working in the squad."

"True, but you were a great help and saved us some time the night you were here." As he pointed to a chair next to his desk, Stattler continued, "Flynn is somewhere in the building, so grab a seat."

Mike was pleased that yet another squad detective accepted him the way Joe Johnson did. Trying not to appear overly anxious, he calmly asked "What do you have?"

"We have ballistic reports that confirm several things. First, that the shots were fired from a distance of three to four feet from the victim. Second, the rounds were 38 caliber 158 grain hollow points, real killer rounds. Third, the ballistics show, that judging by the barrel's lands and twist, it was probably a Colt revolver, maybe a Diamondback with a 2 1/2 inch barrel. We need the actual gun to match it to the rounds and convict the shooter, if we ever get him."

Mike didn't wait for Stattler to continue. He quickly asked, "What else is there?"

Stattler responded with, "You're gonna like this. The rounds were matched to three other homicides. Two here on the Island and one in Jersey."

Spontaneously Mike said, "Holy crap, the shooter must be a hit man."

Stattler continued, "The two found here were both body dumps, you know, shot at a different place from where the body was found. One was found under the Goethals Bridge near the water's edge and the second was found somewhere in the old freight yards in the Howland Hook area. The freight yard shooting is three years old and the one from the bridge was two years ago. They happened before I got here and they're both open with no leads. Flynn has the folders in his office just in case we get lucky. The Jersey case has never been solved but the assigned detective requests ballistic reports from open cases from the tri state area and sends them to his department's ballistic unit and the State Troopers for comparison. We need men like that in our department. Right now, you're the only chance we have to nail these down because, from an investigative and prosecutorial prospective, you're an eye witness to the newest one. With the Capria shooting, that's gives us a known total of four from the same gun. One day we may get lucky."

As Romano and Stattler began exchanging theories about where the killer might be from, whether or not it's a man or a woman, Sergeant Flynn walked into the office, "Mike Romano, happy to see you again. What brings you here today?"

"I had some time on my hands today Sarge and I wanted to stop in and see if there was any progress on the case."

"Nice to see that there are actually cops out there that are interested enough to want to solve crimes instead of just riding around in their cars doing as little as possible. Keep it up Romano; you'll make Detective before you know it. I'm sure that Bill filled you in on the latest developments on the highway shooting."

Mike was beginning to feel better than he had in days because of the praise he was receiving; it put his head in a better place, and he answered, "From your mouth to God's ears Sarge, thanks for the compliment."

Flynn responded with a chuckle, "Well Mike, I'm sure God heard our conversation but what He does is his business. We, on the other hand will try to keep you up to date on the progress of the case. Naturally, if we ever solve it, your testimony will be needed. Thank you again."

"Thanks very much Sarge, I appreciate the thought. Is it Ok if I visit from time to time?"

"Mike, I told you before; you can visit and have coffee in my squad room anytime. You're always welcome."

With a smile that went from ear to ear, Mike responded, "Thank you again, but I have some errands to take care of, so I'll excuse myself." He reached out and shook Flynn's hand then left the Squad Room.

***

Being the kind of person that could not leave things that he was interested in take their normal course, Mike headed for the Latent Print Unit and Lieutenant Stonner. He walked into their office announcing the purpose of his visit, "Officer Mike Romano here, is the lieutenant in?"

From across the large room, in the far corner, Lieutenant. Stonner stood up from his desk, "Romano, yes I remember. You borrowed our magnifying glass for your boss about a week ago. How did that all work out?"

"Great. The case is progressing well, but unfortunately, he's not my boss. I was there just for that one tour. I'm a patrol cop in the Two Three, but I have hopes."

Stonner, always friendly to almost everyone he meets answered; "Anyway, what can we do for you? I'm sure you'll make it someday.

Well Lieutenant, I was wondering about supplies for lifting latent prints in the field. Back in the Three Two I learned how to lift prints at burglary scenes and I planted a seed in my commander's ear, Captain Anderson, about making me the latent officer in the Two Three. I told him that I would be able to requisition supplies from the Department Quartermaster or your office. How far out of line was I?"

Stonner smiled as he answered the question, "In my opinion, not out of line at all, but why the request. Most of the busy houses have uniform print units but we never had any on the Island. The Property Squad detectives usually go out and attempt to recover prints on burglaries that they feel merit the time and effort."

Mike continued with, "That's just it Lieutenant, the Two Three has plenty of burglaries every day, sometimes as many as four or five a day. That's a lot for an area that's almost strictly residential. From what I've been able to determine, there has not been any collars in the command in the last two years as a result of latent print identification. I want to change that and right now I have no steady partner so I could spend time at the scene and do a righteous job of recovering prints to the best of my ability."

"That's the kind of initiative I'm talking about," Stonner almost shouted. "Romano, I'll go a step further and call Anderson and recommend that he starts you off the first chance he gets. Right now, let's go over to our supply cabinet and get you the basics. What do you say?"

"There's nothing to say except, yes and thank you." Thirty five minutes later, Mike was sitting in his car with everything he needed to begin recovering latent fingerprints. It had been a fruitful visit to the One Two Oh and Mike was feeling good, and planned to sleep the afternoon away.

***

Romano awoke at 9:30 p.m.. reasonably well rested and hungry. He fixed some stir fried vegetables with beef strips adding his own concoction of soy sauce, hot red peppers and three chopped cloves of fresh garlic into a wok-like frying pan. When he thought that he cooked it enough, he removed it from the heat and let it cool while grabbing a shower and a shave. By 10:30 p.m. Mike was at the Two Three, anxious to store the booty he received from Lieutenant. Stonner.

"Anxious to begin your tour Mike?" asked the desk officer, Sergeant. Walowski, as Mike walked past The Desk.

"Not really Boss, I generally don't like midnight tours but tonight I'm well rested. By some chance, is the captain in?"

"No, but he told me to inform you that he'll be in at 0800 and wants to see you before you leave in the morning. He also wanted me to tell you to please wait for him in case he's a few minutes late. Must be important, is everything alright?"

Mike Romano, aspiring Print Officer was elated, "Sure as hell it is Boss, yup, sure is and thanks."

Before suiting up, Mike went down to the basement to kill some time and work out in the worst station house gym he had ever seen, but it did have a decent set of free weights. He had the room to himself and stayed until 11:30 p.m., climbed to the third floor locker room, took a three minute shower and got ready for roll call.

Sergeant Hogan called the roll, assigning only four patrol car teams. Mike's old friend, Jerry Sullivan, being new to the command, drew the job of guarding a prisoner at Richmond Memorial Hospital. Mike was assigned to RMP 2240, Sector Charlie with Joe Cavaleri, a young, bright kid, just approaching three years on the job. The hospital was in Sector Charlie and Mike told Sully that he would give him a ride to post and pick him up at end of tour.

"That's great Mike, I was going to take my own car, but didn't know if there would be any flak. Now I don't have to worry about that. Thanks. See you outside at your RMP."

"No problem Sully, Mike said and he turned toward Cavaleri, "Joe, you get a portable, I'll grab the car as it comes in and meet both of you outside."

No sooner did Romano get down the station house steps, when RMP 2240 pulled to a stop at the curb. As he exited the driver's side, Hank Capelli shouted, "OK guys, who wants my RMP, bidding starts at one dollar."

Capelli's steady partner, Vinnie Sandi opened the passenger door and laughingly stated, "Hank's wrong, we accept nothing under a sawbuck and no credit cards."

Mike responded with, "You got the five, but have to wait until payday; I spent all my money on my kids. Please toss me the keys."

Capelli flipped the keys to Mike, "Hey Romano, have any good meals lately?"

Still in a good mood from his trip to the Two Three and the expected positive meeting in the morning with the Captain, Mike answered, "Yeah, some guy took me to dinner a few days ago, hope he does it again." Actually, Mike wanted to visit the Lamplight again only to see if Bryan showed up, but he didn't want to go with anybody, especially another cop.

Capelli chuckled and answered, "It's a date Romano, soon as my wife gives me permission to date a man."

After dropping Sully at the hospital, Romano and Cavaleri began their routine patrol.

On a midnight tour, there was little auto traffic in the confines of the command and if they received a call for service, the team could respond almost anywhere within minutes. They expected a quiet night, so Mike decided to do a little exploring within the command and headed for the area around Clay Pit Pond Park.

***

Baggs thought enough time passed since he had his "conversation" with Paul Capria and decided to go check the fuel level in his Bronco. He was in such a hurry to escape the scene and return his truck to its hiding place last Wednesday, that he felt it to his advantage, should he need gasoline, he could slide into New Jersey, fuel up and return under cover of night with very little risk.

Baggs pulled his new blue Lincoln into a dirt road just off Arthur Kill Road in the Charleston section of the Island. The road was just south of the Park and led deep into the wooded area. The big sedan slowly rocked into the abyss, its parking lights being the only illumination to guide it along the winding route. There were several roads that shot off into the darkness, but Baggs knew exactly where to drive, having been there many times in the last two years.

Deep in the wooded area, just about two hundred feet before reaching the water, Baggs reached a large weeded clearing with two old Quonset hut buildings, the smaller one once served as the office of an old freight company that folded over thirty years ago. The larger building had two barn-like doors on both ends that in the past must have housed trucks or served as a warehouse, and now it secreted a killers' truck, Baggs' Black Bronco. Baggs drove his large sedan around to the rear of the building, parked and locked it after removing a three cell flashlight from the truck. He walked to the front doors and used his light to find the almost invisible cover that protected his padlock from both the weather and more importantly, discovery. After lifting the discolored rubber flap, he removed the lock and opened the doors. His truck was, as always, safe and sound. He climbed into the drivers' seat, inserted his key and lit the dashboard. The fuel gage indicated that he was almost on empty. Baggs regretted not gassing up before he visited Paul last week, now he would have to make a quick run into New Jersey just to get gasoline. It was his habit, to lessen his exposure, to always have enough fuel to make his rounds for

Johnnie Eyes quickly and efficiently. On the infrequent occasions that he was asked to “speak to people”, he certainly wanted a full tank. He had made an error last week and vowed that it would not happen again.

Baggs drove out of the building, stopping to close the doors, and headed towards the paved road and the bridge for his quick fuel run in New Jersey. He planned to put his truck back in the Quonset building within forty minutes.

***

It was now 2:00 a.m. and Romano and Cavaleri were slowly headed north on Arthur Kill Road from Richmond Valley Road when Mike spotted a black Ford Bronco swing onto the road about three hundred feet ahead of him. “Holy crap, Joe, is that a Bronco ahead of us? It could be the one from the shooting last week on Wednesday.” Mike’s heart was pounding as he fought an impulse to race ahead with lights and sirens going. He heard thumping in his head, he thought, *Saint Michael, are you with me?*

Joe Cavaleri responded with, “Take it easy Mike, I don’t know, it’s too far away, but we can follow it and pull it over where there’s room, Ok?”

As the RMP passed under one of the few streetlights on Arthur Kill, Baggs, seeing the glow of headlights behind him, looked into his rear view mirror and saw them. Knowing that the cops would stop him at that time of the morning, he slowly increased his speed. As he rounded a turn and was momentarily out of their line of site, Baggs punched the gas and shot ahead.

Moments later Romano rounded the same turn and saw that the Bronco had sped away increasing the distance between them. Mike reached over and hit the roof lights as he mashed down on the gas pedal, “He’s running Joe. If it’s not my Bronco, we got something anyway. Let’s get him.”

When he saw the roof lights behind him, Baggs knew that he had to lose the cops and not lead them to his hideout, so he headed into Clay Pit Pond Park and hoped to lose them there.

Turning off the truck's headlights, Baggs used his flashlight to see whatever he could and drove like a madman to get deep into the park.

"Shit, he's going into Clay Pit, I don't know if we can follow him but I'm gonna try," shouted Mike. As he turned into the park at high speed, the rear of the RMP fish-tailed, wildly spewing gravel everywhere. Mike almost lost control but managed to straighten out. "Joe, do you see anything?" he shouted.

"Not a damn thing. He must know the woods and is driving without lights" was the response. Joe continued, "Do you want me to call for backup?"

Mike was still forging ahead and struggling with the wheel as the car's rear wheels slid sideways and the right wheel began spinning. The car was now stuck. The Bronco had gotten away. Mike hit the steering wheel with his fist, "Shit, it must have been him. It must have been. No, don't call for any help, he obviously knows the area and we'll never find him. Besides, I don't want the guys to laugh seeing us stuck here. It's my fault, so you get behind the wheel and I'll get out and see if we can get going again."

Joe rolled down the car's window and shouted to Mike, "Let me know when I should put it in gear and watch for anything that might snap back at you. I'll be gentle with the gas."

As Joe was speaking, Mike was looking around for something to put under the right wheel. He found some small tree limbs about three inches in diameter and placed several against the wheel. He shouted to his partner, "Joe try going backward very gently to get up on the limbs that I put under the wheel. When I yell for you to stop, please do it at once and I'll put some under the front of the wheel. When I tell you to go, give it hell and hopefully the car will claw its way out of the rut it's in and back onto the gravel." Mike moved away from any spray that might come flying in his direction and said, "Now Joe, gently and slowly." As the RMP slowly mounted the branches, Mike shouted, "Stop." Joe held the car in place.

"How are we doing Mike? Think we'll get out?"

"Yeah, Joe. Give me some time to put some trees in front of the wheel."

Joe responded, "Sure thing Mike. Let me know when I can rip forward."

Mike was getting winded from walking around and dragging timbers back to the car. It took him several minutes to place them where he thought was best. He then moved to the side of the car, looked up at the sky, saying a silent prayer, and told Joe to "Let 'er rip."

The tires squealed in protest a little as the car mounted the timbers and the car bounced back onto the gravel. The two cops verbalized their elation.

Mike, while attempting to brush debris from his uniform, asked Joe to notify the dispatcher that they would be 10-62, out of service for personal necessity. He wanted to return to the station and clean himself up. Joe notified the dispatcher as Mike climbed into the passenger seat, "You drive, I've done enough damage tonight."

Joe responded with, "No problem, it's almost time to switch anyway. How are your hands?"

"Dirty. Take us in, I gotta clean up. Thanks."

***

Having eluded his pursuers, Baggs was sitting in his Bronco, deep in the center of the park with his lights off and the engine silent, thanking his lucky stars. In the early morning, in the quiet of the park, he was able to hear the patrol cops skid off the road. In addition Baggs was also able to hear most of the conversation between his pursuers and knew when they had freed their vehicle. His thoughts were tactical, *now that those two Bozos are gone. They probably went to clean up and hopefully, no other cops will show up. Then, I can slip back, stash the truck, climb into my Lincoln and go home. I'll wait about fifteen or twenty minutes to be safe.* Exactly twenty three minutes later, Baggs locked his truck into the old Quonset building and was tooling along Hylan

Boulevard on his way to his comfortable home in the Arrochar Section of the Island where he lived with his wife and two children.

***

After Mike changed into a clean uniform, he and Joe took their meal hour and returned to patrol. The remainder of their tour was uneventful. While Joe drove, Mike excused himself from idle conversation, feigning fatigue and put his head back as if in a light sleep. Actually, he was thinking about the Black Bronco they had chased earlier and what he could possibly do to find it. After exhausting several scenarios, his next thoughts were about his early morning meeting with Captain Anderson and the possibility of being designated as the latent print man for the command.

Mike and Joe Cavaleri signed off duty at 0800 hours and were not asked for the keys to the RMP they had used for their tour. Joe hung the keys on the appropriated hook next to the front desk and Mike went upstairs to change and get his thoughts together before he met with Anderson. Returning to the station house lobby and seeing the Captain's office door closed, Mike walked up to the desk officer, Lieutenant Delaney and said, "LT, the Captain asked me to see him before I left this morning and his door is closed. Is he here?"

"No Romano. Are you going to wait for him? I expect him within half an hour."

"I'll be downstairs in the lounge Sir. Please have someone notify me when he gets here. Thank you."

"Go ahead, I'll send somebody down to you when he arrives."

Twenty minutes later, Mike was standing before his captain. "Romano, please sit down," Anderson stated as he pointed to the chair next to Mike. "It seems that you have a fan in the Two Oh. Coincidently, I had decided to try you out as a latent print man after we last spoke and was going to talk to you anyway. Lieutenant Stonner phoned yesterday and spoke to me about you.

It seems that you visited his office during your swing and gathered up some equipment that would be necessary to properly do the job. He added that he is very friendly with Sergeant Flynn, whom you also impressed, when you spent last Wednesday with his squad after witnessing the shooting." Anderson paused for effect.

Mike seized the moment to respond, "That's very flattering Sir. Thank you for telling me Sir."

Anderson continued, "Well Romano, I looked in your folder and there was only glowing reports from the Three Two, including your activity concerning latent fingerprints. I did find something that puzzled me though; you began in MTS in uniform, served in plainclothes and ended in uniform before your transfer, yet again only glowing reports. Rather odd. Care to explain the circumstances to me?"

Mike was taken by surprise by the direction of the conversation. His mind raced, *what does Lars know about the Pumpkin? Am I going to lose the print assignment? Did Bryan somehow speak with Lars?* "No Captain, just a little personality conflict. I left the command on a friendly note and even said goodbye to my CO over pizza and stuff the day my transfer was effective." Mike was getting anxious inside. "Is there anything else Sir?"

Anderson smiled as he spoke, "Yes, there is Michael, after your current set of tours; I'm putting you on a scooter chart, one week of days followed by a week of four bys, no more midnight tours. You will be the designated Latent Print Officer for our command. You'll work with a partner if someone needs a partner on any given tour, if not; you'll drive a solo RMP with a shotgun and be assigned to a regular sector. If all sectors are covered with two men, you'll take a scooter and be assigned to an area of patrol. The scooter will keep you mobile so you can respond to past burglaries, your primary function. Recover what latent prints you can and submit them for identification. Eventually collars will be made and our command will look good to the people in One PP. You begin in four more tours. Hope you're pleased and do a good job."

Mike smiled as he replied, “Not to worry Captain, I’ll give it everything I have and thank you.”

CHAPTER NINE

It was 11:00 a.m. when Baggs arrived at the home of his cousin, Rocco Lucelli in Bay Ridge, Brooklyn. Rocco had telephoned him after their meeting in Johnny Eyes home. The Sanducci's had another job for him to do. "Baggs, everyone was pleased the way you handled the Paul Capria thing. Don Costello now has something he would like you to take care of on a regular basis, there's a situation that only you can safely do for us. It involves making a drop at a cop's house every Friday sometime during the night. The guy will leave his blue Buick sedan in front of his garage on the right side of his driveway, his right front fender will be just under some shrubbery, you are expected to place an envelope inside the wheel well, on top of the tire, so it will not be seen by anyone except the man you are leaving it for. The bush hides everything from sight."

Baggs had done many things for his cousin and Johnny, but going to a cop's house unnerved him. He responded, "Rocco, just who is this cop and why do I get the job? I don't really like going up to a cop's house. Can't someone else handle it?"

"Listen, the family takes care of you well because you can be counted on. You are sharp enough not to ever get caught, so do this little thing without complaining. Don Costello himself asked Johnny to have someone trustworthy beyond doubt to do this thing. Johnny chose you."

"I don't like it, but I guess I can do it. Who is this guy anyway that he gets such special treatment?"

His name is Bryan, commander of the Midtown South Precinct in the City that covers 42nd Street porn and the Garment Center. Last year his brother-in-law, Brian Wilkey, took care of his payments, but some cop named Romano killed him. Actually, The Family was getting tired of him. The guy was a child molester and if he wasn't such a high earner, we would have popped him ourselves. That Romano guy did us a favor. Anyway, after that

Bryan walked his command and made most of his own collections, but now, for some unknown reason, he's paranoid and won't touch any money, so we gotta deliver his payoff cash to him. Some of our people say that he's afraid of Romano. He's nuts if you ask me. What can a street cop do to a big boss? But, not to worry, you'll be alright. You never even have to see him."

Baggs was adamant when he answered, "I hope not, it would kill me." To make light of his reluctance, Baggs smiled and added, "Nothing as good as a bad cop is there? What if it rains, the money will get wet?"

"Very funny, wrap the damn thing in plastic. I'm sure you can handle it."

"Yeah Rocco, I'll take care of the drop. Tell Johnny, everything's ok. At least I don't have to talk to him like I did with Paul. I would have trouble with that; I never "had a conversation" with a cop before and don't ever want to. Anyway, is there any problem with this guy Romano that I should know about?"

"Don't worry about Romano, I told you he did us a favor. If you ever run into him, not that you would, leave him alone, he's nobody. Nobody wants that kind of trouble, especially you."

Rocco slapped his cousin on the back and using his birth name said, "Ok Enrico, Baggs' real name, enough of business. How about an early lunch if you have the time? My wife, Lucille, has some fresh baked bread in the kitchen and we have lots of cold cuts, fresh mozzarella and calamari salad. I can open some Chianti or we can go out. If we stay here, it'll be like old times. What do you say?"

"What Italian can turn away fresh baked bread? Not me, let's eat".

The two men ate their fill for about an hour without any mention of Rocco's latest request instead, they reminisced about their childhood. Baggs returned to Staten Island by 2:00 p.m.

***

That very same day, Romano arrived at the Two Three by 11:00 p.m. and was anxious to begin his tour of duty because it would leave only three more to do before he could begin his new assignment as the latent print officer. He was suited up and pacing the muster room within ten minutes. Slowly the men that would work the tour began to file into the room.

Sergeant Hogan entered the room by 11:30 p.m. and slapped his hand down on the small podium to get everyone's attention, "Ok listen for your names and assignments."

Mike looked to his left and saw Sully slide next to him. "Hey Mike, overlapping tours again, maybe we'll work together tonight. Ok by you?"

"Sure Sully, no problem. I have three more to do after this one; maybe we can team up for the rest of my set."

Hogan began, "Listen up people; we have only four cars tonight. Every team is covering double sectors." He assigned the eight men that stood before him and gave Romano and Sullivan sectors George and Henry. Mike turned to his partner and quipped, "Hey, at least we have a great place for coffee and breakfast in our sector. Have you ever eaten at Russo's Diner since you got here?"

Sully replied, "No Mike, I haven't. What's so great about it?"

"Mike chuckled as he answered, "For one thing, the food is excellent and the clientele is varied to say the least. You'll love it. The cops refer to it as The Cantina."

Sully asked, "Is it a Mexican place?"

Mike was having fun, "No, it's like the cantina in the Star Wars movie; full of colorful and sometimes, rather odd people. Something is always happening there." He paused for effect before continuing, "It never closes either. You're gonna love it."

The first half of their tour was almost without any calls for service. The team answered only two false burglar alarms and one lock-out. By 4:00 a.m. they were bored and looking for something to do.

Sully spoke first, “Hey Mike, I heard about the view of the ocean from the top of the old orphanage, Mount Loretto. Could we take a ride there?”

Mike quickly answered, “Sure but we should wait until the sun comes up in the morning, and it’s kind of cool at that time. I go there sometimes when I’m wound up with my divorce problems. It calms me down.

“OK, It’s a date”, Sully chuckled.

The radio dispatcher came on the air, “In the One Two Three, report of a theft at Russo’s Diner. Unit to respond?’

Mike turned to his partner, “That’s our sector Sully, pick it up.”

Sully keyed the mike, “Two Three sector George-Henry, that’s in our sector Central, we will respond and advise, K”

“Now you’re in for a treat,” Romano told his partner as he stepped on the accelerator.

Once inside the diner, Sully turned to his partner and commented on how crowded the place was, “Wow, even back in the city, there’s not this many people in a place at this time of the morning. Is that music coming from the dining room in the rear?”

Mike said, “Yeah, there’s a full dining room and a bar in the back, it’s one great big room. The owners sometimes rent it out for parties and stuff, usually though, its just locals having fun.” Romano walked up to the lunch counter just inside the door and spoke to the girl at the grill who stood about 5’-8” and beneath her long apron, one could see that she was built like Daisy May in the old Al Capp comic strip, “Hey Marge, how’s it going? Did you call us?”

Sully poked Mike in the ribs and whispered, “She’s beautiful. Is she seeing anyone? If not, I apply for the job.”

Romano turned, smiled and said, “Later.”

Marge answered Mike, “Yeah, hold on a minute. The guy is in the back. She turned to the other counter girl, Carla, and asked her to call the complainant out front.

With the style of a fish monger, Carla shouted, Hey Kenny, the cops are here. Move it they ain't got all day." She then turned to Mike and Sully, "He'll be right out."

Sully was shaking his head in amazement as Marge asked, Mike, do you and your buddy want something to eat? There's two stools back there on the end, near the grill."

Mike looked at his partner, "We will probably be here a while, it's almost time for our meal break, we can get a head start and the burgers are the best on the Island, but Margie will make anything you want. For me, Marge, I'll have a hamburger steak, medium, two eggs over light right on top of it and a mountain of home fries. Oh and don't forget, rye toast with that and if you don't mind Margie, I'll start with a black coffee. Thanks."

Marge asked, as she turned to the grill, "And you, Mike's partner, tell me what you want and your name and I'll put it together for you."

Sully gasped as he saw one of Marge's assets, she wore hip hugging shorts, just tight enough and cut short enough to properly accent her curvaceous derriere and long legs. Marge turned her head and asked, "Well, did you go mute? Speak to me," she ordered as she shook her hip.

After what was probably several seconds, Sully answered, "Sorry, I was thinking what I wanted to eat, I'll have the same as Mike, but my eggs are sunny side up please."

Marge clunked two cups of black coffee on the counter in front of two empty seats, "Have a seat boys, be ready in a minute."

Carla shouted into the dining room again, "Kenny, the cops are here for God's sake. Get your ass in here before they leave."

As she finished, out walked a senior couple about 75 years old. They both looked like they had slept in their clothes for the last three weeks and were hugging and kissing as they teetered out the door. They were followed by a four foot tall, silver robot with flashing eyes that turned right and whirred up to Sully and said, "Hello."

Sully could do nothing but say, "You were right Mike, this place is the Cantina."

Scant seconds later, a large man with the look of a farmer walked over to the two cops. “Hi, I’m the one who called. I was robbed.” In his hand he carried a remote control pack with a small telescoping antenna. “Some guy in a white van took one of my robots and drove off. They cost me fifteen dollars each.”

Romano, still reveling in the thought of being the latent print man, turned to his partner, Sully, you drive after this call, and I’ll take the complaint.” Pulling a blank complaint form from his memo book, Mike asked, “Ok sir, Kenny, can you tell me what happened?”

Kenny began, “Well, you see this robot, its cool and I’ve been selling them to make some extra money. I pay $15.00 dollars each for them and sell them for anything between $25.00 and $40.00 each. I know that they’re expensive, so I thought that I would start now, even though Christmas is still three months away. If people can’t pay for it now, I’ll take an order and a down payment and give them a robot when they pay me in full. I only have two, this one here and the one that was stolen. I always have two to show people.”

Marge put their plates down in front of them, “Here you go boys, eat up.”

Mike picked up a fork, put a chunk of hamburger with fried egg on it and popped it into his mouth. He then turned back to Ken, “Sorry, please go on.”

“Yeah, you guys eat and I’ll talk, you can write everything down after you eat.” He reached down and picked up the robot, cradling it in his arm. Turning it sideways, Ken pulled a stopper on the back of the robots bulbous head and deflated the upper portion of the toy.

Sully although not looking at Ken asked, “Sir with all the people in here, how did the man steal such a large object without being seen and caught? Was that one deflated?” as he enthusiastically devoured his meal and followed Marge’s every move with unblinking eyes.

The complainant continued, “Well, I had brought both of my robots into the back room because I knew there would be lots of customers there and was demonstrating how they worked. You see if it's turned on and you say, 'Starman, come here', that's the robots name, it moves toward you automatically.. You can turn it right or left, back and forward with the controller. When you stop it in front of someone, you push a button and it says 'Hello' or 'Hello, I'm Starman' depending which button you push. The guy that took it asked if he could take the control and walk it out here from the dining room and show the people at the counter. We were all having fun with the other one, so I said yes, and he walked it out the door instead. By the time I realized what happened, he jumped into a white van and drove off down Hylan Blvd. Carla and Marge said that he was in here before but didn't know his name. Anyway, I want to make a report and maybe you can put an alarm out for the van."

Mike had almost finished his meal by the time Ken was finished with his narrative and put down his fork, picked up his portable radio and keyed the mike, "Two Three Henry-George to Central, K."

"Go Two Three Henry."

"Central, please be advised that at Russo's, 4518 Hylan Blvd., we have a missing robot. The missing subject is approximately four foot tall and answers to his name, its Starman. He was last seen leaving said location accompanied by a white male driving a white van, direction of flight unknown. It seems that the driver of said van kidnapped the radio controlled robot from his rightful owner. A 61(complaint form) is being prepared and will be recorded in the Two Three should a recovery and/or apprehension be made. Please acknowledge, K."

It was obvious that the dispatcher held back a guffaw as he repeated Mike's transmission. He ended with, "Henry please notify when you're back in service."

Mike answered, "Henry is 10-63 on meal at this time Central, K." Romano completed the complaint report as he drank another cup of coffee.

"Ken asked, "Do you guys think that you'll find the guy and my robot?"

Sully answered, "Well, you heard my partner put it over the radio and the dispatcher repeat it. We can only hope."

After their complainant left, Mike turned to his partner, "Sully, come take a look at the dining room, I think you'll find it interesting."

The cops walked into the large room. It was occupied by at least twelve patrons and a bartender that was cleaning up after last call. Not a single person seemed uneasy that there were two uniformed cops in the place. The bartender even shouted, "Did you guys help Kenny out? We all feel bad about what happened."

Mike shouted back, "Yeah, we took a report and put out an alarm. Maybe he'll get it back."

As his partner was having a quick exchange with the barkeep, Sully was slowly moving toward a particular wall of the dining room and a life sized rendering of Chewbacca, Hans Solo's huge Yeti like alien sidekick in the Star Wars movie. Next to it was a movie poster for the film. Scattered around the other walls were small framed caricatures of aliens depicted in the film's cantina scene.

Mike, noticing his partners interest, asked, "Well, Sully, what do you think? Which place came first, this place or the one in the movie? Personally, I think this is one of those mysteries of the universe."

"I think you're right. This place is fascinating, so is Margie. Tell me about her."

Mike chuckled then spoke, "Did you see the Corvette outside, parked under the sign as we came in? That belongs to her. She does all the maintenance herself. From what I've heard, she can break down an automobile engine and put it back together faster then most professional mechanics. I heard your heart pounding as you looked at her, don't fall in love, she's gay. She was married once, a bad one and after the divorce, she went over to the other side, some people call it the dark side, like in Star Wars. Sorry pal."

Sully thought that he was in love, "Wow, what a shame. But maybe I can convince her to switch back. She used to like guys."

Romano patted his friends back and said, "That's the dream of almost every man that meets her, many men have tried and none have succeeded as far as I know. Good luck. Let's go back out front and hang out for the rest of our meal hour. You can sit there, watch her move and dream."

After they left the diner, the rest of their tour passed slowly and without incident. At about 6:00 a.m. the sky lightened up and Mike told Sully to drive to Mount Loretto. Once inside the grounds, Mike asked Sully to follow the gravel road up the hill all the way to the red brick building at the top. He explained that it used to house the Monsignor and administrative offices.

Mike being a naturally inquisitive guy had previously researched the history of the place and in an effort to help pass the time told some of the story to Sully. "The man who started the Orphanage was Father Christopher Drumgoole, there is a street here, Drumgoole Blvd. named after him. Anyway, he worked in an orphanage in New York City back in the late 1800's and took in kids off the street. After he outgrew a ten story building some twenty years later, he bought this and some surrounding property. At one time Mount Loretto was the largest orphanage in the United States. I hear the kids used to farm it, cows and everything."

"It sure is a beautiful spot Mike. Look at the sunrise," Sully exclaimed.

"Yeah,' Mike replied, "See that beautiful church over there, Saints Joachim and Anne Church. The original one was used in the Godfather movie. Anyway it burnt down back in '73. Few years later it was rebuilt and that's it. Enough, I'm getting depressed. Enjoy the view. By the way, some of the guys are wacky enough to come up here in the early morning hours and fire their handguns, so I'm told. Before you ask, I've never done it."

"Not you Mike, not Mr. Straight and Narrow."

Mike felt compelled to answer, "You bet. Let's go back to Russo's for breakfast before we end our tour. You can dream about

Margie and maybe we can get an update on Starman. What do you say?"

Sully swung the car around as he answered, "Yeah, maybe I can get lucky and Marge is ready for a guy like me."

Sully lusted over Marge as the team ate some breakfast as the end of their tour drew close. Once at the station house, Sully thanked Mike for an interesting tour and the two men parted.

Romano went home and spent the morning doing mundane chores like shopping for some food and visiting the local Laundromat to wash some clothes. It was about 3:00 p.m. and he was just about to crawl into his bed when his telephone rang. Mike was tired and really didn't want to answer it. After five rings, he picked it up, "Hello?"

On the other end was Rocco Banducci with information about Dennis Bryan. "Michael, I have your information, the man lives in Grymes Hill, the working man's answer to Todt Hill, an exclusive residential area of Staten Island. He has one of those houses tucked in the hill next to Saint John University. I didn't want to push for the address, but it's on Arlo Road. Does that help?"

Mike knew that his friend was probably on a pay phone somewhere, still he wanted to keep the conversation to a minimum, "Thanks, I know his car, I'll find him. I'm sure you have to go. See you soon. Thank you."

"No problem my friend, be careful," was all Mike heard just before the click of a dropping coin and the phone went silent.

Mike went back to bed all keyed up. Now he knew where the Great Pumpkin lived, he would catch him dirty someday. He remembered looking at his alarm clock and seeing 4:00 p.m. just before the alarm rang at 10:30 p.m.. Mike cursed the contraption, slapping it into silence; he reluctantly rose out of bed and headed straight into the shower as his first step of preparation for another midnight tour.

***

Mike arrived at the Two Three ten minutes before roll call. He suited up in record time and rushed into the roll call room. Sully greeted him with, "Hey Mike, made it in time I see. Never knew you to be late for anything. Had a rough day?"

Romano answered, "No Sully, just overslept a little," as he settled into a rickety old chair.

Ten minutes later, Sergeant Hogan assigned Romano and Sullivan to adjoining sectors George and Henry again with the comment, "Maybe you two hotshot crime fighters can recover Starman tonight." The room erupted in whistles and applause.

Mike answered, "Ten-four Sarge, we'll give it our best shot."

Mike and Sully had a very uneventful tour that Thursday morning. By 8:20 a.m. both men left the station house. Mike however did not go directly home, first he drove to Arlo Road in an effort to locate the Buick belonging to Dennis Bryan. After negative results, he drove to his apartment and thought about his children and how much he missed them. Mike remained at home that day busying himself with some mundane chores going to bed at 2:00 p.m. and rising at 10:00 p.m. to get ready for another tour.

Once again he was assigned to work with Sully. The tour was as uneventful as the previous one with one exception, when the two men stopped in at Russo's for their now repeated breakfast just before the end of their tour; Margie relayed a closing story regarding the "Starman Incident."

It seemed that the man who made off with the toy two nights before had left a twelve year old bottle of scotch for the salesman. It had a note attached that stated he was sorry he had stolen it but wanted very badly to give it to his son and had no money on him at the time. The reluctant thief had heard thru friends that a police report was made and hoped for forgiveness. The scotch was a peace offering. Marge stated that Kenny retrieved the scotch and called it a fair trade even though he was still upset at being duped.

The two men parted at the end of the tour, each man going directly home.

CHAPTER TEN

It was 6:30 a.m. on Friday morning when Baggs pulled his big sedan behind the Quonset hut where he kept his Bronco. Friday and Saturday were his collection days and he was free until midafternoon. He decided that he would get an early start, do most of his rounds on Friday and leave himself a shorter Saturday collection. After all he did have a family. He hoped to return his collections to Johnny Eyes by lunch time and be able to go to his job of record; the one that his friends and neighbors knew paid his bills. After all you couldn't be a bagman for the mob and put that as your employment on your tax returns or your kids' school records. Later that night, he was scheduled to make his first drop at the home of Dennis Bryan, to him, just another dirty cop on the Family payroll. After pulling the Bronco out of its lair, Baggs drove out to the intersection of Arthur Kill Road and cautiously entered the paved road after he was certain that he would not be observed. He then headed for the Outer Bridge Crossing into New Jersey. He would make his collections through Jersey City, Newark, Secaucus and Bayonne before returning to Staten Island with his "bags" or "drops" to his cousin Rocco's house. There he would be paid for his work and in keeping with his new assignment, be given the envelope that Don Costello personally made him responsible to deliver to Bryan. Tonight was to be his first drop and he was nervous and undecided as to which vehicle to use for that little trip. Baggs pushed the thought out of his mind and began his rounds as usual.

By 1:30 p.m., as Baggs entered Rocco Lucelli's kitchen, he was surprised to see Johnny Eyes was chatting with his cousin. Johnny spoke first, "Enrico, or do you like Baggs better, one of our best associates. How the hell are you? You've been well this week? Are you ready to bring that fat bastard Bryan, his payoff?"

It took Baggs a few seconds to recover, "Yeah Johnny, I'm your guy. Anything for you and our friends, but can I ask a question?"

"Sure Baggs. What do you want to know?"

"Well, I'm not sure how to put this, so I'll ask outright. You and your father have Bayonne and the area around it. Why are we giving your hard earned money to a cop from Manhattan anyway? I know that we were asked by Don Costello and all, but how come someone from New York isn't taking care of it?"

Eyes first frowned as Baggs was talking, but broke into a smile as he began answering the question, "Well Baggs, as to Don Costello, we all share with the Don. As to why you were chosen, first and foremost, you are blood to this family, you are one of us and Rocco's first cousin. Second you're hungry and can't live on the money you earn legitimately. Third, you have proven yourself to be trustworthy and fourth you are careful because if you get caught, we are not the people you have to worry about. You have to worry about the time you would spend in jail, with your background, it would go hard. You're good at what you do because you are always careful to protect your own ass."

Baggs didn't like being reminded about his position, always straddling the fence between the criminal and straight world. To help himself shake off what Eyes had just said, he responded with, "I gotta run, can you guys please give me the package for Bryan, I have some things to do? I'll make the drop tonight."

Rocco answered him while Johnny Eyes just smiled, "Baggs, take it easy, nobody is wishing you a bad time, we know that we chose the best man for the job."

Ten minutes later, Baggs left Rocco's and was on his way to secrete the Bronco, pick up his sedan and be on time for his legitimate employment.

After work, at 1:30 a.m. Baggs snaked his personal sedan along Arlo Road and parked at the curb in front of Dennis Bryan's house. He left his engine running, exited his car, gently closing the door to eliminate any loud sound and stood still, leaning against the car. After looking around to make sure he had no onlookers, Baggs quickly walked up the driveway to Bryan's blue Buick sedan. Just as Rocco described, the auto was very close to some shrubbery, almost covering the right fender. After looking around once more, Baggs quickly bent down on one knee and placed the brown, rubber banded, paper sack containing Bryan's payoff money on top of the tire. Gently he tapped the package to make sure it would not fall off before it was retrieved. After he was satisfied that the bundle was stable, he quickly rose and almost sprinted to his car anxiously wanting to leave as fast as possible. Baggs had done many things, including murder for his mob family, but standing in front of a Police Department Official's home shook him to his core. He hurried home.

CHAPTER ELEVEN

Mike was in uniform and in the roll call room twenty five minutes before every other cop working that night. He was anxious to finish his last midnight tour and begin working his coveted new assignment as latent print officer.

Sergeant Walowski stepped into the room at 2345 hours and began his litany, "Listen up, here we go.........." Mike and Sully were once again paired up but assigned to sectors Adam, Boy and Charley. The station house was within the confines of sector Adam.

As they entered their patrol vehicle, Mike turned to Sully, "Oh boy, this is going to be one boring tour my friend, nothing ever happens down at this end. All we have is some residential areas, the woods on both sides of the Outer Bridge and the Conference House and the woods around it. Of course we can tour the woods on Page Avenue; it's kind of interesting in there."

"What's in there Mike, Leprechauns and fairies?"

'It's a big area that runs from Page and Hylan up to Sharrot's Road, at Mount Loretto and over to Amboy Road. Of course we can't get a patrol car every place in there, but it can kill some time. If we don't get any calls, we can drive thru there for almost an hour and not see another soul except each other."

Sully responded with, "What a horrible thought. Do you think I can bring Margie along, to fill in the dull moments?"

"Stop being a wise guy. You drive first and head for the Conference House on Hylan; I'll show you where we can back in and maybe catch some kids drag racing. Sometimes they show up on Friday nights."

"Will do Mike," Sully stated as he put the car in gear. Sully drove slowly down Main Street towards Hylan Boulevard, turning right towards the Conference House at the end of the Island.

As they approached the concrete barrier at the end of the road, Mike pointed to their left and stated, “Sully, there’s a small dirt road about fifty feet before the wall, back in about twenty feet and shut the engine. We’ll wait and see what happens.”

Sully complied. As they settled in to wait for possible drag racers, Sully asked, “Mike, you’re the Staten Island historian what can you tell me about the Conference House?”

Mike, always ready to tell a story, began, “The conference house is a rubble stone building built late in the 17th century, probably about 1680 or there about.”

“Damn, it’s that old huh?” Sully commented.

Mike continued, “The land it sits on was called Billop’s Point and belonged to a Captain Christopher Billop who served in the Royal Navy. He received the land as some kind of grant, about 950 acres and later another 1000 acres. He called it Bently Manor. The Captain’s grandson, also named Christopher Billop, was the owner during late 1776 when the British rowed across from New Jersey, then in British control, and had a conference with some famous members of the Continental Congress, Ben Franklin and John Adams were two of them. General Howe and his brother were trying to make peace with the American upstarts. They were unable to reach any agreement and the war continued.”

Sully was captivated, “Wow, the place has history alright. I’m almost honored to even look at it. Now I have to make sure I go inside someday.”

Mike quipped, “Glad you like the story, let me continue.” After mockingly catching his breath Mike continued, “Our local residents still believe that down in the basement is a large stone hearth that reportedly has a tunnel that leads out to the Raritan Bay. Story goes that one day, when the British heard that Lafayette and Washington were there, they raided the place and did not find them. The story is that they escaped thru the tunnel to the water and got away. Personally, I have my doubts because history books state the property was under British control throughout the war.”

Mike was on a roll now and was enjoying his captive audience of one. During down time his mind usually wandered to his personal problems, now, for awhile, he forgot about them and continued, “Tottenville legend claims that ghosts haunt the place. Inside there’s supposed to be at least one female and one male spirit that has been seen on the stairway that leads upstairs. The woman reportedly was stabbed to death, possibly by the man. Some say it’s Billop. I’m not sure of the facts. Several people that live in Tottenville now claim that they have seen the apparition of a woman in white moving across the grounds, usually near the water.” He smiled and added, “That’s all I got.”

“Wow Mike. That was some story. Tell me do you actually believe any of it?” Sully asked.

Mike had been focused on the small piece of roadway that was in their field of vision while he had been spinning his Conference House tale while they waited for some possible racers. As Sully spoke, four cars, two 60’s Corvettes, followed by a shiny black, ’57 Chevy Nomad station wagon, and a 1958 blue Impala Convertible rumbled past them, turning around just before the concrete barrier. They were unable to see the four cars turn around, but saw the two ‘Vettes line up with the headlights of the larger cars shining brightly behind them. Mike gently tapped on the dashboard to get Sully’s attention. To Romano, it was obvious that the two sports cars were about to race. In the limited light of one lamppost, the car closest to the cops appeared to be gold or silver in color, the other, an early Stingray, looked red.

Sully whispered, “We got ‘em” as he reached for the cars’ ignition.

Mike reached over and held up his hand saying, “Let ‘em race. They’ll come back and either line up to do it again or hang out to wait for more cars. That’s when we come out and get them. Open your window when you see them come back so, if we’re lucky, we can hear the engines cut off. I sure don’t want to race them down Hylan Blvd.”

Sully’s heart was thumping, “Sure wish we could watch the race Mike. Do you think Margie ever brings her car down here?

I'll bet it can beat both of these machines. She's so hot; bet her car is as hot as she is."

"No, I don't think Marge races her car, she babies it from what I'm told, so get her out of your head, and you stand as much chance of getting her as a snowball does in Hell." As Mike finished talking, the two Corvettes throttled their engines. Between them stood a tall lanky guy holding up a bandana in each hand. He could be heard shouting a countdown, "Ten, nine, eight.........one," and on one, pulled the bandanas down almost to the street. Amid smoking tires and roaring engines the two cars jumped down Hylan Blvd.

Mike turned to Sully, "Now we listen for their engines to shut off when they come back."

As Mike predicted, the throaty rumbling of the two sports cars could be heard as they returned and once again crossed the teams' field of vision.

"Ok Sully, when you hear their engines shut down, quickly get our car going and I'll hit our dome lights as we come out of the trees. Don't use headlights until we hit pavement, then hit the high beams. They'll be confused and blinded. You position our car to block the Vettes; we don't want them to even think about running. Got it?"

Seconds later the two racers were again facing the vastness of Hylan Blvd. They were not lined up for another run but did shut their engines. Excited voices could be heard extolling the merits of each car. Sully said, "Here goes," as he launched the patrol car forward toward the pavement. Mike hit the roof lights as they bounced onto the paved road and Sully brought their car into position in front of the Corvettes. The two cops bounded out of their patrol car as several of the young people danced and shouted expletives yet remained in place as if deciding whether or not to take off on foot.

"Mike Romano helped them decide by shouting, "Run and we call for a tow truck to take the cars." They all froze. He continued, "Everybody calm down and get ready to hand my partner your IDs, Driver Licenses, Insurance and proper registration papers for the cars. As soon as that's done, we'll all talk."

As Sully gathered identification from the group, Romano reported their location using the portable radio. Less than sixty seconds later, Fitzsimmons and Logan zoomed up in another car with their dome lights flashing. The place had begun to take on a carnival atmosphere.

Logan shouted, "I see you guys have lots of paper in your hands, we'll take the kids, and you guys do whatever you have to and don't worry about watching them." He and Fitz began herding the group towards the concrete wall. "Ok guys, sit down and don't move unless one of us calls for you." Once the entire group was seated, Fitz went to each car and removed ignition keys placing the collection on the hood of his patrol car. The lights and commotion resulted in the residents of the two homes adjacent to Satterlee Street spilling out onto their lawns. The spectators chatted amongst themselves as they watched the show.

Romano and Sully sorted through the papers they had gathered and decided that Sully would have first go at the kids. Sully stood next to the red Stingray and loudly asked, "Will the driver of this fine automobile please come forward?"

Hesitantly, a male about twenty years old stood up and slowly walked towards the cop. The young man held his arms out as he walked. After some unintelligible mumbling he spoke, "That's my car officer. All my papers are in order. What did I do?"

As Sully began speaking to his young person, Mike stood next to the second Vette and called out, "Will the driver of this fine machine come here to speak with me?"

"That's my car officer, coming," shouted a tall thin guy as he anxiously and quickly approached Romano. "I know you're gonna write me a speeding ticket. Aren't you?"

Mike was beginning to enjoy himself. "This is a fine car you have here. Wish I had one like it, and yes I'm going to give you a speeding summons."

"I'll beat it because you guys are not highway cops and you weren't behind us, so write away."

The kid had just twisted Mike Romano enough to bring his darker side closer to the surface. “Write away I will you young smart ass. I don’t need to follow you to know that you drove a speed in excess of the posted speed limit. You also engaged in a speed contest, that’s summons number two and number three is that your speed and race constituted reckless driving. That’s summons number three and is returnable in Criminal Court. Don’t forget to bring the other ones with it. When one is returnable in Criminal Court, then all summonses issued at the same time are returnable in Criminal Court. The judge will be thrilled to hear your side of the story. Maybe he would like a Corvette too and impound yours. Any further comments?”

The wind was taken out of the guy’s sails. He began shuffling his feet side to side as he answered, “No Sir. Please don’t take my car.”

Mike gently patted the cars fender as he answered, “Not yet young man, not yet. Now go back and sit down while I do some writing and decide what to do with you.”

Without saying another word, the young man turned and returned to the wall. One of the females gently caressed his hand in an effort to comfort him.

Sully had been gesturing toward his partner during Mike’s litany. He also sent his kid back to the wall and began writing his share of summonses.

It took the two cops fifteen minutes to complete their respective summonses. When they were finished, they jointly walked to the waiting youths. Each officer handed his man the three summonses with a caution, “If you come back again, at any time, we will take your cars. See you in court.” Mike added, “Stay right here a few more minutes until we decide to let you go.”

As Romano and Sully finished their respective soliloquies, a fairly loud burst of applause could be heard from the residents watching the little drama from their lawns. Feeling silly at that moment and wanting to annoy the kids, Sully and Romano looked at each other and in unison, almost as if rehearsed, gently bowed to their appreciative public. The young people, still gathered at the barrier wall murmured their disapproval at the gesture. Romano and Sully turned to the group and waved to them in a dismissive manner. Slowly the kids climbed into their respective autos and drove off with Fitzsimmons and Logan following them. After several blocks, the patrol car could be seen turning off the boulevard.

Mike and Sully made the appropriate memo book entries and notified the dispatcher that they were now resuming patrol and drove off.

Sully turned to Mike and remarked, "Wow Mike, you sure know how to have a good time. That was fun. I'm going to miss working with you."

""Thanks Jerry, I'll miss your company too."

***

After leaving the vicinity of the Conference House, Sully drove up Hylan, past Mount Loretto, to Wolf's Pond Park on the water side of Seguine Avenue. The park was fairly large and hosted many outdoor activities including rock concerts. On the far side of the unpaved parking area were a few dirt roads that gently meandered into the park woods. Mike directed Jerry to head for them. Sully asked, "What's going on there Mike? The kids can't hot rod in there, can they?" He laughed at his own silly question.

"No, they can't race, but from time to time, somebody gets their ass kicked in there. I personally found a kid beat up in there several months ago. Poor guy almost died. Since then I check it from time to time just in case and it relieves the boredom."

After spending some time in the winding roads and finding nothing out of the ordinary, the team resumed their regular patrol.

The remaining hours before their meal break were quiet and uneventful with the exception of one call for a ringing alarm at a hardware store on Richmond Avenue to which three patrol cars respond because it was such a slow night. It wasn't a break in, just an alarm malfunction that the service company responded to. At 3:00 a.m., Sully piloted their car to Russo's for their meal hour.

Mike headed for the rear dining room and sat in a corner booth. Feeding his infatuation with Marge, Sully sat at the lunch counter and chatted with her a few minutes before joining his partner in the rear.

Agnes, a weathered old waitress, took their orders, Delmonico steak, medium rare for Mike and a double cheeseburger for Sully. Naturally they both ordered potatoes and a salad to go with it. Both men had a soft drink to wash it all down. They remained there for their entire meal hour before returning to their patrol car. As was customary, Mike now climbed into the driver's seat. As Mike started the engine, Sully asked, "Mike, are you going to take us down around Arthur Kill road where we lost that Black Bronco? If you do, you have my blessings. Have at it my friend, it's slow and your last night with a partner. Maybe we'll get lucky."

Yeah, thanks Jerry. This could be the night," Mike responded as he put the car into gear.

The team rode into Clay Pit Pond Park as far as the dirt roads would allow them to. Mike did not want a repeat of the night they chased the Bronco into the park and got stuck. Their Dodge Diplomat had adequate ground clearance, but was only a standard rear drive vehicle. It had its limits. Having no success the team resumed regular patrol in their assigned sector for the remainder of the tour. Mike and Sully dropped their Conference House summonses into the box on the Desk as they entered the station house, and then stopped at the small receptionists' desk to sign out at end of tour. By 8:15 a.m., Mike was in his car and on his way home. He wanted to call his kids and try to spend some time with them before he returned to work on Monday and began his new assignment.

The next day the two old friends were teamed up again for their last tour of the set, Friday night into Saturday morning. Once again the tour was uneventful. At 8:00 a.m. on Saturday morning, Mike and Sully exchanged pleasantries and wished each other well, Sully telling Mike, "Go get 'em print man. I'm here if you need me at any time."

Mike was anxious to collect all the equipment he had gathered from his locker and bring it home to set it up in an old attaché case he had. He responded with, "It was nice spending time with an old friend and I would like to chat some, but I want to get home and see my kids today, sorry."

The two men shook hands and left the station.

***

Later that morning Mike telephoned his kids. "Hello Daddy, its Annie, Donnie and Mom aren't home. They left early to go to Aunt Kelly's house and I got to stay home because I'm going to be picked up by Frankie's parents later to go to a movie in New Dorp with them. Mom and Donnie will be home some time tonight."

Mike had forgotten that his daughter was old enough to begin dating. He wasn't comfortable with it, but the two kids would be with Frank's parents so he shook it off.

"That's real nice Annie; I keep forgetting that you're almost a young woman now. Do you have any time to see your old man before you go?"

"Sure Daddy. What are you doing right now? I'll be picked up about 1:00 this afternoon."

"Well Annie, I just got off work. Let me take a quick shower and I'll be there in less than hour. See you soon."

"I miss you Daddy," was her response as she hung up.

As he put the phone down, Mike's eyes misted over and he sobbed as he answered his daughter after the line went dead, "I miss you kids too."

Within ten minutes, Mike was showered, dressed and in his car driving to his old house to pick up Annie. As he pulled up into the driveway, Annie bounded out of the house and ran towards his car. Mike had all he could do to slam the gearshift into park and jump out to meet his daughter's embrace. "Daddy, Daddy, I miss you so much it hurts. Donnie is in pain too, sometimes he cries while he sleeps," she said softly into her father's ear.

Mike attempted to speak but when his lips moved, no sound came out. He was thankful that Annie couldn't see his face. After a loud grunt, that he used to mask his emotions, he continued with, "Ouch you're going to break my neck with your hug," he grunted again and continued with, "I hurt too sweetheart, I wish there was another way, but we can't all be together."

Annie's grip on him began to subside, allowing Mike to regain most of his composure, "It's a shame you kids have to grow up so fast, but we all have to keep moving forward. Just remember, I'll always be your Dad. If ever you or your brother need anything, just ask and if it's in my power to give it, you'll have it because I love you guys."

"We love you too Daddy." In a typical young person fashion, Annie switched gears and continued with, "I'm hungry, can we go get something to eat?"

"Sure can kiddo," he answered. "Jump in the car and let's go."

Mike always felt comfortable eating in diner style restaurants. One of their favorite places to eat as a family had been, The Colonnade Diner on Hylan and Clove Road. Mike asked Annie, "The Diner kid?" She quickly gave her consent and off he drove.

After they each ordered a gargantuan breakfast of pancakes, eggs, Italian link sausage, home fries and toast, along with juice and coffee, Mike decided to catch up on his daughter's social life and began, "Annie, tell me about this boyfriend of yours, is he a boyfriend or just a friend? Know anything about his family? I should know too because you're going to be with them later. Where do they live?"

"Wow. You sure want lots of answers and all at once too."

"Take your time Baby, but answer it all. After all you're my daughter and I gotta know that you're safe."

Annie smiled and almost blushed as she spoke, "Well, we met through a friend of mine who lives near this diner. Frank is a senior in New Dorp High School and just completed Drivers Ed and got his Driver's License. The family lives in New Dorp and his father owns a paving company, Panzaro Paving, they do roads and driveways and stuff here and in Brooklyn. Frank has one older sister who lives at home and has a car that he sometimes gets to borrow. She's in college at Saint Johns. Mom has met him and thinks that he's real nice and polite too." Annie was always comfortable with her father and jokingly asked, "Anything else that I might have missed?"

The waitress brought over their food and both of them wolfed down the meal and the only conversation exchanged between them as they ate was related to which one of them ate like it was his or her last meal. Between laughing, choking and giggles, they managed to eat almost every morsel.

When they were outside, Mike asked, "How about we go home and I wait around to meet Frank and his folks? Is that alright with you? I want to know who my daughter is going to be with. Ok?"

"Sure Daddy. I told them all about you and I'm sure they would like to meet you too."

They arrived back at the Romano house by noon. Mike parked his Chevy at the curb, leaving the driveway for the people that would have the responsibility of watching over his daughter for the balance of the day. He remained outside relaxing as best he could with his daughter by sitting in his car or on the front lawn.

The Panzaro car pulled into the driveway at 12:55 p.m.. Mike was sitting out front on the steps of his former residence. He had found some strange comfort at being there with his daughter. In some small measure it was like turning the clock back to a time before the fateful night that he found his wife with her lover. As the car emptied its cargo onto the driveway, Mike snapped back to reality and rose to greet them. "Hello. You must be Frank," he said as he extended his hand to the young man who stood before him.

"Yes sir, I am, and this is my Dad, Frank Sr. and my Mom Carmella. My sister Dotty wasn't not home today, she went out with friends."

The older Frank Panzaro extended his hand, "Mike, it's a pleasure to finally meet you. Little Annie has had some wonderful things to say about you." He then turned and pointed to his wife, "Carmella thinks Annie is just terrific, it's like we've known her for years."

Tough Police Officer Romano, had butterflies in his gut. Mike had never imagined what it would feel like when he met Annie's first boyfriend, plus his parents at the same time, and was convincing himself that it was better to meet them all at once to better gauge what kind of people they were. In his head he heard the pounding of wings, *not now Saint Michael. I haven't heard from you in a while. Now you come, it's Ok. I got this one.* Beneath that armored exterior, Mike Romano was just a caring sensitive human being. He quickly took inventory of the boy's parents, Carmella's expensive well-made clothing, Frank's expensive suede sports coat, and the expensive looking shoes on the feet of both parents, plus a brand new Mercury Grand Marquis, one step below a Lincoln Town car. Well, the guy appeared to be successful. The heir apparent, young Frank was neat, clean and well groomed and appeared to be muscular like his father.

Shaking the elder Panzaro's hand Mike said, "My pleasure folks. I'd invite you in for a drink and some conversation but,…"

Before he finished, Panzaro said, "It's Ok, Annie explained what's been going on. It's fine, maybe some other time."

Mike was now getting uneasy and wanted to be alone again. "Well I have something important to do. I just wanted to meet all of you. I gotta go." He turned to young Frank, reached out to shake his hand and said, "You seem like a nice guy Frank and when you're with my little girl, always take good care of her. Okay?"

"Yes Sir, I will."

With that exchange concluded, Mike turned and kissed Annie tenderly on her forehead, "I love you Annie. Have fun and take care. If you need me just call, I'll be home all night from three o'clock this afternoon." He turned, shook hands with the Panzaros and left. As he pulled away, Mike looked at the group in his rear view mirror and thought, *if Betty hadn't been a cheater, we could have all been one big happy group as our kids entered adulthood and began dating. Damn her to hell.*

Mike went to the Laundromat, opened his trunk and removed two bags of dirty laundry that had been sitting, getting ripe in his trunk for two days, then went inside and paid the attendant to process the clothes. He then went next door to the supermarket and shopped for some groceries. Later, when Mike returned to his apartment and tried to sleep, he found it impossible. The earlier meeting with the parents of his daughter's boyfriend kept him visualizing what might have been. After two healthy glasses of scotch, he finally fell off to sleep.

***

Mike's dreams were a kaleidoscope of the recent past. The Ford Bronco, the beating he gave his wife's lover, the trip to the zoo with his kids and the day each one was born. The visions he saw all passed his mind's eye simultaneously, capping off with his promotion to Detective.

The constant ringing of his telephone seemed like part of his dreams at first. The persistent sound finally shook him from the grip of Morpheus and he sat bolt upright, reaching for the receiver and knocked his empty glass from the nightstand. Groggily, Mike inquired, "Hello, who is this?"

He snapped to full alertness as he heard, "Daddy, it's me; come quick some guy is trying to kill us."

Over the shock of his daughter's plea, Romano could hear a loud, deep pounding sound that was almost overpowering the sound of his Annie's frantic words.

"Where are you and what is going on? Are you hurt? Where the hell is Frankie?"

"We're together, in the phone booth outside the diner we were at today. Come quick a guy is trying to get in and hit us with a baseball bat. Frankie is in here with me and he's holding the door closed."

Blam, blam, thud, was all he heard above his daughter's shouts. "I'm on my way. Don't leave the booth." As he sprung out of his bed, the drumming of wings in his head became louder and louder as he pulled on a pair of pants, grabbed his revolver and car keys and ran to his car.

Mike, out to save his daughter, reached the diner in record time and raced into the parking lot, narrowly missing two cars that had been in an accident and almost totally blocked the entrance. He paid no attention to them as he screeched to a stop and focused on the big guy who was still trying to reach Annie by pounding the phone booth with a baseball bat. Mike slammed his car into park and jumped out shouting, "You son of a bitch, that's my daughter. I'm gonna shove that bat up your ass after I beat you to death with it," as he ran toward the man. The big man stopped pounding the booth and charged at Romano swinging the bat as he ran. Mike retreated backwards and felt himself bounce against a car. In an instant he assessed his adversary, the man was much taller than he was and at least thirty pounds heavier, but it didn't matter. The man swung again, Mike managed to avoid being hit and planted his big fist directly in the center of the man's face. The bat crashed to the ground as the big man staggered to regain his balance. Mike was as quick as an enraged tiger as he grabbed the man's right arm, pulled him towards himself and tripped him as he struck the man on the side of his head. In one motion, the would be archangel slammed his assailant down on the hood of one of the automobiles, twisting his hands behind his back and handcuffed the man. The guy was yelling in pain. To the protecting Italian father within Mike Romano, it seemed like the entire battle lasted less than five seconds.

Mike was about to pull his prisoner to an upright position as he felt his two arms being restrained while someone behind him shouted, "Cuff that madman." He twisted his head sideways to see several uniformed police officers around him and his adversary, one of them was a Captain.

As the shock of being handcuffed reached his brain, all he could say was, "Police. I'm on the job. That guy was trying to kill my daughter."

One of the cops holding him pulled Mike's revolver from its holster and shouted, "He's got a gun. We have a live one here."

Another cop shouted, "Holy crap look at this guy." He was referring to the man Mike just grappled with. The guy's face was a disaster area.

Annie and Frank came running out of the booth, Annie was shouting, "Don't hurt my Daddy. He was helping us. We hit that guy's car and he went crazy." Two uniformed officers stood in their way.

"Search him for ID and if he has none, put him in a car and read him his Miranda Warnings," shouted the Captain.

When Mike heard the orders, he panicked and began to struggle as he repeated, "I'm one of you, I tell you. I'm a cop and came to help my kid. I just got out of bed and forgot my ID."

One of the cops said, "Yeah, yeah we heard it before pal. Get into the car."

From somewhere in the mayhem came, "Release him, the man's one of mine. He is a cop damn it, and a good one too. I'm Detective Sergeant Flynn of the Two Oh Squad and that man works with me."

Mike was elated when he heard the friendly voice and yelled, "Sergeant Flynn, Get these guys to release me. Thank God you're here."

Flynn continued, "Officer, release this man at once. Captain, you're obstructing an investigation. Are you sure you want to do this? You know Captain that shit could hit the fan if you continue?"

The Duty Captain, unsure of himself and intimidated by Flynn, didn't want to risk banging heads with a Detective Squad Commander and had no idea what Flynn was talking about. He quickly ordered, "Release that man at once. You heard the Sergeant."

While the handcuffs were being taken off Mike's wrists, an ambulance roared onto the scene and two medical techs jumped out. They quickly assessed the big man's face. One of them said, "Captain this man has severe facial damage. He has to get to a hospital now. If he's under arrest, send a cop with him. We gotta go."

The Captain pointed to a radio car team, "One of you jump in the ambulance and ride with the prisoner and the other man, follow them in the patrol car. When he's treated and released, bring him to the One Two Two and process the arrest, you guys have the collar. Now get the hell out of here while this gets sorted out."

Mike, still in shock at the turn of events, embraced Flynn and thanked him. Ignoring the Captain's attempts to talk to him, Flynn pulled Romano to his own car and ordered, "Climb in and tell me what the hell happened."

Mike told Flynn, "In a minute Sarge. First I have to speak to Annie and her friend." Frank walked over to his daughter and gave her a hug. "Listen Annie, I have to sit with the bosses for a few minutes and explain what happened, then we can get Frankie's car towed if it needs it and I'll take you home. Please go inside and wait. Order whatever you guys want and tell the waitress that I'll be in soon. OK?"

"Sure Daddy. Wow, I never saw anything like that. I knew you were tough, but wow, you sure beat the crap out of that guy. I still can't believe it. That guy you caught with Mom is lucky he's alive." She quickly realized that she probably struck a nerve by mentioning that particular incident and Annie quickly added, "You're the best Dad in the world," as she jumped up and hugged her father around the neck.

Frank sheepishly walked up to Mike, extended his hand and said, "Thank you Sir, he wanted to kill us. I'm sorry I got Ann into this."

Pointing to the cars, Mike answered, "Well son, accidents like that one could happen to anyone, I'll square it up with the cops, and you take Annie inside. Your car belongs to your sister, right?"

"Yeah my Dad and her are gonna kill me."

After watching the kids go into the diner, Mike returned to Flynn. "Ok Sarge here's what happened, "I was sleeping and the phone rang........... and that brings us up to this minute." Still puzzled by Flynn's threat to the Duty Captain, Mike asked, "Sarge, you sort of straight out threatened the Captain, what investigation would he be holding up by arresting me?"

Flynn smiled broadly as he answered, "Why the Bronco shooting naturally. You're my star witness and we need your help. It worked, didn't it? The guy backed off like someone put a match to his balls." He laughed at his own joke, "I like you Mike, and I hope to have you under my command someday."

"He sure did Sarge. What happens now?"

"You my friend are a complainant in this little escapade. The guy with the new face is the perp. I'll stop in at the Two Two and make sure one of those uniform cops processes the collar. You may have to sign an affidavit for the DA, someone will call you. Now go home, take care of your kid and call my office tomorrow and someone will give you the arrest number of Mr. Beautiful and the accident number for the boyfriend's insurance. Glad I was here to help." With a big grin, Flynn added, "You sure are something Mike Romano", and turned to walk away.

Romano had almost forgot to tell his new friend an important bit of information and shouted, "Sarge, I know where the Bronco is from."

The Sergeant spun on his heel and almost tripped on his own feet in his excitement to get back to Mike, "What where?"

"Well, a few nights ago, my partner and I came across it on Arthur Kill Road near the prison, between it and Clay Pit Pond Park. The driver ran when he spotted our car and we chased him into Clay Pit where we lost him because he went deep into the woods and we got stuck. We never found him, but I look for the truck every chance I get."

Flynn excitedly said, "Mike, that's great. Do you think he's holed up somewhere in the woods? Is there a shack or something in there?"

"I don't think so because the command would have heard about it. Kids use the park as a lover's lane and hikers go in there as well as the Boy Scouts. We would have heard. "I'll bet he has a place to hide real close though. Someday I'm gonna find it and get him."

Flynn answered, "Great work Romano. I'll have the area checked by my men, hell; I'll go too, whenever we have a chance. It's your command, so keep an eye out and call right away if you think there's reason. From a guy as sharp as you, I'll know it's not smoke and we'll respond ASAP."

As Flynn spoke with the uniformed Captain, Mike walked into the diner and found the two kids sitting in a booth near the door. Frank spoke first, "Mr. Romano, my father's coming to take me home and I told him what happened and what you did. He says to please wait, he wants to thank you personally and he has a tow truck coming to take the car to a friend's shop. Please wait."

Mike's only concern was to make sure that the kids were ok, he smiled and answered, "Sure Frank, I'll be happy to wait."

Outside, the flashing yellow lights of a tow truck danced through the windows as the senior Frank Panzaro walked up to the little group. Frank was all smiles as he reached for Mikes hand and pulled him to his feet. "Officer Romano, Mike Romano, my family thanks you for saving our son from harm. Is there anything I can do for you?" Without waiting for an answer, he then turned to his son and hugged him.

After some more friendly exchanges, Mike excused himself and Ann stating, "You know that I have to get her home to her mother, not a pleasant task, I'd like to get it over with. We can talk another time. Please excuse us, Frank, happy that I could help."

Once outside, alone with his daughter, Mike's knees began to shake as the avenging angel took his place in the rear of Romano's psyche and the events of the last half hour sank in, leaving in its place, a father who was just happy that his daughter was safe.

Annie, on the other hand could not hold herself back, "Daddy, did you know that your eyes glowed red when you grabbed that guy? It was scary. Do you know that you pushed his face into his car windshield so hard that the window broke?"

Mike was surprised at the comment. "No Honey, I don't remember." Embarrassed at not being able to recall his own actions, Mike tried to make a joke, "And no, I didn't know that my eyes glow red, it must have been your imagination or the reflection of the cars tail lights, but I was real upset."

"Well, anyway, I'm glad that I'm your daughter and you love me. God help the person that pisses you off, like that child molester you shot when I was little. Please take me home now. I already called Mom and she's home."

He pulled up to the house within ten minutes. Mike walked his daughter to the front door and waited for it to open. Donnie was the first one outside, followed by Betty. Donnie jumped up to hug his Dad, then his sister. Mike put his hand on Donnie's head to get his attention, "Give me another hug will you kid?"

Don snapped around, "Sure thing" and again jumped into his fathers waiting arms.

When Mike put the boy down, he looked up at Betty who coldly spoke, "Thank you for bringing her home safe. Come inside now kids, talk some other time." Even icier in tone, she continued referring to her ex, "He," not even saying Mike's name or using Daddy, "has to get home now, say goodnight."

With a mixture of sadness at having to leave his children and rage building up at the sight of Betty, Mike feigned a cheery, "Good night my children and God bless you. I gotta go."

"Good night Daddy", they each said in turn.

Mike quickly returned to his car and drove home.

Once he was safely in the sanctuary of his apartment, Mike poured himself four fingers of Dewar's, settled into his leather recliner chair, the one luxury item in his place, turned on the TV and began staring blankly at whatever was on the screen while, in his mind, reliving the fight at the diner, the shooting on the highway and his pending divorce. He wished the guy he put into the windshield was his wife's paramour and thought, m*aybe for a second, that's the face I saw and that's why I hit the bastard so hard.* It was 3:30 a.m. when Mike placed his glass down on the table next to his chair and fell asleep.

***

Mike, still in his lounger, was awakened by constant ringing of his phone. Forcing himself to rise quickly, his body aching and stiff from not sleeping in his bed, Mike quickly grabbed the phone and tried to be alert as he asked, "Hello, who is this?" Without waiting for an answer, he added, sorry, I just woke up, got to bed late."

It was Annie, "Yeah, me too Daddy. Sorry to call but, I just wanted to tell you that we won't be home for a few days. Mom is taking Donnie and me to Aunt Kelly's for a week." In typical fashion, she continued without waiting for a response, "She says that she'll square it with our schools, and Donnie's just a kid and my school has some kind of teacher conference for two days so I'll only miss three days. Be back next week end. OK?"

Mike was fully awake now, "Why for a week? What's up? Is there anything wrong?"

"No Daddy, she just wants us off the Island because of last night. She says that I need the time to calm down from the trauma and you may be irritable and nasty because you got in trouble with the cops. She wants you to straighten it all out without us around. She says that if everything returns to normal, then we'll come home and you can see us again."

"Listen honey, I don't want to see her, just you kids. She's just breaking my back, the divorce and all but not to worry. I'm not in trouble with the Department and I'll see you in a week. Have fun."

"We love you Daddy." The phone went dead.

Mike was pissed, he thought, *now she's using the kids to break my balls and stress me out. I can't wait to get away from her.*

Mike was fully awake now. He quickly fixed himself a breakfast of scrambled eggs and some rye toast, washing it down with a glass of orange juice, as he thought of how to spend the rest of the day. It was 10:10 a.m. when Mike was showered, shaved, dressed and ready to run into Saint George to the DA's office and check on the results of the arrest at the diner. He also planned to stop in at the Two Two and gather any information he could not get from the DA's Office.

It was 10:45 when he found a parking space near the Two Oh and walked the two blocks to the District Attorney's Office at 230 Richmond Terrace. After identifying himself to the security officer, Mike found ADA Williams working the complaint room and asked about the arrest from the diner incident. Williams informed him that Raymond Grillo, thirty five years old, from Mariners Harbor, was arrested for felonious Assault on a Police Officer, two counts of Attempted Assault First Degree with a weapon, a baseball bat and Criminal Mischief as a felony, to wit, the phone booth that was no longer serviceable. The complaint was sworn to by the arresting officer, PO John Murray of the One Two Two on his (PO Michael Romano's) complaint. The ADA added that there were witnesses in addition to the two teenagers. Williams offered Mike those names. Wanting to forget that he almost killed a man in an uncontrollable rage, he declined.

Mike asked, "What kind of sheet does this guy have? I know it's kind of early, but has he seen a judge yet?"

Williams answered, "He has an extensive record for assault and he's a cop fighter. Currently he's on parole for beating and injuring his wife. I think he'll cut a quick deal and be re-incarcerated. He owes three years and our office wants nothing less then three to five added to his sentence if he pleads guilty to last night's charges. By the way, do you want to see the booking photo?" he asked as he handed it the Mike.

With a mixture of horror and pride, Mike remarked, "I did some job on him, he looks like he went head first thru a meat grinder. I hope all that heals."

Williams quipped, "Remind me never to get on your wrong side Officer Romano and thanks for coming in. Now please excuse me, I have to get back to my work. We'll call you if we need you but I doubt that it will be necessary. Have a good day."

The two men shook hands and Mike left. He had learned all he wanted to, making a trip across the Island unnecessary and decided to return to his apartment. After attempting to relax for several minutes and being unable to do so, Mike called his attorney, Arthur Slotnick on the chance that he was again working on a weekend, just like the fateful day Mike walked into his office. After several rings, an answering machine clicked in and recited the office hours, then requested that the caller leave a message. Mike did so, "Mr. Slotnick, this is Mike Romano inquiring about the current status of my pending divorce. My soon to be ex-wife is really beginning to annoy me. I'm getting anxious and short tempered and don't want to hire you as my criminal attorney. Please call me back at 555-0347. I'm working days this week, Monday to Friday and should be home after 4:00 p.m. Thank you."

The balance of Romano's time off was uneventful. He didn't know that he would be sent out on his first past burglary job as soon as he arrived at the station house that Monday morning.

CHAPTER TWELVE

Mike attended the eight to four roll call and was gently kidded by Sergeant. Hogan as he spoke, “Romano, Latent Prints. What the hell is that Romano? I haven’t heard that term since I attended the Police Academy. Noted here on the sheet is Scooter if no RMP unit is available. Have you become a celebrity over your swing?”

There was a ripple of laughter as the sergeant finished speaking. Mike answered, “No Sarge, I’ve just been assigned as the print man for the command. I’ve got skills.”

Hogan chuckled, “I’m sure you do Mike. The command was notified about that little incident at the Hylan Boulevard diner the other night, I’m sure you have skills. Poor guy, you almost killed him. Hey what’s in that case you have there, your lunch?”

There were whispered questions heard from around the room at the announcement. Hogan, realizing his error in mentioning Mike’s flirt with an arrest situation, covered with, “Just trying to get a rise out of you kid. Good job that night and good luck with your new assignment. Oh, and by the way, stop at the desk, Holy Child of God Church has been hit. Someone broke in and took Sunday’s collection money. Happy hunting! The rest of you guys, get out there.”

Mike strode up to the desk officer, “Lieutenant Cassidy, Sergeant. Hogan informed me that you have an assignment for me. What is it, a burglary?”

The desk officer smiled, “Here you go Romano, your first official print job, but be advised that the property Squad was already there before you came on duty. It’s at Holy Child of God Church. Somebody stole the Sunday collection money.” As Mike reached over the high desk, Cassidy handed him a copy of the burglary complaint and added, “See if you can get lucky son, the squad said that they could find nothing worthwhile.”

"Thanks. I'll get right on it. By the way, what vehicle should I use?"

Cassidy quipped, "Whatever you want, a scooter or an RMP if one is available. Just let me know what you take so I can enter it on the work sheet and don't forget to notify the radio dispatcher. Go get 'em kid."

Mike checked the peg board next to the desk and found two patrol car keys still on their respective hooks. He removed the key for RMP 1535 and signed out a portable radio. "Lieutenant, I'll be using 1535 today." The desk officer only waved. Mike checked his radio, "Two Three Latent Print car to Central, please acknowledge, K."

The dispatcher waited for the ohhhs and ahhas to subside, Latent Print, what auto number are you? K."

"RMP 1535. Be advised Two Three Latent will be on assignment and ten-sixty two out of service at 4700 Amboy Road, K."

"Ten Four, Two Three Latent, advise." was the return response.

Mike was looking forward to his first job in his new assignment. He was totally consumed with the thought of finding finger prints left behind by the person or persons who stole from a church and was able to push his personal problems related to his divorce to the back of his mind, even the black Bronco could wait. He wasn't assigned to a patrol sector so he felt no need to take a shotgun as it was his option.

As Mike pulled his car from the curb; he remembered something his friend, Leona, from the Annadale Luncheonette had said to him during one of his coffee stop conversations. Leona had told him that Michael Guggalarie, the kid that hangs out near the train station and "helps" old ladies by picking up their purses is rumored to also be a burglar. Mike pursed his lips as he thought about the young punk breaking into a church, but quickly brushed it aside, *I'm being ridiculous, Michael G is just an opportunist, but why not stop in to see Leona anyway?*

Mike drove down Main Street, turned left on Amboy Road, quickly drove to the intersection of Annadale Avenue, and made the dog leg left that lead to Annadale Square. He parked directly in front of the luncheonette and strode inside. Leona was behind the counter picking up the last remains of somebody's breakfast and didn't look up as the little bell on the door tinkled to announce that someone entered.

Mike was pleased that there were no other customers as he spoke, "Leona, how about two eggs with bacon, rye toast and coffee for your favorite cop?"

Without looking up she cheerfully responded, "Sure thing Mike, how do you want your eggs?"

Mike sat down at the farthest counter stool from the door as he answered, "The usual, over easy please, thanks."

Leona put two eggs and some bacon on the grill, walked over and put a large mug of black coffee in front of Mike. She smiled, reaching for his hand, giving it a caress and gentle pat, "Nice to see you in a good mood for a change. Did your divorce come through?"

"No not yet. Actually, I'm reasonably happy because today, I'm officially the latent print cop for the command. I'll be going to past burglaries in an attempt to recover finger prints left by the bad guys, submit them and hopefully get a positive identification so an arrest can be made. I was one of the cops who did it in my old Harlem command, it's challenging and fun. With no steady partner, I usually ride alone and right now, with my personal life all mixed up, it's a blessing. Most people are trying to be courteous when they ask, 'How's your divorce going?', but it's just salt in the wound. You went through it, and you know how it feels."

Leona quickly realized that she still was holding Mike's hand and embarrassingly pulled away as she answered, "Yeah, I know just how it feels. You want to block the pain and anguish and somebody reminds you. Anyway, I have to flip your eggs."

Mike watched her as she moved, gathering his breakfast. He thought, *I wonder, no I'm not ready. Damn it Sully, you planted the thought in my mind. No time, got too much going on.*

Leona placed his plate in front of him along with some flatware as she asked, “You look like something is on your mind. Can I help?”

After putting black pepper on everything, Mike answered, “Well, you know that kid Michael Guggalarie, the kid you would like to see arrested? Well, if you see or hear anything more about him, please call the station and leave a message for me to stop in. Right now, I have to go to Holy Child of God Church as soon as I’m finished. It seems that they were burglarized last night and somebody got the collection money.” In his head, Michael heard the beating of wings and added, “I don’t know why but I’ll bet Michael knows something about it.”

She looked surprised as she answered, “Sure Mike, if I hear anything, but I can’t believe that even a bad apple like him would break into a church. Do you know how they got in?”

“No, the complaint report says that the place was locked and responding detectives found no evidence of a break in. Maybe somebody connected with the church did it. I’ll talk with the pastor and see what he thinks.”

“Good luck Mike. See you soon?”

“Sure Leona, I’ll be riding alone most of the time now and don’t have a partner that I have to convince to stop here. You’ll see me again, and thanks for the delicious breakfast.” Mike placed a five dollar bill on the counter and left.

***

Romano piloted his patrol car to the parking lot at the rear of the church. The lot was set back behind the building and not very visible from Amboy Road, the “front of the church”. In actuality, the main entrance of the church was accessed from the parking area. The building was not designed like most other Christian Churches, in the shape of a crucifix, if seen from the air. Holy Child of God was a modern building and built in the round, with no visible “arms or appendages” visible. Mike thought as he parked, “*this place is certainly different and paradoxical*; *the front is in the back. Where did the bad guys come, in the back- front or the front- back of the church?"* and chuckled at his own humor. Grabbing his print kit from the seat next to him, Mike left his vehicle and entered the church thru the huge glass doors facing the center of the lot. Once inside, the curvature of the building was evident because Mike could see no corners and was unable to see the end of the main corridor. The walls were constructed of large concrete blocks and painted a glossy beige color. It was stark but pleasing to the eye with liturgical type wall hangings tastefully spaced along the walls. Mike pulled one of the four huge oak doors that were directly opposite the entrance. It was unlocked and he walked thru entering what was obviously the worship area because he saw row upon row of pews and an attractive altar. The altar stage was elevated with light blue drapes behind it, also curved and spanning a approximate fifty feet sector of the circular design. Hanging over the actual altar in the traditional sense, was a huge crucifix, its suspension magically defying gravity, as if hanging there by the will of God. Close inspection revealed thin, almost invisible wires holding it in place. At the top of the perimeter walls, were striking stained glass windows, and above them began a huge domed ceiling. It was all very modern, yet pleasing and maintained a slightly traditional flavor. He was impressed. After a quick scan of the area and seeing not a single person, he returned to the corridor and began walking in the direction of Arden Ave. As Mike walked thru the hallway, he noticed that there were several standard size doors to his left, putting other rooms and offices along the perimeter of the building, leaving the major center portion of the building the exclusive bastion of the cavernous worship area. He wondered if it was referred to as a chapel, worship area or sanctuary. Holy Child was not like any "church" that he remembered as a young Catholic.

Lost in his thoughts as he walked, Mike did not notice the frocked figure approaching him before the man called out, "Hello Officer, I'm happy to see you. Your command told me that they would send a uniformed man to follow up the early morning visit from the Property Detectives."

Mike held out his hand in greeting as he spoke, "Good morning father, I'm Michael Romano. Are you the pastor by chance? I'm sorry for your trouble. Who in their right mind would break in to a church? It's like stealing money from God."

The priest's smile was luminescent as he exchanged a surprisingly hardy handshake, "Yes, Officer Romano, I'm Monsignor Scala and I'm the pastor. I see that we are in good hands; The Lord has sent me a fellow Italian. Please call me Vincent or Father Vincent, my title always sounds so pompous."

Since he was a child, Mike had always been slightly uneasy when around clergy of any kind, yet this time, the easy and friendly mannerisms of the man that stood before him made Michael relax and instilled a deeper than normal desire to give this particular assignment more than his all. The avenging angel inside him was crying out for results. Mike "knew" he only heard his own heartbeats, but it sure sounded like the beating of wings.

Mike thought for a moment before he answered, "Father Vincent, I don't know if God did you a favor by sending me, but as a long retired altar boy, I promise that I'll do my best for you."

The priest answered, "Come with me my son and I'll show you where the crime occurred" and led Mike to a set of double steel clad doors. Father Vincent continued, "In this room we keep athletic supplies, missals, the collection baskets themselves and other assorted paraphernalia. We also have a large heavy double door cabinet that we use to store valuable things. Sometimes we keep our collection money inside the cabinet overnight until two people; usually I and another person can make a bank deposit the next day. Last night, someone violated the cabinet and took Sunday's collection. The detectives that responded checked for fingerprints but said that there was nothing of value because everything was smeared. You'll see powder over everything." As Scala unlocked the right hand door, he entered; still holding the doorknob and standing to one side he spoke, "Michael, the cabinet is over there on the right against the corridor wall. I haven't touched anything. The only people who touched anything in this room were the detectives and of course the thief or thieves."

The first thing Romano did was to look at the entrance doors. There were no jimmy marks on or around the lock/latch mechanisms, and no residue of fingerprint powder left by the responding detectives in an attempt to recover any prints. He asked, “Father Vincent, did you or any of the staff clean these doors since the detectives were here?”

“No Michael, since the first police response, nobody entered the room or touched anything until now. Why do you ask?”

“Well Father, there seems to be no attempt by the detectives to check the doors. I can see that they felt it was unnecessary because there is no sign that they entered your room thru the doors; however I can see that they spent lots of time on the cabinet. Those tools on the floor, do you think that the burglar left them behind?”

“No my son, we always have tools in here. Our maintenance people use this room to store various items and necessary equipment and so does our priests and staff. As you can see, there’s a myriad of sports equipment and office supplies here too.”

Mike continued, “Well sir, it is my suggestion that you relocate anything that may be used to pry things open. Your staff unwittingly assisted the bad guys by giving them tools to work with. I forgot to ask, has this happened before?”

“Seemingly surprised by Mike’s question, the priest answered, “Yes it has, twice last year. You didn’t know?”

Mike was embarrassed by his lack of knowledge and tried to cover with, “No sir. I just began this assignment, this is my first job and I haven’t had time to review all past burglary reports.”

Mike began to look around the room with an investigators eye and asked, “Father, is it possible that besides the obvious, can you tell me if there is anything moved or is there anything different about the room since the last time you were in here. By the way, who put the collection money into the cabinet?”

The congenial cleric looked guilty as he answered, “Sorry to say that I did it yesterday, Sunday, at about 3:00 p.m. after it was counted and entered into our books. I have the only key to the cabinet and I was alone. Yesterday our parishioners were generous and our collection was slightly in excess of thirty six hundred dollars. I feel like a fool. We should have bought a safe after the first time."

"Please Father, you're a man of the cloth and not trained to think about things relating to security, especially in a church. I personally can't believe that God allowed this to happen at all let alone three times. It amazes me that someone would even do this."

The priest smiled gratefully and answered, "Thank you young man for trying to make me feel better. Now, how can I help you do your job? I cannot say that I see anything different about the room."

Mike moved around the room slowly, digesting everything he saw and mentally attempting to get inside the burglar's head, *if I broke in here, what would I have touched? How would I get in without messing up the door?* It was then that he saw a possible entry point. Up high, near the ceiling, were three horizontal windows, hinged at the top, one was wide open. He heard his heart beating or was Saint Michael speaking to him? Quickly he asked, "Father Vincent, that window at the top of the shelves, are you in the habit of leaving it open?"

The response was quick, "No, we have opened it from time to time, but I always insist that it be closed and locked. My staff has standing orders never to leave any window open. But it's very high on the outside and too small to get through. The responding detectives agreed and did not climb up to look at it because there was no evidence of a ladder or any other means to reach the window from the outside. They wore suits and one of them was rather overweight. Do you think that's how the thief got in?"

As the priest was asking the question, Mike was pulling a step ladder over to the shelves adjacent to the outer wall as he answered, "I don't know, but I intend to check. Do you have a tape measure in here? That window looks kind of small for an entry point."

"I don't know, but you do your thing and I'll get my maintenance man. I'm sure he has one. I'll call him from my office next door."

As Romano mounted the step ladder, he looked carefully at the shelves. There was dust settled on and around each item stored there. Only on the lower shelves did he see footprints in the dust along the front edges indicating that someone had climbed on them. Carefully, Mike climbed to the top shelf. He couldn't believe his own eyes. There on the flat surface of the shelf, below the open window, in the disturbed dust, he could see what looked like palm prints. It was obvious to him that they would be of little use because they were overlapped with each other and smudged. Police Officer Romano, on his first assignment as the Two Three print man, had found evidence of a burglary on his first assignment. Carefully he climbed back down and retrieved his finger print equipment and returned to the lofty perch to begin the process of trying to recover useable prints.

As Mike was setting up, Father Vincent returned with a tape measure and called, "Be careful my boy, don't fall. Here, I'll toss up a tape to you."

Mike looked down, smiled and said, "Sure thing Father, just make sure I don't have to reach for it. I don't want to lean over the edge. I don't think you'll be able to catch me." The tape was tossed up and caught. Mike continued, "They, I say they because I think there was more than one burglar based on what I see, definitely used the window to leave this room and because of nothing on the door, maybe enter it also. The multitude of prints up here indicates lots of activity. I'll be awhile."

Because he had to disturb the prints on the shelf to reach and to work on the window, Mike first dusted the shelf area. It was a messy business, kneeling on top of the shelf, barely wide enough to hold him and his equipment without disturbing whatever evidence was still usable. Using white powder because the shelves were dark gray, Mike managed to raise a partial palm print and two fingers. Carefully he applied the transfer tape, lifted the prints and put them on glossy black cards, drawing a small diagram on the back of each card indicating where he recovered that particular print from, numbered and signed them all.

Father Vincent stood on a step stool and watched Romano with great interest. "Officer Romano, would you like a couple of dust rags to clean off that awful stuff afterwards as you proceed to another area? Your uniform is getting quite soiled." Mike was concentrating and didn't answer immediately. The priest was returning with two rags as Mike answered.

"Yes, that would be a great help. Thank you." After "cleaning" the area where he just worked, Mike turned his attention to the window. Using his flashlight to cast contrasting shadows along the surface of the glass, Mike was able to see finger marks both inside and outside the lower edge of the glass. Before beginning his work, Mike measured the window opening and shouted the results to the priest, "Ten inches high and thirty inches wide, kind of tight to squeeze thru. It's amazing that they got in this way, I see prints on both sides of the glass."

Mike began working the inside of the glass with white powder, carefully taping and lifting four fingerprints, and transferred them to white glossy cards. Mike also drew a diagram of the recovery location and signed the reverse side of each card. As he gathered his equipment in preparation to climb down, Romano asked, "Father, could you have your man meet me outside, under this window with a ladder? I want to check the outside of the glass too."

The pastor responded with, "Certainly Michael, you're a very meticulous and efficient person, aren't you? I'll bet you're a better investigator then those detectives that were here earlier."

Mike answered, Thank you for the compliment, but it's the only way to do the job."

After using the supplied ladder and checking the outside of the window, Mike recovered only two partial finger prints and one partial palm print. The window frame did not appear to be forced but indicated that it must have been pried from the outside with either a knife blade or a small screwdriver. As Mike finished, he turned to the ever present Father Vincent. "Father, can we go back inside, to your office, I'd like to properly mark all this stuff before submitting it to the Latent Print Unit in Saint George? Usually I would take elimination prints, but I don't think you climbed the shelving in the storeroom, and the prints from the cabinet door were from the inside from where the metal was pulled back."

The cleric chuckled at Mike's joke as he responded, "We can Michael. Leave the ladder, my helper will put it away. Come, I'll put a pot of coffee on in my office." He waited for Mike to acknowledge the offer and led the way.

Once in the pastor's office, and seated with a cup of black coffee set before him, Mike continued marking the cards he gathered. On the rear of each card he put the date and location and numbered the cards 1 of 9, 2 of 9 etc. As he worked, Mike asked, "Father Vincent, if you are not in the habit of leaving the storage room windows open, please tell me who has access to the room? It seems to be that someone released the window lock and somehow the burglar reached the window and climbed in. I think that the burglar is a young person because of the small opening. Do you have any ideas who may be leaving the window unlocked? Are there any kids who have access to this room?"

"We have many young people who come and go in this room. As you can see we have lots of sports equipment in here. When our youth activities are going on there are many times that we send the kids in here to get items that we need. Usually the room is locked and only opened by a staff member of our church. I don't even want to think that one of our parishioners is responsible for the break in."

Mike saw the hurt look in the priest's eyes at the suggestion that one of his flock was responsible for the theft. However, he continued, "I realize how hurtful it would be if one of your own did this Father, but there seems to be no other explanation unless someone is an expert lock picker and your building is left unlocked without a security system. Do you lock the entire building at night and employ an alarm?"

Father Vincent took a few seconds to reflect on the prospect that one of his church members was the thief or in league with the actual thief or thieves. Vincent was losing his calm demeanor, and answered Mike in an agitated tone, "This hurts a great deal Officer Romano. Yes, we lock the building every night. I usually check the doors myself and there is an alarm that is set with a key. It is set from the outside and I can also operate it from my office if I work late. There are only three keys to it, I have one, my Assistant Pastor and our church Sexton have the other two. Once the alarm is set, we have one minuet to close the main doors before the alarm arms itself. If we forget to turn the alarm off before entering the building, we have 90 seconds to either go outside and turn off the alarm or run to my office to shut it down before it alerts the police. All our doors are on the system. I personally set the alarm last night."

"Sir, Father Vincent, it was not my intention to upset you, I'm sorry, but it is obvious that there was no forced entry into your church. The thief got in without setting off your alarm. That leads me to believe that he either used keys or climbed in through that window in your store room. I think the window is where he entered. If it is normally locked, then someone that had access to the room unlocked it to set up the break in. If you have no further questions, I'd like to leave now and forward these prints to the Latent Unit. Maybe we'll get lucky. Thank you for your time and please have the window locked. If there is any identification, as a result of these prints, I'll personally let you know."

Monsignor Scala thanked Romano for his work and shook his hand. Scala then made the sign of the cross and blessed Michael before he departed. Mike humbly thanked the priest and returned to his car. After putting his equipment case into his vehicle, Mike returned to the subject window for a second look at it. As he stood below it, Mike concentrated at the height of the window above the ground and tried to imagine how anybody could reach it, balance himself long enough to pry it open, and assuming it was closed but not locked, open it and then enter through such a small opening. Mike estimated that the window was eight to nine feet above the ground, and made a mental note, *I'll add a tape measure to my kit tomorrow.*

Mike's portable radio crackled ending his examination of the area under the suspected entry window, "Two Three Print car, what's your condition? Are you still out of service at the church on Amboy Road and Arden? K."

Mike responded with, "This unit is just returning to his auto and is 10-98, available. Do you have another assignment? K"

The dispatcher answered, "Negative Two Three Print, but 10-1 your command."

Mike had just been requested to telephone his command and responded with, "10-4 Central. This unit will be out of service for a few minutes on that 10-1, K."

Mike walked back inside the church and went directly to Monsignor Scala's office, knocked on the open door and walked in. "Sorry to bother you sir, but the dispatcher just notified me to call my command, they want to speak with me, may I use your telephone?"

With a smile, the cleric answered as he slid the instrument toward Mike, "Of course my son, and call me Father Vincent if you must use a title."

"Thank you. I won't be but a minute." The call was answered on the second ring, "One Two Three Precinct, Lieutenant Cassidy speaking. Can I help you?"

"Romano here, responding to a 10-1, Sir. What's up?"

Mike was surprised at what his lieutenant had to say, "Mike, we have another church burglary from last night. This one is at Saint Luke's Lutheran at 6100 Amboy Road. Somebody was busy last night. We just got the call here at the desk. Please respond, make a 61(complaint report) and try to raise some prints. We have to get this jerk that breaks into churches."

"I'm on it Lieutenant. I'm on my way." Putting the phone down, Mike turned to Father Vincent and said, "Another one at Saint Luke's Lutheran Church. Maybe it's the same guy..

The cleric made the Sign of the Cross and said, "Heaven help us, not even a house of God is safe. Good luck my son."

Mike arrived at Saint Luke's three minutes later. He had seen the church during normal patrol, but now he stopped in front for a moment to really look at it before pulling around the back to park. The building itself looked as if it went as far back as the Island's colonial days. The exterior consisted of wide wooden boards and stucco, much like old Tudor buildings he had seen in photos of old England. The double entrance doors were constructed of massive dark wood that looked like hand cut oak. Atop the slate roofed building sat an old fashioned belfry right out of a Currier and Ives picture. After making a memo book entry, Mike pulled his car around to the small parking area. As he walked up to the church, he saw that a side door had fresh marks along the edge where it met the latch side of the door jam, and slowly entered the building through that door.

Once inside he was struck by the contrast of that interior compared to Holy Child's. The ceiling had exposed wooden beams that were without any finish at all and had been left to age naturally, the rough interior plaster walls were painted white. The rows of wooden pews for the worshipers were also dark oak with a patina that only age and years of use could apply to the finish. It all was pleasing to the eye. At the front of the church sat a modestly decorated altar, in the center of which was a very beautiful golden colored tabernacle, its door bent and ajar. Hung on the wall behind the altar was an ornate old looking crucifix. Mike called out, "Police, anyone here?"

From a doorway behind the altar, out walked a tall man dressed in black and wearing the classic Christian type liturgical collar, "Yes, hello Officer, I'm Reverend Roger Blithe, the pastor of this little congregation. I'm happy that you responded so quickly."

Sensing the incredulous tone in the man's voice, Mike attempted to ease his pain with his response, "Got here as soon as I heard about your misfortunes Reverend and you are the second house of worship broken into last night. Holy Child was violated also. I'm here to do what I can to find out who did this."

The pastor stared at the name tag on Romano's chest before he spoke, "Officer Romano, as you can see, during the night one or more people broke into our church by forcing the side door and then damaged our tabernacle while taking a gold chalice that has been with our church since it began in the late 1880's. Sadly, we are not a wealthy parish and do not have an alarm system. We may be forced to get one installed now." As he spoke, Blithe turned and gestured towards the altar, "The piece is not worth much as chalices go, but it has great sentimental value to us and I pray that it can be recovered. If you look around, you'll see that two poor boxes that we have near the church entrance were cracked open too, however, I believe that they were emptied last night before the break in."

Mike walked to the entrance area and examined the damaged boxes. They too were fabricated out of old wood and were probably as old as the building. The slotted lids were caved in leaving the small ornate padlocks hanging down in front.

"Sir, these boxes can't be dusted for fingerprints because they are made of wood, but that tabernacle should reveal lots of prints. I'll get right on it. Do you have something that I can use to cover the altar vestments? The process is not the neatest thing to do.

"Certainly, I'll get something right away."

Minutes later, Mike covered the vestments and began his work.

CHAPTER THIRTEEN

While Mike Romano was diligently working in his capacity on Staten Island, Enrico, aka Baggs, was working too. As he usually did, Baggs stashed his big blue sedan in the rear of the building where he stored his black Bronco at 6:30 AM and traveled to New Jersey. He was the most trusted collector for Johnny "Eyes" Sanducci and began snaking his way through the businesses that paid regular tribute to the Sanducci Family. Baggs began in Perth Amboy and traveled north ending in Paterson.

By noon, he was standing in front of the former place of employment of Paul Capria, the Fucini Meat Packing Company in Jersey City. Baggs entered the building thru the street level loading dock. Across the entrance were heavy clear plastic ribbons hanging down to the ground that served a dual purpose, to basically close the large opening and yet still allow quick entry to the building work area where the walk-in refrigerators were. Three men who were milling about inside, stopped and stared at Baggs as he entered, then quickly returned to going about their business as if they never saw him. Baggs, noticing their uneasiness at seeing him shouted, "Hey, where's Paul, you know, the manager?"

There was mumbling between the men and the most Baggs could make out, without being able to determine who said it was, "Not here."

In his most demanding, no nonsense tone, Baggs asked, "Well then, who's in charge now? Someone get him for me."

One of the men, a large man with the bloodiest apron Enrico had ever seen, shuffled away and entered one of the walk-ins. Within seconds, out walked a tall rough looking man about 40 years old, "Hello, I'm Jim Fucini, how can I help you?" he asked in a slightly nervous tone.

Baggs knew that he had everyone on edge and was not about to ease the pressure. He answered, "I'm here on business for Johnny Eyes. My name is Baggs. Where can we talk?"

As Fucini approached, he fumbled for a clean spot on his apron and wiped his hands, then extended his right hand, offering a handshake.

Baggs reluctantly shook his hand and said, "After you, please, lead the way."

Fucini entered a small office that was remarkably clean considering the surrounding environment. There was a small bar, a rather large desk, behind which was a large high backed, maroon leather chair. It looked comfortable. Jim Fucini started to sit as Baggs closed the office door, but thought better of it, Please, Mr. Baggs, sit here and be comfortable."

"No, I prefer to stand. I'm here on business and won't be here long. Now let's get to it. As you know," Baggs wanted to keep the conversation on a sharp business edge and continued, "Mr. Sanducci has been receiving his money, for his managerial skills, every week for the last six years. Your former manager, Paul Capria was not forwarding the proper amount for quite some time. It is Mr. Sanducci's desire that I deal directly with you from now on. He assured me that there would not be errors in the payment calculations if you personally handle what Paul used to do. We feel that it would be better for all concerned. Are we correct in that assumption?"

The tone of Enrico's little diatribe and the almost direct threat to his personal safety made Fucini very uncomfortable and nervous. His mind wandered, *is this the guy that whacked Paul last week or is he only the bag man? How the hell do they know what we take in from the book* (illegal gambling) and our business? He began, "Baggs, if I can call you that?"

"Baggs is good Jimmy, everyone knows me by that name."

Fucini was sweating even though the office was air conditioned, "I don't know about Paul holding money back. I guess that's why I'm his replacement and it makes sense since I'm one of the owners. My brother John is the other one. Anyway, we are aware of our obligation to Mr. Sanducci regarding the weekly tribute regarding our business. As to the 'other enterprises', you know that amount varies." Baggs was slowly getting annoyed with his groveling.

"Listen Jimmy," Baggs began, "I can't spend lots of time here and I have other people to see, so if you have something for Mr. Sanducci, give it to me and I'll be on my way.Ok?"

Big Jim could feel the irritation emanating from the collector that stood before him, "Baggs, if you can give me an amount that Paul took from Mr. Sanducci, I'll replace it in a show of respect."

Baggs smiled, "No, that won't be necessary. Paul paid what he owed. You just continue being straight with us and things will be fine. Now what do you have for me to take back to Mr. Sanducci?"

Fucini was still standing and had to sit down as he opened a small safe inside a false panel in his desk. Baggs was scaring the hell out of him, so to play it safe, he announced his moves, "Sure thing, I just have to get the envelopes from my safe, that's all."

For effect and to humor himself, Baggs put his hand inside his jacket as if he was about to pull his weapon. Jim's eyes widened. As he straightened up, he announced, "Here you go, two envelopes, clearly marked, the shop and the other stuff."

Baggs took the envelopes and stuffed them inside his jacket pocket as he spoke, "Mr. Sanducci thanks you Jim, and I thank you for listening. See you next week." For effect he added, "It's a shame what happened to Paul. I knew him for some time. See you." As Baggs left the office, he could hear a sigh of relief from Jim Fucini and he knew there would always be a full amount in the weekly collection from that day on.

Baggs continued snaking through his collection route and completed his rounds by 4:30 p.m., just as the evening traffic began. It took a full hour to return to his Staten Island lair and put his Bronco away. Once inside, as usual, Baggs dumped the money that was collected on an old wooden work bench that was next to the rear door of the Quonset building. After emptying each envelope or paper sack he put them aside and counted the money separating the bills by denomination and recording the amounts of each contributing individual or business on a slip of paper that he would later turn in along with the money. It was fairly warm inside the building and Baggs opened the rear entrance doors to allow some air circulation. He had just bundled the bills when he heard some noise outside in front of the building. Quickly he put the money into a satchel he used for that purpose and threw it under his work bench. Instantly, Baggs drew his weapon while exiting the rear door and quickly, but cautiously, moved alongside of the building towards the front.

What he saw made him chuckle, two large raccoons were wrestling and thumping against the building. He picked up a stone and threw it at them, hitting one. They scampered into the brush. What he didn't know was that one of the paper bags and empty envelope that remained inside was whisked from the bench by a gust of wind and into the brush. Baggs returned to the bench, grabbed his satchel and gathered the discarded envelopes and paper bags, stuffing them all into one of the remaining bags for disposal into the first dumpster he passed. After locking the hut, he put the trash package on the front seat of his car along with his satchel containing the week's proceeds; it amounted to a total of $352,000.00.

Forty minutes after securing the Bronco and the Quonset building, Baggs arrived at Rocco's house. The two cousins greeted each other with a handshake and a "man hug", an Italian tradition.

"Cousin, I'm happy to see you Enrico. Once again Eyes and I thank you for your service. Did you have any trouble at Fucini's?"

Baggs grinned as he answered, "No, I actually enjoyed my visit. One of the Fucinis, Jimmy to be exact, was elevated by me to the position of our new liaison. He'll now be the man held responsible to seeing that we always receive the proper tribute and he understands that he must always submit the proper amount. Jimmy was polite, overly cooperative and even willing to pay whatever Capria owed us. I explained to him that Paul Capria has already paid his bill. You should have been there, he almost pissed himself. We'll never get shorted again. Some of my other stops acted nervous too, but never said anything. I had a good time today."

"Well, once again you have taken care of business. Do you have time to sit and have a drink?"

No, I have to get home. I promised Pat that I would take her out somewhere special tonight. Gotta go."

"Fine, I'll see you Friday so you can make Bryan's delivery. Take care."

"Sure thing, but I still wish there was somebody else that could do it. It gives me the willies."

"It's your job cousin, direct from Mr. Sanducci and Mr. Costello."

CHAPTER FOURTEEN

Mike Romano had completed his first work week as the Latent Print man in the Two Three and had submitted ten sets of recovered prints to Lieutenant Stonner's unit in the Two Oh. His two day swing between tours was uneventful and rather boring. He began to agonize over the loss of easy contact with his children since his estranged wife took them to her sister's. Mike busied himself with doing mundane chores like doing his laundry, washing his car and making sure to pick up clean uniforms from the dry cleaner. Mike even took a walking tour of Clay Pit Pond Park in an effort to find any clues about the driver of the Black Bronco that he and Sully had followed and lost inside the park.

His first set of four to twelve tours as print man began that Monday at 3:30 p.m. After roll call, Mike signed out his department issued equipment for the night, portable radio, RMP 1134 and a 12 gauge Remington model 870 shotgun. It had been Romano's choice to carry a shotgun during the day tours, but regulation decreed that a solo patrol car officer must carry the weapon during four to twelve and twelve to eight tours. As per protocol, Mike went over to the bright red heavy iron goose necked, iron pipe loading station with six inches of sand on the bottom and inserted the gun's barrel into the padded opening and turned the weapon over. After sliding the pump back, he chambered five double '0' buck rounds and slid the pump forward, checking that the safety was on and was now ready for anything that might arise.

After stowing his print kit on the floor behind the driver's seat, Mike turned on the car's ignition and reached for the hidden release button for the shotgun rack. He put the Remington into the rack; barrel pointing away from the operator and locked it in. The rack was designed to prevent any mishaps if the operator accidently left a round chambered and grabbed the weapon in haste, setting it off. The passenger door would sustain all the damage along with the eardrums of the officer.

The first two nights of his set of tours was rather uneventful. Romano responded to several past residential burglaries, usually obtaining and submitting latent prints. He always finger printed the residents so that Lieutenant Stonner's men could eliminate any prints that belonged to persons rightfully allowed to be inside the violated locations.

On Wednesday afternoon, Mike arrived at the station house early with the idea that he would call Stonner's office and inquire if his work at Holy Child bore any fruit. When he got Lieutenant Stonner on the phone, the lieutenant informed him that there were workable prints from both Holy Child and Saint Luke's and that he had both good and bad news. Stonner explained that the prints from both churches were from the same person, but there was no match on file, indicating that the burglar had not been entered in the system, yet. As Mike heard the news, his heart raced and he again heard the beating of wings as he thought, *with the help of Saint Michael, I'm gonna get this guy.*

Mike then called the office of Sergeant. Flynn. "Hi Sarge, its Mike Romano."

"Hello Mike. What can I do for you? Do you have any new information?" Without waiting for any answer, Flynn continued, "I have something new for you. Yesterday, Secaucus PD called and notified us that they found a body with rounds that matched the weapon used by your Bronco shooter. It looks like he did another one. That makes four we can tie him to, three here and one in New Jersey, if we can ever get him and his weapon."

Mike was silent for a second before answering, "Sorry to hear that another human being lost his life but happy that when we get this guy, we'll get him good. Another question I never asked, do any of the victims have gangland ties?"

Flynn's voice had a slightly elated tone as he answered, "Every one of them my boy, every one. Why do you ask?"

"I really can't put it into words but by the remote locations of the two old Staten Island bodies, out of the way, yet findable and the Bronco hit, a normally heavy flow of traffic and getaway woods nearby, it tells me that the hits are from a real professional, like the guy is spiting in the cops' faces."

"That's an interesting theory, Michael. Keep your eyes open, I have faith in you and call at once if anything odd happens."

"I sure will Sarge. Excuse me, time for me to go to work. Have a safe tour, Boss."

"You too Mike," Flynn answered. The receiver clicked. Mike smiled, replaced his handset and went up to the locker room to suit up. Roll call was due to begin in ten minutes.

***

Romano loaded his gear into the same car that he used the day before, first securing the shotgun before heading out to begin his patrol assignment. On that particular tour he was designated as the Burglary Response Auto and did not get a Sector assignment. Mike was happy that he could roam the entire command without stretching the rules and thought, *tonight; I'll spend some time looking for the Bronco again.*

Within ten minutes, Mike was slowly bumping his way through the passable roads inside Clay Pit Pond Park in an effort to once again locate any clues regarding the Bronco he had followed and lost several days before. The only thing that he found was where he and Sully had used small timber to free their car when it bogged down as they chased the truck. Once back on the paved roadway, Romano decided to check everything that even looked wide enough to allow a car to drive into the brush or woods along Arthur Kill Road, then quickly drove to the intersection of Bloomingdale Road and Arthur Kill, deciding that he would begin his quest by looking in the large, high ground wooded area at that location. Romano doubted that he would find anything because the area was a favorite of horseback riders, but the investigator inside of him dictated that he be methodical in checking all out of the way locations. Twenty minutes later, with negative results, he returned to Arthur Kill Road and headed slowly south towards the Outer Bridge.

Mike had just turned off the paved road onto an almost hidden dirt road when at 1635 hours, his radio crackled, “In the Two Three, silent alarm, possible burglary in progress at 4550 Redford Ave, just south of Richmond Avenue. Units needed to respond. Alarm company not responding, K”

As Romano reached for the mike to respond, he heard, “Two Three Frank on the way,” followed by, “Two Three John, K” He keyed his microphone, “Two Three Latent Print Car responding also, K.”

Central added, “Be advised two Three units, we don’t know if the perps are inside. A guy walking his dog also called it in. K”

What Mike Romano did not know, was that prior to the radio call, he was about to enter the road that led to the storage shed of Baggs’ black Ford Bronco. It might have made his day because the truck had been in the building.

Mike hit his lights and shot to Page Avenue, cut a left to Hylan Boulevard and left again, arriving just as the first team was exiting their RMP. Romano stopped his car on Hylan and exited with his tour partner, the Remington 12 gauge, in his hands. As he focused his attention on the building, he noticed a small basement window without glass and whistled to alert the cops. The second team had arrived at that point and indicated that Mike should cover the rear door of the house. Sector Frank notified the dispatcher that all units were on the scene and they would “check and advise.”

Once it was established that all exits from the house were secure, Bill Grange, one of the Sector Frank officers, notified the dispatcher that, “4550 Hylan Blvd. appears secure at this time. Please have a supervisor respond, there is a break of a basement window. K.”

The dispatcher requested the patrol sergeant. The voice of Sergeant Hogan could be heard, “Two Three patrol sergeant will respond Central. What’s the condition?”

Grange answered, “We want to enter, search for perps and secure the premises. K”

Hogan responded with, “Ten Four. Units stand by. Sergeant is on the way.”

When Hogan arrived he was briefed as to what the responding men had done so far. It was explained to him that besides the broken window, all doors appeared to be locked from the inside and there was no response to pounding on the doors. The men wanted to go in through the window and search for a perpetrator or perpetrators. Regulations required that a supervisor be present.

Hogan, a cautious man, instructed Mike to remain at the rear of the house and assigned a cop to the front door. He then instructed two men to enter the house through that basement window after he first directed a cop to look over their shoulders and guard them as they dropped thru the window, making sure that nobody was present to compromise the cops' safety. When his men were safely inside, Hogan also dropped thru the window into the house.

After checking the basement and finding no one, Hogan flicked a wall switch to turn on the recessed ceiling lighting and directed his driver to replace Romano and tell him to bring his fingerprint kit into the house and join the search. He instructed his men, “First, we all go to the highest floor of the house and work down. Touch nothing; Mike will be dusting for latents once we know the place is secure. Let's go and be careful.

The top floor contained only what appeared to be three bedrooms and another room that may have been used as a huge closet and a large bathroom. The ‘closet room’ contained stacks of shoes, several wigs and a closet of ladies clothing. It was ransacked as were all the bedrooms. Below, on the main floor were a kitchen, living room, another bathroom and what appeared to be a home office. There was no burglar hiding in the house. Whoever broke in apparently left thru the same basement window before the cops arrived.

Mike had secured the shotgun and was now in the house. Hogan turned to Mike, “Ok Romano, do your thing. Where are you going to start?” Hogan advised that he would stay behind as Mike did his work because, in essence, he would also be searching the premises for valuables and it was required that a boss be present during such a search as an integrity safeguard.

Noting the time of day and assuming that school was out and most people were usually starting to return home from their jobs, Hogan notified the dispatcher, "Two Three Sergeant to Central. This unit and Latent will remain on the scene until arrival of owners, all other Two Three units are ten- ninety eight, and resuming patrol. Has the alarm company contacted the owners? Sergeant and Latent will be ten- sixty two (out of service) at this time. K"

Turning to his other men and speaking to no one in particular he ordered, "My driver and I will remain; you other men can resume patrol."

The dispatcher replied, "Unknown Two Three Sergeant."

Mike spoke, "Sarge, I'd like to do the toughest room first, while I'm fresh, the room with all the shoes."

Hogan smiled and said, "It's your call. Lead on."

Returning to the 'closet room', Mike moved directly to the glass topped dresser, carefully putting some loose items on the floor then he dusted the entire surface of the glass and raised several sets of finger prints. From experience, Mike knew that the prints that showed up clearer were probably new and might belong to the burglar. He then carefully applied the transfer tape to protect them for later removal and recording. Next he began to open the dresser drawers looking for any jewelry boxes or such that might reveal prints and was surprised to find dozens of fishnet panty hose and bras. Inside some of the bras were "falsies" or artificial foam breasts.

When Hogan saw the items, he laughed loudly and said, "Holy crap. This is where he lives."

Mike asked, "Who Sarge?"

"The Red Rider, that's who!"

"Who or what is the Red Rider?"

"I'm surprised that you don't know. For years, there's this guy who is supposed to be a high powered chef in some fancy New

York City hotel and he likes to dress up as a woman when home. He's married and I'm told even goes to church on Sunday with his wife and wears women's clothes. We're in his house!"

Mike expressed his surprise, "No shit! He's married and by the look of the rooms, has kids too and the pinball machines in the basement must be theirs. How did he get the name Red Rider?"

Hogan was having a good time. "I've only seen him from a distance a few times and he had on something bright red. I'm told that he always wears something red. The guys in the command first referred to him as Red Riding Hood. Over time it got changed to Fishnet Red, because he usually wears fishnet stockings and a skirt along with something red. I have no idea why his nickname got changed to Red Rider. I'm staying here until he gets home so I can see him up close."

Mike responded with, "Well Sarge, get comfortable because we're gonna be here awhile. I think that I'll recover lots of prints though, and I'll still have to take a set of elimination prints of all the family members, so enjoy."

Hogan had moved over to the room's closet and found the sliding door was slightly open. He pushed it back and saw some clothes were on the floor along with ladies shoes. Hogan reached in and pulled a leather skirt from its hanger and held it against himself, "Hey Mike, how do I look? It looks like it could fit me, so it must be his. All the clothes look too big for a woman, unless his wife is built like a New Jersey milk cow."

"Romano couldn't help himself and quipped, "Wow, you sure look hot. Your new nickname can be Hot Hogan."

"Hey, you're forgetting I'm your Sergeant; a little respect is in order." Both men laughed and Mike said, "Excuse me, Sergeant Hot Hogan."

Hogan's driver, Lenny, got into the act by announcing, "Hey guys, the shoes in these boxes are all huge. I hope they belong to the Red Rider and not his wife, if she can wear these things, I don't ever want to meet her."

After a few more chuckles, Hogan brought the room back to a professional demeanor, "Lenny, you know not to touch anything, especially never opening boxes. Assist only if asked."

Lenny, slightly embarrassed, only responded with, "Sarge."

Mike pulled a pair of patent leather shoes from the closet by hooking them with his fingers and placed them on the dresser away from the previously taped over prints. After using his flashlight to cast ever so slight shadows of any prints that might be present and finding several, he got them ready for dusting. After dusting the shoes and determining the latents to be of possible value, Mike applied the transfer tape. Turning to his supervisor, he announced, "This is gonna take some time Sarge. We still have to check the other rooms before we go downstairs."

It was several minutes before Romano transferred all the taped prints to cards and marked them. When he had finished, he then led Hogan and Lenny thru the other rooms. They appeared untouched, except the master bedroom. The cops remained for almost forty minutes while Mike worked and recovered only three usable lifts before he announced, "I got what I could on this floor, we can move down now Sarge."

Hogan responded with, "Keep at it Mike, I trust you completely. Lenny and I will be sitting in the living room. Call out if you need me."

Romano checked out the main level of the house. It appeared that nothing was disturbed. He notified Hogan, "Sarge it seems that nothing on this level was touched. I'm going down to the basement."

"Fine Mike, have fun. Some family member should be home soon. We'll wait here."

After descending to the basement, Mike first looked for a piece of window glass that he felt was large enough to contain a finger print, and found nothing he could use. The floor of the basement was covered with floor tiles that were hard underfoot. Whatever glass was not broken when it dropped to the floor was now broken into small pieces by the cops, including him, entering through the window. Mike found no usable piece even though the other teams had used the front door when they left the premises. He was getting tired and after doing a cursory check of the small half bath and a laundry room, Mike turned his attention back to the main room of the basement.

On one side of the room was a small dry bar and under the counter was a small refrigerator. Carefully he opened the door and inside was several cans of beer and soft drinks. The smooth surface of the fridge yielded several prints. After transferring them to cards and properly marking them, he remained at the bar and tried to think like the burglar. Across the room were four expensive arcade type pinball machines that were all lit up as if they had recently been played, Mike immediately walked over to them to get a better look. Underneath two of the machines were beer cans accompanied by the all too familiar odor of spilled beer. Mike thought, *these little shits played pinball and drank beer. They must have been here all day and were only seen when they left. Wonder how come the alarm company took so long to notify us? The doors were never opened. Maybe these guys were worried about a door alarm?* First he carefully retrieved the beer cans and put them on the bar to allow then to dry enough to be worked on after he printed the pinball machines.

When he had finished his work, Mike tallied up all the lifts he made in the house, he had a total of eighteen, of what he thought were workable prints.

By the time Mike finished marking them all, it was 6:35 p.m. and Sergeant. Hogan called out, “Officer Romano, the owners are here.”

Mike’s curiosity about the Red Rider was about to be satisfied, “On the way Boss,” he replied as he hurriedly gathered his equipment and the recovered prints and put everything into his kit.

***

Four people were gathered in the living room in addition to Hogan and his driver, a male that appeared to be about forty years old and three females, obviously the wife and two daughters. They all wore casual, but expensive clothes. Romano was disappointed, the guy looked normal and stood about five-nine, with a full head of neatly groomed black hair and was of medium build. The woman was shorter, appeared slightly overweight and in Romano's opinion, was once very attractive. The girls looked like carbon copies of their mother and were probably still in high school.

Hogan spoke as Mike put down his gear and nodded an acknowledgement of their presence, "Mr. and Mrs. Gabriel, this is Officer Romano, our finger print expert. He has recovered some prints that he believes were left by the burglar or burglars and needs your cooperation. Now that he has finished his work, he will take a complete report from you as to what you believe is missing. My driver and I have been here for some time now, and as we are no longer needed here; I will leave you in this officer's capable hands and return to my duties." He added, "Sorry to meet you like this. We'll do our best to catch them." Turning to Mike, he said, "Romano, when you're finished, please notify me and I'll meet you at the command. Carry on." Hogan tapped Lenny on the shoulder and walked to the front door.

Romano began with, "Mr. and Mrs. Gabriel, I too am sorry to meet you folks this way," he held out his hand in greeting. Mrs. Gabriel took it first saying, "Mary, please officer," followed by her husband, "Oscar, hope you can help Officer Romano. He swept his hand past each of his girls and announced, "Mary and Alice, 15 and 17 respectively. Where do we start?"

Mike said, "If you will please walk thru your home with me, beginning upstairs and tell me what you think is missing, I'll record it in my memo book as we go thru all the rooms, then we'll go downstairs and I'll fill out a complaint report. Please, I must apologize about any print powder that is left behind; I tried to be as neat as possible. I always advise people to use a vacuum to remove it from any furniture surfaces before using any spray on cleaners. When those powders get wet they become pasty and very hard to remove. The black is finely ground charcoal and the white is usually manufactured from powdered chalk. We all can remember our school days."

Oscar replied, "We understand Officer, follow me."

"If you folks insist on first names, please call me Mike. Thanks. By the way, how long have you used your alarm company? I think the thieves spent some real time in the house before leaving; they even played with your pinball machines and had a couple of beers. When we arrived, there was no one present and your doors were all locked. You should get a new alarm company. Your current one dropped the ball."

Oscar cursed and mumbled as his wife looked around in the master bedroom. The girls ran to their respective rooms squealing and groaning. Mike and Oscar remained in the doorway, as Mary called out, "My diamond and ruby ring is gone. Oh my God so is mother's gold bracelet. Oscar what are we going to do?"

Mike recorded the items in his book. Oscar tried to calm his wife down by saying, "Don't worry, Mike here, Officer Romano, will catch them with his finger prints."

Mary was distraught and asked, "Can we add to the report tomorrow after we check everything?"

Romano smiled and answered, "Of course, but I need the obvious items to list on my report. Mr. Gabriel, Oscar, let's move to another room please."

The Red Rider led the way to the room containing the oversized lady's clothes. As Oscar and Mike entered the room, Oscar looked nervously around, turned to Mike and said, "Mike, thank you for not laughing or making fun of what's in here. Yes, its mine and Mary and the kids are good with it."

Slightly surprised by Oscar's candor, Mike answered, "You're the victim of a crime, I'm not here to judge you, only to help and try to catch the bad guy. You're personal life, as long as no laws are broken is not my business. Can you determine what if anything is missing?"

The cross dresser buried himself in the closet and began spewing items out behind himself like a dog digging a backyard hole. "Thank God it's still here. They never found it." He then backed out holding a small grey lock box. “This is from my very lucrative side business in the East Village, where I teach culinary arts and can wear the garments that you see here without fear of ridicule. I don’t declare the money. Guess tonight’s class is canceled.”

Romano’s answer started a quick exchange, “You mean that you come home and then run into The City the same day?”

“No, I carry a change of clothes in my car. I change in the restroom of the garage where I park and take a taxi to my class.”

“Wow, that must cost a pretty penny.”

“I make a great salary and my culinary arts class is a cash business. Mary has her own little business too. We’re doing well.”

Shortly after Oscar’s confirming revelation in “his room”, Mike went downstairs to explain why he had to make elimination fingerprint cards for the entire family and submit them with the recovered latent prints. Mike further added that he would contact the Gabriels in the event that there were any prints of value resulting in the identification of one or more perpetrators, quickly adding that there would be identification only if the bad guys had been arrested before, or their prints were in the system for any other reason.

As Mike gathered up his gear, both Oscar and Mary shook his hand and thanked him for his diligent service and again thanked him for his courtesy regarding their unusual life style. Once in his RMP, Romano radioed the dispatcher that he would be returning to his command to file his reports and submit his findings to the Latent Print Unit.

***

Sergeant Hogan was standing on the steps of the Two Three, as Mike pulled up in his patrol car. He quickly walked down and met Mike at the curb.

“Well Romano, what happened? Did Gabriel admit to being a cross dresser? Is he gay? Come on, let’s hear all the details.”

"Well Sarge, I got lots of prints, four sets of elimination prints and yes, he admitted to the fact that he is a cross dresser. It appears that his family doesn't mind although it was never explained. Mrs. Gabriel has her own business and besides being a high end chef, Mr. Gabriel has a side business where he teaches a cooking class in the Village, and always dresses in drag. The guy changes from normal clothing to women's clothing where he parks his car, then goes downtown by taxi to teach his class. Both of them thanked me for not making fun of their family situation. Outside of dressing weird, the guy is alright."

The sergeant was hanging on every word. When Mike was finished, Hogan responded with, "Suspicions confirmed. Gabriel is the Red Rider. Guess it takes all kinds to make the world. Good job Romano."

An hour later, Mike signed off duty.

CHAPTER FIFTEEN

Many weeks had gone by as Romano settled into his new assignment. He began to get notices from Lieutenant Stonner that a few of the prints he had sent in produced some identification. The prints that he recovered from the house burglary at 4550 Hylan Blvd. (the Red Rider's home) belonged to two guys from Great Kills. They were actually brothers, Jim and Frank Anderson, seventeen and nineteen years old respectively. They both had long juvenile records and they each had two previous burglary arrests. Currently, they were both on parole and their parole officer had been notified. Stonner told Romano that he would be called to court if the boys elected to go to trial. Property Squad Detectives have been in contact with the Gabriel family who assured them that they would be at the District Attorney's office to press charges when notified that an arrest had been made.

Mike's soon to be ex-wife and children returned to The Island from their extended stay at her sister's in Queens. His divorce date had drawn nearer and Betty grew increasingly bitchy. Mike's attorney cautioned him not to do battle with her and to have as little contact with the woman as possible. Subsequently he managed to visit with his children only once or twice on a week day and that was when he worked his four to twelve sets, and Betty was at work. Mike did not like having to sneak around his own home and could hardly wait for the judge to bang his gavel and say, "Divorce Granted."

To avoid dwelling on his personal problems when not with his kids or working, Romano would drive past the houses on Arlo Road in a so far, futile attempt, to find Bryan's blue Buick in one of the driveways. His timing was always off. The persistent cop also visited every small roadway he came upon while driving along Arthur Kill Road in an attempt to locate the elusive black Bronco.

Believing that the truck was hidden somewhere within the confines of Clay Pit Pond Park, he often parked his RMP and walked around in earnest, the results were always negative. Mike never knew he was less than a quarter mile from the Bronco's hiding place and sometimes Baggs personal auto, one that he would recognize at once. Even Sergeant Flynn had nothing new to tell him about the case relating to the Bronco.

***

Mike Romano, Two Three Print Officer, was beginning to grow more impatient with the lack of results, concerning what he deemed important, when the hand of providence moved again. On a Monday morning at 7:00 a.m. Monsignor Scala opened the church doors and walked to the store room where the parish kept Sunday's collection money. The pastor was anxious to prepare a bank deposit slip and be at his bank when the doors opened at 8:30 a.m. After entering the room, he was shocked to see his "safe cabinet" door bent and wide open once again. Before he even walked up to it, Scala began muttering a prayer. Vincent Scala felt that he just knew his cash box was gone and chastised himself for not listening to Officer Romano. The cleric immediately looked up at the windows and saw the infamous window open. By 7:15 a.m., Monsignor Scala was composed enough to phone the Two Three desk and ask for Michael Romano without even a thought about dialing 911. When told by the Desk Sergeant that Romano was unable to come to the phone because he wasn't even in the station house yet, the pastor said, "Well, I only want him to respond here. I'll wait and don't send anybody else. Please send him here as soon as he arrives. It happened again, they got us again."

As the sergeant began to ask, "What happened Monsignor???"

The distraught priest said, "Thank you. God bless you," and hung up the phone.

Romano walked past the desk officer five minutes later and in keeping with his respectful personality gave the desk a "See" (a quick salute of respect to both the American Flag that hung on the wall and the officer in charge). The Sergeant quickly returned the salute and added, "Romano, Holy Child was burglarized again over night. The pastor called for you and only you to respond. Get there as soon as you stand roll call. Put the job over the air. Got it?"

"Sure thing. Will you please notify the roll call sergeant that you're directing me to go?"

Twenty minutes later, Mike walked into Monsignor Scala's office. "Good morning Monsignor. I've heard about your troubles and I'm here to help."

"Thank you for coming so quickly my son," was the reply from the priest as he stood and shook Romano's extended hand. Scala continued, still gripping Mike's hand, as he moved from around the back of his desk, "Please follow me into our store room. I'm afraid that I never took your advice and obtained a proper safe. We lost our Sunday collection again. Did you get a match on the finger prints from the last time?"

"Yes sir, we did. The prints belong to the same person who broke into Saint Luke's Lutheran Church and desecrated their tabernacle, taking religious objects that were part of the church since its founding. There is no identification yet. I would like to see the room please and then suggest an idea with you as to how we can catch the person or persons responsible."

As he led the way, Scala mumbled, "Yes, yes, let's go see the room so we can then sit and talk." Once in the room, Scala excused himself to, "Go back to my office and think about what to do."

Romano spent an hour in the storeroom dusting for prints and managed to only recover several partials, as if the perpetrator had wiped any area that he touched. He carefully tagged and recorded them for processing, then went back to Scala's office to take a proper report and discuss his idea with the old man.

"Father Vincent," Mike began, trying to be as friendly as possible because he wanted the pastor's cooperation. "I believe that I may possibly know who keeps breaking into your church."

The cleric almost jumped out of his chair saying, "Please tell me Michael and I'll beat the crap out of him." As his words became airborne, Vincent Scala looked astonished at the sound of his own voice and said," God forgive me for that slip, but I'm so angry. Please excuse me. That was very un-priestly."

Mike smiled inwardly and acted as if he didn't hear what the priest said and answered his question. "Well sir, I would like to spend some time inside the church on a midnight shift over a week end and hopefully catch this bum in the act, if my captain gives me permission. Will it be alright with you? I'll need a key to the church and the alarm. Easter is coming and you'll probably be getting more than the usual donations and I'd like to do it then. How about it? Can I count on you?"

"Yes, yes, you can do whatever you like. How can I help?"

"Father Vincent, is there a room where I and a partner can spend the night that is adjacent to the store room, one that shares the same wall?"

"Yes, come with me," Scala answered as he pointed to a door on the far wall of his office. "Behind that wall is a small room that I use to rest in when I want to hide from the world. It has a couch and armchair and shares a wall with the store room. What do you want to do Michael?" he said as he opened the door and flicked a wall switch, bathing the room in light.

"With your permission sir, I would like to drill two small holes thru the block wall, hide in this room and wait for the bad guys to enter the store room. If you give us a key to that room, we'll enter the room as they bang away at your cabinet and catch them in the act. They can never wiggle thru that window before we can grab them. What do you think?"

"Yes you can make a hole, two holes or one big enough to crawl thru, I don't care, just get them."

"Ok sir, Easter is two weeks away, I'll try to convince my boss and then we can set it up. Thank you. I'll file a burglary report and send in these prints, I'm going right back to the command when I leave here."

The pastor replied, "Yes, Easter would be an ideal time for a thief to try to rob us again. But this time my own Saint Michael will be waiting."

Mike was surprised that the cleric compared him to The Archangel. The last person to use those words was his soon to be ex-wife Betty back when their marriage was solid, before she strayed into extra marital sexual liaisons. Quickly regaining his thoughts, he replied, "No sir, I'm not Saint Michael, but I try, and I'm not a saint by any means, but thank you for the compliment."

"Not at all my son. The Good Lord sent you to our church for a reason and I believe it is to catch the thief. I will pray for that end and Bless you."

As Michael reached the office doorway and was about to leave, he turned and said in a slightly humorous manner, "Better pray that my captain allows me to change my tour and sit inside the church and wait for a burglar that may not come. Convincing the Boss is going to be tougher then grabbing the bad guy. As soon as I have his answer, I'll come by and tell you. Have a good day Father."

Captain Anderson wasn't on duty when Romano returned to the station house and his idea about the church burglaries would have to wait. After filing his report and forwarding the newest prints from Holy Child, Mike put himself out for meal, notifying both the desk officer and dispatcher, then drove to the Annadale Luncheonette for a quick meal and a visit with Leona. She always made him feel good and maybe she had info on Guggalarie.

"Hey Leona," Mike shouted as he walked into the luncheonette and parked on a stool at the far end of the counter.

"Well, hello Michael. I haven't seen you for some time. Has you new assignment kept you too busy to stop by?"

"Kind of, when not lifting prints, I'm obsessed with that little shit Michael Guggalarie and when not chasing him, I'm always looking for the black Bronco I told you about. Then there's my divorce. Betty is making it her personal business to keep me on edge by using my love for my children against me. But you don't want to listen to that stuff. Anyway, how have you been?"

"Great Mike and my two girls are terrific too. You know, sometimes I think, what if we met years ago? Would we both be alone? Could we have been more than friends?"

Mike was startled to hear the words that had passed thru his mind many times. He replied, "Well Leona; that is a question that is filled with probabilities. At this point in time let's just enjoy our friendship and the what-ifs. What do you say?"

Leona smiled at him with a faraway look in her eyes and replied, "Sure Mike. Are you always this tactful when you answer a loaded question?"

It was obvious to both of them that they were playing a word game and flirting like school kids as he answered, "Only when I speak to a good person and care enough to keep the door open to whatever might happen someday." Seeing the look of hope on her face, he added, "But right now I don't want to walk thru that door. I'll stay on the friendship side." As soon as he heard his own words, he wished that he never said them but said nothing about it.

"Fine Michael, I'm here if you ever want to walk thru that door. What can I get you today, a hamburger, a salad, breakfast? You name it and if I have it, it's yours."

"Just a ham and Swiss on rye bread with mayo, some coffee please and some conversation." As Leona turned around to prepare his sandwich, Mike asked, "Has Guggalarie been around lately? Holy Child was broken into again sometime Sunday night and I still think he had something to do with it. The Lutheran church also was burglarized and the unit in Saint George tells me that the same person did both churches but there is no record of the prints on file."

"Actually, he was in here this morning with his buddy Tommy Perino and another kid whose name escapes me. Michael paid the bill for all of them. Oh yes, I almost forgot, last week Michael and Tommy were riding very expensive new bicycles. Does that help?"

In Romano's head, he heard something that sounded like the beating of wings and it startled him. "Did you hear that Leona?"

"Hear what?"

"Never mind, it's just nothing. It must be my imagination working overtime, happens sometimes", he answered as Leona put his coffee and sandwich on the counter.

Other customers came in; requiring Leona's attention leaving Mike alone while he ate his lunch. By the time he was finished, Leona was busy as a one armed woman at a wall paper hanging contest. Mike left six dollars on the counter and said goodbye as he left the restaurant.

The rest of his tour was uneventful except for two past house burglaries that he responded to. By 3:00 p.m. he was back in the Two Three completing his paper work and packaging the recovered prints for transport to the Two Oh and Lieutenant Stonner by whatever cop was chosen to deliver the daily department mail during the midnight tour.

After signing off duty, Romano headed directly to Andersons office. The captain was in and motioned for Mike to enter as soon as he saw him.

"Romano, I've been told how busy you've been with your fingerprints. I've also been notified by the Boro Office that you have recovered the same prints in two churches within our command. That's excellent work even though there has been no match to date, however I'm also told there has been arrests as a result of other jobs that you responded to. I thank you. You make our command look good. Now, what can I do for you? I assume you're here for a reason, what is it?"

"Well Captain, in case you didn't know, there has been another burglary at Holy Child this weekend. I was there today doing my thing and forwarded some more prints. I suspect that they will match the prints of the last two church break-ins and I have an idea on how to catch the perps and would like to get your approval to go ahead with it."

"I know about the break in. Ok Michael, let's hear your idea. If it makes sense, maybe we can do it."

"Ok, here goes. There's a kid in Annadale who is reputed to be a purse snatcher and burglar. I'm told that he may and may not be old enough to take a real collar and be printed. I had the squad run his name and they tell me the boy has no record. Maybe that's why we can't get an ID on the prints."

The captain was interested, "Go on."

"Well Captain, Easter is two weeks away and people usually give a larger than normal contribution to their church at that time and at Christmas. If I'm right, our burglar will hit the church again. I'd like to spend the night of Easter Sunday into Monday morning inside the church, with a partner of course, and catch the little creep in the act. I have the full cooperation of Monsignor Scala. What do you say Captain?"

"Give me a few days to think about it Romano, it's a rather unusual request for a patrol officer. How do you propose to watch the subject room?

Mike excitedly answered, "Well, the pastor, Monsignor Scala, has an inner room adjacent to his office that shares a wall with the room where they keep the money. He'll let us drill a couple of holes thru the cinder block wall to monitor the room. If the bad guy or guys enter, we'll be able to see and hear him. Scala will give us keys to enter the church and a key to enter the room before the guys can get away. It's a good plan Boss."

"Sounds like it might work, if the burglar decides to break in the night that you're there. Do you have a partner in mind for the work?"

""Yes I do and if possible, I'd like Jerry Sullivan with me for the stake out."

"Ah, yes. You two guys were partnered up for a while weren't you? That's fine with me. Romano, you know, as we're discussing this thing, I've thought about it. It's a go. Go talk with Sullivan and set it up with roll call and Lieutenant Cassidy, the Executive Officer. Please keep me informed. Oh, by the way, did you get any prints from the church today?"

"Yes Sir, I did and sent them in. They probably will be a match to the sets from the last burglaries. Those guys think that they can do whatever, and whenever they want to it. If I can help it, that's about to stop." Romano thanked his Captain for agreeing with his plan to catch the church burglars, left the office and drove home.

Back in his apartment, as he was pouring three fingers of his "celebratory scotch", Mike saw the flashing light of his answering machine. After taking a sip, he listened to the message, "Romano, it's Arthur Slotnick, your divorce date has been assigned. It's a few weeks away, Thursday, May 3rd. Please call me and schedule an office visit to go over any last minute details. There's no rush, but it should be no later than a week before the court date. Talk to you." Mike raised his glass to the heavens, said, "Thank you", put the glass to his smiling lips and finished the golden liquid in one gulp.

***

While Romano began relaxing at home, Baggs was having a conversation with Joe Plegesi in his Jersey City butcher shop. "Joe, Mr. Sanducci relies on me to collect the fees from the various merchants that belong to our organization. The amount of our share is based on our estimates that we calculate for each particular business based on years of experience. We understand if there is a small fluctuation on a weekly basis because we know your customer participation varies a little, but you as a business man, realize that if your noncommercial related customers are off count, you are responsible to supplement our share with money from your retail customer base and we expect the same amount every week, with an occasional variant of maybe a hundred."

Beads of sweat were running down Plegesi's forehead as Baggs spoke. He was only capable of an occasional nod and a soft, barely audible, "Yes". He had heard rumors about Baggs, that sometimes, after a visit laced with conversation, people have disappeared or are found shot to death. Today was the first time that Baggs had ever said more than, "Hello, thank you" and "see you again", or "have a nice day", in three years of collections and he was scared shitless.

After what seemed to him like an eternity, Joe Plegesi was able to find his voice again, "Baggs, there has been a falloff in customers with the numbers bets and poker players, added to the fact that I've had extra family expenses, please tell me what must I do to set things right with Mr. Sanducci."

Baggs enjoyed when someone groveled. He liked it almost as much as killing a man, maybe more, because he didn't have to worry about leaving clues behind. He decided to keep playing with poor Plegesi and reached into his jacket as if going to draw a weapon. Joe almost turned white as he lost his balance and thumped against the wall. Baggs enjoyed the scared man's reaction and instantly decided to prolong Plegesi's anguish by moving his hand around for a few seconds, ending with, "Ahhh, that's better, had an itch." Baggs then smiled, withdrew his hand and said, "No problem Joe, just increase your weekly contribution by ten percent and things will be good. OK?"

Plegesi regained his composure and replied, "Sure Baggs, just let me know when you see that the back money is paid up. OK?"

Softly and menacingly, Baggs replied, "There is no need to keep a tally of back payments; the ten percent addition is from today on, any problem with that?"

The expected reply was forthcoming, "Sure Baggs, tell Mr. Sanducci I thank him for understanding. It won't happen again. I'll see you next week. Please tell him."

Baggs smiled, patted Joe on the shoulder, left the shop, climbed into his Bronco and moved on to his next collection stop.

***

Two days had passed since Mike had sent in the second set of prints from the Holy Child burglary. When he checked his station house mailbox, he found a notification from Lieutenant Stonner that both sets of prints recovered from Holy Child were indeed from the same men, but again no hit. After roll call, Mike drove directly to see Monsignor Scala.

As usual, the priest was happy to see him and met him at his office door, "My Saint Michael. What brings you here today? Do you have any news?"

"No Father, not really except the last set of prints match the first. But, I have been thinking about the window in the storeroom. Can you give me a list of church workers, both on the payroll and volunteers?"

"Sure Michael. What do you have in mind?"

Mike was eager to share his thoughts with the old priest, "Here's what I'm thinking Father, because the guy or guys always get into the church through the same window and it's in the storage room where you keep the collection money, I believe that there's a trusted person or persons, who have daily access to the storage room and that it's that person who leaves the window unlocked or maybe even open."

The cleric had a shocked expression on his face as he answered, "Michael my son, I find it hard to believe that one or more of my parishioners are involved in such a heinous thing as robbing from God's House. I'll have a list prepared for you but truly hope you are wrong. Please return here after the noon hour and I will have your list for you."

Mike replied, "Thank you Father." Seeing the concerned expression on Father Vincent's face, Mike attempted to lighten the conversation with, "I've got to actually do some work now and earn my paycheck by doing some patrol. Please excuse me. I'll be back after lunch time."

As Romano turned to leave, Scala gently put his hand on Mike's shoulder and brought him around to face him saying, "You are a good cop and a good man Michael Romano. May the Good Lord bless you and always keep you safe." The old priest then raised his right hand and blessed Mike in Latin.

Michael bowed his head in embarrassment, expressed his thanks and left.

The rest of the morning was rather easy for Mike, he had only one past burglary call and that was at a residence in the Woodrow area of the command. When he arrived at the house on

Sinclar Avenue, Michael was surprised to be told by the lady of the house, Mrs. Cassidy, that there was no apparent break-in. Her husband left for work at 7:00 a.m. and she lounged around until 9:30 a.m. before showering and getting dressed. She had planned a day out with girlfriends and when she reached into the dresser drawer where she kept her jewelry, she noticed several pieces missing. Romano checked all the entrances to her home and came to the same conclusion as the woman, that there was no apparent break-in.

The woman was a fastidious housekeeper and the place was neat and clean, making the fingerprinting of the master bedroom easy. Before he began, Mike alerted her to the fact that there would be powder left behind and it should be vacuumed up before she attempted to polish her furniture and clean up the remnants of his labor. After dusting the dresser top and finding no prints, Mike, by Mrs. Cassidy's direction, carefully removed the small jewelry box that she kept her valuables in from a drawer under some neatly folded blouses. It had a highly polished finish and he knew that it would yield good prints. After recovering many, Mike asked her to submit to printing for elimination prints. It was at that time that she asked, "Officer, do you need prints from my husband and son too?"

In his mind Mike chastised himself for neglecting to ask her how many residents lived in the house, especially because of the lack of any signs to indicate a break-in, shaking it off, he responded, "Yes, when can I return and obtain their prints? I'd like to do it today before I get off duty if at all possible."

She replied, "My son returns home from school by 4:00 p.m. and I'll call my husband to make sure he's home by that time. Do you think that the crook will be caught?"

Mike tried to reassure her, "Well most of the time, if the prints are on file and those that I recover are good enough, we get a hit, that means a positive identification and an arrest is eminent. When that happens, you will be notified to respond to court. However, I will say that sometimes, I personally get notified when identification has been made and if that happens, I'll call you and let you know as soon as I find out."

"Thank you Officer. Please return by 4:00 p.m."

As Michael reassembled his equipment and prepared to leave, he said, "Thank you for your cooperation and I will probably be here by 3:30. I'll see you folks then."

Being relatively close to Annadale, Mike decided to spend his meal hour in Leona's place. As he started his patrol car, he keyed the mike, two "Three Print, ten- sixty two meal at 896 Annadale Road."

The dispatcher responded, "Ten Four Three Print"

As usual, once inside the luncheonette, Mike took the last seat at the far end of the counter and also as usual, Leona walked over and with a broad smile and suggestively asked, "Hello, what will you have today? Is there anything special that you would like today Officer Mike?"

Romano smiled back at her and said, "Hi Leona, the list is long and I only have an hour so I'll start with coffee please."

Leona quickly returned with the coffee, placing it before him on the counter and gently touched his hand as he reached for it. Mike's mind raced, *Wow, here it comes. Decision time and I'm not ready for this. I want to shed that bitch of an ex-wife first before I even think of someone else.* As he looked down at her hand, she quickly withdrew it as if she was as surprised as he was.

Mike ordered a tuna salad plate and they chatted about mundane things whenever she had a few seconds to spend at his end of the counter. Mike finally asked for the check as he rose from the stool and Leona waved him off saying, "My treat."

Not wanting to allow any chance of their relationship progressing beyond what it was at that point, he left a five dollar bill on the counter as he left, smiled and said, "See you again."

Romano drove directly to Holy Cross and picked up a sealed envelope from the Monsignor's assistant. Once in his RMP, he opened it and reviewed the list. He quickly spotted James Guggalarie as one of the steady volunteer workers of the church. He was not too surprised. Now all he had to do was tie him and his son to the burglaries. He decided to keep the information from Scala.

The second half of Romano's tour was completely uneventful, that is until he returned to the morning's burglary scene on Sinclar Ave, arriving at exactly 3:30 p.m. and found Mr. Cassidy already home. Their conversation was strictly business centering on who might have a key to the house and who would ever have reason to go into the drawer where Mrs. Cassidy kept her little jewelry box. According to Cassidy, only he and his wife would ever go into the top dresser drawer and that he "almost never even opens the drawer."

Romano and the Cassidys were in the kitchen having a cool drink when the younger Cassidy walked in. When Mike turned around to look at the kid, young Cassidy froze and said, "I know you. My friends pointed you out to me. They say that you always harass them and pick on them. Now you're in my house. I didn't do anything and you better not start on me. My parents are here and will give you lots of grief."

Mr. Cassidy spoke first, "Watch your mouth John. This officer is here to help us. We were broken into and he's here for our fingerprints. Hopefully that will help catch the person."

Mrs. Cassidy was next, "John, apologize to the officer and mind your manners. Right now he is a guest in our house."

In Romano's mind, the sound of beating wings began as he heard the words spewing out of young Cassidy's mouth. They got louder as the youth's parents chastised the boy. Mike snapped, "Listen young man, I'm not used to taking crap from kids unless I'm arresting them, so calm down. Try to be as gracious as your parents or do you have an attitude because there's something to hide? What's your friends names and don't lie to me because I'll know?"

The senior Cassidy spit his words at his son, "John, before I slap you, answer the officer and be nice about it or he'll be arresting me for assault."

The kid answered, "Mike and Tommy."

Mike quickly asked, "Mike and Tommy what?"

"Sir," was the response.

"That's not what I want. There is no need to call me Sir, Officer will do. I want their full names. What are they?"

Mr. Cassidy felt the need to say, "Now John, answer the man."

The kid was obviously nervous as he spoke, "Officer, their names are Perino and Guggalarie."

Cassidy told his son, "Tell the man who's who."

Mike jumped in, "That's unnecessary Mr. Cassidy. I know the boys and they're not the best kids for your son to hang out with. Now, John, please let me take your fingerprints for elimination."

The kid was reluctant but submitted without saying a word. As Michael took the boy's hand, the beating of the wings in his head grew louder. He sensed what the outcome would be after the prints were sent to Lieutenant Stonner but said nothing to the Cassidys. He thanked them for their cooperation and returned to the Two Three by 4:15 p.m. After compiling his report and forwarding it to Stonner, he put in an overtime slip and signed out. Mike knew that in a few days, he would receive notification as to the results of the Cassidy burglary. As usual, he took Arthur Kill Road to Richmond Avenue, looking for the elusive black Bronco, then turned right and crossed the Island to his apartment. The daily ride took him an extra twenty minutes at end of tour but he felt that one day he would get lucky and see the Bronco.

The remaining work days of his current set of tours were just more of the same, respond to past burglaries and sometimes recover latent prints. There were only two significant incidents. First, on the last day of his tour, in his mailbox, was notification that the prints on the Cassidy's jewelry box belonged to Mrs. Cassidy and young John Cassidy. Now he had to convey the findings about their son to the couple, it would be delicate to say the least. He decided that it could keep until he came back for his 4x12 set after returning from his two day swing.

The second noteworthy incident was when he ran into Michael Guggalarie and his friend Tommy Perino just before end of tour. Romano was driving back to the station along Amboy Road and came across the boys at the service station on the corner of Annadale Road and Amboy. He stopped his car, got out and slowly walked up to the two youths. They acted as if they didn't have a care in the world. When he was within three feet of the boys, he began with, "Michael, I see that you're still best friends with Tommy Perino, how nice."

Romano then turned his attention to Perino, "Tommy, do you know John Cassidy?"

The reaction to the question pleased Romano, the kid actually twitched. All he could say was, "Why. We didn't do anything. Is he in trouble?"

Romano chuckled and answered, while looking directly at Guggalarie, "No, not yet but he will be, same as you guys."

The smart mouth challenged as he spoke, "Yeah Romano, we know that you don't like us but you'll never get us. We're just kids. Hell, I'm just only gonna be sixteen next week."

The words were music to Mike's ears. His mind raced; *Finally, I'll get the little shit and put him where he belongs. Holy Child is gonna be his undoing. Now I'll just push him a little.* "Hey Mike, your brother Robert used to be a pain in the ass too. Last month he died in a car accident, didn't he?"

The kid had a painful look on his face as he asked, "Yeah, why bring that up?"

Romano smiled menacingly and silently asked God for forgiveness as he answered, "Do you really think it was an accident?"

Guggalarie turned white, "Why did you say that? It was just a car accident. He drove too fast on Amboy and hit a tree on a turn."

Mike smiled again as he asked, "Really?" and turned to walk back to his car. The two boys remained quiet and still as statues as Romano entered his car and then turned around and shouted, "See you soon boys. You can count on it."

Holy Saturday (Catholic Church Holy Day, the day just before Easter) finally arrived and, right after roll call, Romano drove directly to see Monsignor Scala to finalize plans and hopefully catch the church burglars.

Scala was pleased to see him, "Officer Michael Romano, Holy Child's own Saint Michael, I see you're here to make ready to catch the bad guys and, with God's help, bring them to justice. I am here to assist you in any way."

Mike was eager to discuss what would occur the following night. "Well Monsignor, I have a partner for tomorrow night and we'll enter the church before midnight. As we discussed earlier, we plan to spend the night in the dark, inside your inner office and wait for the thief to enter the storage room. At that time we'll go around and use our key to catch them in the act of attempting to break into your cabinet and reach the cash box. We'll have them cold!"

The pastor was getting into it and excitedly asked, "But don't you want to drill your spy holes first, right now? I have the electric drill our maintenance man uses and some drill bits."

"That's great. Let's get on with it," Mike answered. Where is the drill?"

"I have it inside the storage room. I thought that you could drill from that side so you could pick where you feel is a good spot. There are no obstructions on my side of the wall so you can't damage anything. "Let's go Michael", the priest said as he excitably led the way.

Once inside the adjacent storeroom, Romano picked two places to drill through and into the pastor's inner office. The first hole was drilled low and next to the subject cabinet. Mike had decided that the burglars wouldn't spot a hole in the wall if it was well below their waists as they concentrated on their target. The second hole was almost behind a shelf that held some cleaning equipment. After that hole was drilled, Romano carefully re-arranged some items so that the hole was blocked from possible viewing of anyone standing in front of the cabinet. The two men joined forces to clean up any debris from the work. Romano also ran his hands across the floor in an effort to dirty them and then rub them across the drilled areas to make it appear that the holes were probably once used to mount something should they be seen, Mike was taking no chances. Mike turned to the cleric, "All that I need now Father are a set of keys. Do you have them ready for me?"

"Yes my son. Let's go back to my office."

Back inside the pastor's office, Scala spoke first, "Here you are," he said as he reached into his desk and pulled out a ring with three keys on it. "The big key unlocks the front door of the church, the second, the round key, shuts off the alarm, and the third key is for the storage room. Is there anything else that you may need?"

Romano took a few seconds to think before answering, he said, "Yes Father, your blessing and God's help in catching those thieves."

"You have it my son," he then signed a blessing toward Mike and promised to pray for the capture of the church burglars.

"Thank you Father. I have to go back on patrol now. See you on Monday morning with two in custody, I hope." Mike then left and went back on patrol.

***

It was twilight, about 5:15 p.m. when Romano, and all patrol members in the Two Three heard the dispatcher, "In the Two Three we have a silent alarm reported at 100 Petrus Avenue. Units responding?"

Sectors Frank and Eddie responded in turn, Mike keyed his radio, "Two Three print car is only a few blocks away and will also respond Central."

The dispatcher answered, "Acknowledged, all Two Three units. Don't shoot each other, K."

Romano hit the dome lights of his vehicle and was off like a shot. As he neared the premises, he keyed his radio, "Print car on the scene and will take position in the rear." He exited the car with the 12 gauge Remington.

The dispatcher answered, "Acknowledged, Print car. Frank and Eddie advise that they are approaching the scene at this time."

As the second car screeched to a halt in front of the residence, two officers from the first car jumped from their vehicle and in their excitement, slammed the car doors shut making a loud thud. Even though he was in the rear yard, Romano heard the loud noise and knew what might happen. He had just braced himself and watched as the sliding glass doors leading to the yard loudly shattered spewing glass and several of the vertical blinds that hung in front of the doors, along with a kitchen type chair that bounced as it tumbled to the ground.

Almost instantaneously, a tall lanky man came bounding thru the remnants of the door and into the yard on a dead run. Romano took an aggressive stance, shouldered his shotgun, and slapped the slide back and forth, chambering a round, while simultaneously shouting, “Police freeze.”

It is said in law enforcement circles that the sound of a slide being worked on a shotgun is the loudest sound in the world. Well, maybe it is because even before Mike shouted, the running man froze in mid stride and slowly turned his head towards the sound. With his eyes opened as wide as the newly adjusted doorway, the man shouted, “Don’t shoot. I did it but I didn’t take anything,” just as Mike shouted his warning. It was almost comical, like a freeze frame in an old black and white cartoon.

Romano slowly approached the man shouting, “Hands on your head and belly down on the ground. Don’t move a muscle.”

The guy complied so fast that his body bounced as he dropped to the ground. Mike lowered the shotgun, placing the stock under his right arm and pulled his portable radio from it’s holder with his left hand. He spoke into it, “Two Three print unit has one under arrest in the rear of 100 Petrus, K”

The dispatcher answered, “One under, ten four, Two Three prints;” just as two other officers came running around from the front of the house, it was Logan and Fitzsimmons. Bill Logan spoke, “Well, Mike Romano does it again, not only does he get prints that are left behind, but sometimes, he even gets the hands and fingers still attached to the perps. Nice going Mikey.” They approached the prone man, Logan holding his handcuffs ready. Fitzsimmons asked, "Your collar Mike, it was our call?"

Romano answered, "No, it's your collar, put me down for an assist and toss the guy, will you? I'll bet he has stuff in his pockets."

Logan cuffed the man while Fitz patted him down, hitting his right pants pocket several times, before pulling him to his feet.

Fitz reached into the pocket to retrieve whatever he previously felt. It was three ladies rings and an expensive men's wristwatch. "Well, well what do we have here?"

"The response was, "Those are not mine. You must have put them there."

Bill and Fitz looked back at Romano who had his shotgun shouldered again. Mike spoke softly, "Ask him again and then take the handcuffs off. It's been a while since I fired this baby."

"Bill answered quickly, "Sure thing. Let's do it. He spoke to Fitz, "Ask him again partner, if you don't like the answer, unhook him and let him go."

The burglar was now shaking, "You people are gonna kill me?! Yeah, I took them from inside the house. Keep the shotgun cop away from me."

Mike smiled and said, "He's all yours gentlemen. I'm gonna put the gun in my car and go inside to try to get some prints to lock him in good. See you back at the house."

The dispatcher was notified that a prisoner was being transported to the Two Three. He reported to the officers that the alarm company had notified the owners and that they would be home within an hour. Romano notified the dispatcher that the Latent Car would remain on the scene to look for prints and secure the premises until the owners arrived home.

It was almost 7:15 p.m. when Mike, by habit, found himself driving back to the station house on Arthur Kill Road. As he approached the Lamplight Restaurant, he saw Henry Capelli's Lincoln turn into the restaurant's parking lot. He thought, *he must go there a lot. The day we ate there they certainly knew him. So what?,* he immediately pushed it from his mind and never gave it a second thought.

As Mike walked into the station house, he was greeted by Jerry Sullivan. "Mike, my old buddy. I can't wait until tomorrow night. It's gonna be like old times, we always had fun. Thanks for requesting me; Sergeant. Hogan gave me the particulars today during the day tour, along with an official tour change. I came in to meet with you and talk before the last minute tomorrow night. How is this going to go?"

Mike outlined his game plan. "We'll be in street clothes, no uniform and we'll each have a portable radio and a good working flashlight."

Sully showed excited interest, "What else?"

I have the keys to the church, alarm and the storage room where the cash is kept. We'll have to bring something to eat and drink and there's no smoking at all. I've drilled two holes through the wall to look into the storeroom; we sit in the dark and no talking, silence is important because we don't want them to know that we're next door." Before Mike could continue, Sully laughed and asked, "What if we have to pee?"

There's a private toilet in the Monsignor's office but we can't flush until morning. We can't risk any sound, are there any other silly questions?"

"Sorry Mike. I'm excited and just trying to be funny. What happens when we know that the kids are inside the room?"

"Well, before we try to take them, one of us goes to the far end of the hallway and quietly calls for backup to respond to the rear of the church. When we're together again, we use our key and we go in and grab whoever is inside."

"This should be fun," was Sully's response.

Mike continued, "If we get them, we'll each formally arrest a single perpetrator, assuming there's more than one."

Sully interrupted with, "Great. Then we go to court together."

"Hold on Sully. We split the collars only if the Boss lets us. They might frown on it because processing and court will continue our tour and they have to pay us both overtime. Personally, I love it and I need the money as you know."

Jerry responded with, "Me too, but maybe we can guarantee ourselves some OT if we each cuff one of them a few feet apart from each other and they separately give 'spontaneous utterances' to the officer who hooks 'em up. The ADA will need each cop to explain what each prisoner said." With a grin he continued, "Being busy and concentrating on our own man, we could not possibly hear what our partner's man said. What do you think?"

Romano smiled and said, "Sounds like a plan. Is there anything else?"

"No Mike. See you tomorrow, unless you want to go to Russo's with me and stare at Margie."

"You and Margie, it's always Margie. I told you that you stand as much chance as an ice cube in Hell."

"Yeah, but she's great to look at, and I can always dream."

"You go; I'm signing out and going home to call my kids. I won't be able to see them later. I usually try to see them on Sundays if I'm not on duty. I've gotta sleep because we have to be alert all night tomorrow. See you here about 2300 hours." Romano changed, signed out and went to his little apartment. Of course it was too late to phone his kids, so he clicked on the tube, poured some Dewars into a tall ice filled glass and settled into his recliner.

Several hours later Romano dozed off but did not really rest. His trip into the Land of Nod was tumultuous at best. Mike's subconscious manufactured a very active dream state. While asleep, Mike was chasing Michael Guggalarie and Tommy Perino after they got away with the cash box from Holy Child of God Church. In his dream, Monsignor Scala was with them but kept falling over the hem of his vestments and landing face down into a muddy baseball field behind the church. Because he was unable to catch Guggalarie, Mike sprouted wings like an angel and flew after him. As he got close, his wings disappeared and he was forced to continue on foot as he fell to the ground. In the dream, Guggalarie got away. The dream replayed several times.

Romano awoke that Sunday morning at 10:00 a.m. with aching muscles caused from moving around during his turbulent dream and the fact that once again he spent the night in his chair. Until he looked at the glass on the table beside his chair, he could not fathom why he had a headache. The emptiness of the glass informed him that he might be experiencing a mild hangover.

After a shower and a shave, Mike felt much better and ate some bacon, eggs, toast and coffee before phoning his former residence. The call was answered by Betty who said, "Hello Michael. It's so nice to hear your voice. It's been a long time."

Mike was not sure if her tone was genuine or she was a terrific actress and was once again setting him up for another verbal attack, as was her practice. He responded cautiously, "Hope you're well Betty. I'm told our legal jousting will soon be over. Maybe we can be friends because of the children. Are they available?"

The hair on Mike's neck bristled as she responded, "I hope so too Mikey. I'll get them for you."

She had used her pet name for him. Mike didn't like it and thought, w*hat are you trying to do? I can't wait to be shed of you. You're nothing but a treacherous harlot and if the kids didn't care about you, I would take Rocco up on his offer to do anything for me;* he wanted to tell her exactly what had just raced through his mind but remained silent for a few seconds. Regaining his self-control, Mike answered, "It's a shame that we wasted all those years, but we did have two great kids. Yeah maybe when our blood simmers down, we can be friends for the children's sake."

Betty, obviously disappointed with his controlled answer, coldly responded, "Please hold on, I'll find the children."

Mike held the phone for what seemed like an hour before he heard static, followed by, "Hello Daddy, its Donald. Are you coming over now?"

Romano tried to hide the remorse in his voice with, "Hey Buddy Boy, its great to hear your voice. Are you taking care of your Mom?"

The cheerful response was, "Sure Dad, just like you always tell me to do. She's fine. What time are you coming?"

Mike felt terrible as he answered, "Well, you know that my job sometimes gets in the way of plans that we make. Well, it did again. I have to catch up on my sleep today because I'm going on a stake out tonight." There was an excited gasp on the other end as Mike added, "All night, until Monday morning. I gotta be alert to catch some bad guys, but maybe we can get together later the next day. Ok?"

Donnie still pumped up at the term stake out, asked, "Is it like television? Will you be sitting inside a room and looking across into a window or sitting in a car and looking thru binoculars?"

"Almost kid. Two of us will hide in a church to catch bad guys who rob the collection money at night."

On the other end of the phone Donnie screeched, "Annie, come quick Daddy's going on a stake out tonight and hiding in a church. It's gonna be better than a television cop show."

By the time that Donnie finished speaking, Annie had pulled the phone from her brother's hand and spoke into it, "Daddy, what is Donnie talking about? What stake out? Are you coming to see us today?"

Feeling like a bigger heel, Mike explained to his daughter why he would not see them as previously planned. When he was finished, Annie, hearing the tone of her father's voice, dutifully answered with, "We understand Daddy. Have fun and get him. I'll explain everything to Donnie. Sometimes you get only one chance to get a bad guy and we get lots of chances to be with you. It's important that you do a good job and don't get hurt. You have to be in top form all night." Not waiting for an answer, she continued, "We love you Daddy. It's all good, we're fine."

Mike's voice cracked as he "I love you kids too. Talk to you soon." As he replaced the receiver, Mike muttered aloud, "That little girl always amazes me." Romano then spent the next few hours running errands and returning to his apartment by midafternoon. After putting away his clean laundry and some groceries, he set his alarm for 10:00 p.m. before going to bed and another bout of sporadic sleep.

***

It was 2300 hours when Romano and Sullivan met at the station house. By 2310, they had secured two portable radios and Romano spoke to the desk officer about getting permission to use one of their own vehicles to drive to the church stakeout. Lieutenant Cassidy, with whom, Romano was very friendly, first denied permission citing regulations. Michael countered, “Loo, tonight is out of the ordinary. If the thieves are watching the church, a marked patrol vehicle near the church might cause them to scrub their break in for tonight. If we arrive in our own vehicle and park on the street near the church, we attract a lot less attention. If there’s an arrest, we’ll call for a transport RMP. The captain gave his approval for this operation tonight.” Without waiting for an answer, Mike continued, “Its good then? We take one of our own cars, yes?”

Cassidy liked Michael, so after twisting his face a few times said, “Fine Romano but you do nothing with your car except drive it there, park it and return here with it. Any police action, transport, chase or whatever is handled by a responding car that you will request from the dispatcher. Got it?”

The two cops answered in unison, “Ten-four Lieutenant. Thanks sir. We got it.”

“I’ll make a blotter entry while you two clowns go stand roll call. When you get to the church, notify the dispatcher that you’re on special assignment and in plainclothes. Don’t forget. I’m going to monitor the radio tonight and if you screw up, I’ll order you to return to command forthwith.” With a big smile, he ended the conversation with, “Now get the hell away from my desk. Oh yeah, good luck.”

Sergeant Walowski supervised the roll call. When Romano and Sullivan’s name was called, the room erupted with comments such as, “Special assignment, I have your special assignment.

From a source in the rear of the room, who sounded remarkably like Fred Collins, "Are you two guys going to take turns in the confessional? Which one of you two is in the booth first? Is that like in the barrel?"

The room erupted with laughter at the last remark. Sergeant. Walowski announced, "I see that I've lost control, now get out there and listen up if these guys call for assistance. That means they have a collar or need other assistance, and I better hear more than one team respond. Go!"

It was decided that Mike's car would be used because it was grey and would be less conspicuous. Mike put his print equipment in the back seat just in case he might need it later. Sully put a duffle bag containing some snacks and drinks to get them thru the night next to the print kit. The team left the station by 11:40 p.m. and drove directly to Holy Child.

The team parked the car behind a doctor's office on the corner of Arden Ave. and Amboy Road. The two cops then walked across to the church, using a wooded area to remain hidden from sight as they approached the actual building. Mike used the keys that Scala had given him to turn off the alarm and enter the church. The interior was light enough to walk without the use of their flashlights. As Mike turned to secure the entrance door, Sully put down the duffle bag and tapped Romano on the shoulder, saying in a barely audible whisper, "Listen. What's that noise? Sounds like the dirt bags are already here."

In a surprised whisper, Mike responded, I can't believe it, they sure are!"

Both cops stood motionless and listened. From the corridor in front of them and slightly to their right, came the distinct sounds of someone trying to open a metal cabinet without using a proper key. Mike turned his flashlight on and motioned towards the sound. Sully responded with hand motions after switching his light on. The two men slowly advanced towards the storage room. Once in front of the double doors, Mike carefully held the set of church keys to prevent them from rattling and slowly slid the storage room key into the keyhole of the door on the right side, while motioning for Sully to have his firearm ready. Also drawing his weapon, and tucking his light under his arm, Mike used hand signals to communicate with Sully, indicating that on the count of three, they would enter the room and apprehend whoever was inside. Sully nodded his head in acknowledgement and Mike slowly turned the key. It made a fairly loud click causing the cops some anguish. They had hoped the sound was not heard over the loud pounding from inside the room. Their fears materialized when the pounding stopped.

Mike, using a forward motion to indicate to his partner that he would be moving forward, slowly pushed the door open. Almost instantly, a figure holding a raised metal pry bar popped from behind the door and looked right at him. Mike Romano was now face to face with Michael Guggalarie!!

Sully couldn't see the kid because of where he was standing. Mike impulsively began to thrust his gun hand forward to prevent his subject from closing the door as both Michaels simultaneously shouted, "Oh shit!" Romano's training and experience immediately kicked in and he remembered never to compromise his gun hand. If he had pushed it forward and the weapon got past the doorway, Guggalarie would have had a chance to bring his own weapon down on his wrist and gotten his gun. Mike instantly backed up and braced himself for a forward rush planning to put his shoulder against the door and bull his way in, but he was too slow. Guggalarie slammed the door shut and clicked the lock. Realizing what had just happened, Sully cleverly shouted, "The guys outside will get them, let's rush the room." He then softly said, "I'm going around. Will you be ok alone here?"

"Mike's responded, "Yeah, I'll keep them inside. You watch the window while we wait for backup. Go."

Sully took off as Mike radioed, "Two Three special assignment at Holy Child church on Arden and Amboy, 10-85 forthwith requesting assistance. We have two perpetrators trapped inside the church and need assistance at this time, K"

Dispatch replied, "Acknowledged. What's your condition? Any officer hurt?"

“No Central. Officers are fine. Just need assistance to block escape of perps.”

The radio crackled with units responding even before the dispatcher officially put the request in. Sergeant Walowski and his driver along with the team of Fitzsimons and Logan announced that they would also respond.

Hearing a racket from inside the room and fearing that they might scramble out a window, Mike withdrew his handcuffs and snapped them around the two doorknobs to prevent the doors from opening no more than a few inches in case the guys inside tried to leave by way of the doors. Wanting to help his partner, he then bolted for the exit that Sully flew thru just seconds before. As Mike hit the doorway, Sully called over the radio, “One just dropped from the window and number two is hanging out.”

Just as Mike rounded the corner of the church and the window came into view, the second man dropped to the ground and Sully was already in foot pursuit of the first man. As the second person hit the ground and darted off towards the woods behind the church lawn, Mike shouted, “Police stop or I’ll shoot.” Not knowing what was happening behind him, Sully dropped to the ground at the announcement. Romano fired two shots in the general direction of the runners. He had no intention of hitting them but hoped that they would stop when hearing the gunfire. The opposite happened; the two youths turned on their overdrive and sprinted away into the trees.

Seeing his partner hugging the ground, Mike called out, “Its ok Sully, let them go. We’ll get them another time.”

As Sully rose, he asked his approaching partner, “My God Mike, that scared the pants off me, did you try to hit anyone?”

“No Sully,” was the reply, “I was trying to scare them into stopping. It’s no problem though as long as Walowski didn’t hear the shots.” There was pounding in his head and Mike didn’t know if Saint Michael’s wings were beating or it was only the sound of his elevated pulse rate from all the excitement. Mike chose to believe the former and continued, “Did you see the guy in the doorway?”

Sully answered, "No. Did you? Who was it?"

Romano's need to administer justice personally and arrest Guggalarie himself caused him to justify a lie, "No, but I'll know him when I see him on the street. I wanted to cuff them to the altar rail and call for transport, now I have to see them on the street or get prints and hope they're in the system." He knew that Michael Guggalarie had recently hit the magic number, 16 years old and his prints now could be used against him. Next, all he had to do was arrest him based on his own personal observation. "Let's go look at what kind of damage they did."

As the two men walked back to the building, Sully commented between long breaths, "You know Mike, I still can't figure out how they got up to that window. One guy must stand on the other's shoulders to open the window, and then pulls himself in. I can understand that, but how does number two get in. The window is too high, right?"

Mike huffed a little too before answering, "You got me on that one. Maybe they can fly. They sure took off when I fired my gun."

Just then, the responding patrol cars screeched to a halt. Sergeant Walowski was the first man to jump out. He excitedly asked, "Did you guys get them? Are they secured?"

Sully, feeling that Mike fired the shots and should answer in any manner that he felt comfortable with, gestured towards Mike.

Mike answered, "They got away Sarge. When we got inside the building, they were already at work. When I opened the door to the room, I was staring at one of the guy's faces. He quickly slammed the door before I could react. That's when Sully ran around back and I handcuffed the doors so nobody could open them from the inside and then I joined Sully. You heard the radio transmissions between us. The guys were too quick and got away. We weren't ready. It all happened too fast. We were just on our way inside to see if they got anything. Sorry we lost 'em."

Walowski answered, "That's alright Romano, and even the best cop in the world can't get them all every time. You guys tried hard. Let's go see what they did." Turning to Fitz and Logan he said, "You and the rest of the guys resume patrol." Fitz and Logan, usually kidders, felt bad for the team and remained silent.

As they entered the store room, Mike flipped the wall switch. The room was bathed in light and revealed a mess. In their haste to escape, Guggalarie and his companion, who was probably Tommy Perino, managed to bend the metal shelves as they hurriedly climbed to the top in their hasty effort to reach the window and make their escape. They had littered the room with sports equipment and cleaning products. The large storage cabinet where the cash box was housed was once again trashed; however the cash box was still there. Lying on the floor was the pry bar that Mike had seen in the hands of Guggalarie along with a heavy claw hammer and a large flat blade screw driver. The most interesting item the two youths left behind was a long length of knotted rope that was tied to an upright support of one of the shelves with a small black canvas knapsack tied to the other end of it. The knapsack looked big enough to hold the pry bar and a hammer. Apparently once one of the burglars got into the room, he lowered the rope to the second man who probably tied on the knapsack and used the rope to climb in. Obviously they never left the rope or the knapsack behind before.

Sergeant Walowski commented, "Well boys, as least now you know how it was done. How many times is it Romano?"

"Four times that I know of Sarge. This is gonna be the last."

"How can you say that? Did you see their faces and know who they were? You never got hits on their prints so either they aren't in the system or they're too young."

Once again Mike waivered from his usual moral code and answered only part of the question, "I got a good look at the guy who opened the door when we were face to face and if I see him again on the street, I'll recognize him, prints or no prints. I just hope he's over 16 years old and not a kid. If you rob a church, you gotta go to jail and not family court."

Walowski gently ordered, “You two stay here and try to get some good prints. Use the pastor’s phone and call the house by landline when you’re ready to return. I’ll notify dispatch that you’re out for the rest of the tour. Any questions?”

Mike answered, “No Sarge, Sully and I are good and have stuff to eat and drink.”

Sully added, “Now that they’re gone, we can even flush the toilet and not worry about the noise.”

Mike asked, “Is it possible that we remain here for the rest of the tour Sarge? We can take our time on the prints, I can use the time to formulate my submission and most importantly, I would like to be here when the pastor comes in. I’ll call him at daybreak.”

“Yeah, I guess it’s fine but won’t you need a voucher for evidence like the rope and the tools?”

Mike looked at Sully and asked, “Sully would you take my car and pick up a voucher from the desk? We can fill it out while we’re here and get a supervisor’s signature at end of tour. While you’re gone, I’ll start dusting for prints.”

Smiling broadly, Sully answered, “Sure Mike, do you want anything from Russo’s? I might as well stop in and get something real to eat.”

Mike laughed and said, “Yeah but wait a few minutes. Hey Sarge, will you please sign our memo books that you were here and the cash box was intact and unopened? You know that there’s nothing like being careful and covering your ass.”

“Sure Romano, soon as you guys scratch something in your books.” Mike and Sully made proper entries into their memo books and Walowski signed each man’s entry before leaving.

When they were alone, Mike turned to Sully and commented, “You know Sully, Margie may not be there but if you really are going to stop and get some food, please bring me a burger with lettuce, tomato and onion on it along with fries.” He reached in his pocket and handed Sully a five dollar bill with, “Thank you.”

"You got it Mike. Just maybe she's there and I might not come back until morning. If that happens, I'll send your food here if someone will make the run for me."

Laughingly Mike replied, "Sure hope I don't have to wait too long." Sully then took Mike's car keys and the keys to the church. After locking his partner in, he tapped on the glass and waved goodbye, laughing all the way to the car.

While Sullivan was gone, Romano began to dust for prints. An hour later Sully returned with food and vouchers from the command, parking in the church lot. Mike was so engrossed in his work that he never heard his partner enter the building and relock the door. So that he didn't startle his partner when he entered the storeroom, Sully called out, "Mike, it's me Sully, don't shoot." Mike turned to see Sully with a feigned look of despair on his face. Sully continued, "Here partner, I got everything I went for except Margie. You were right, she wasn't there and now my day is ruined."

Mike turned back to his work and responded, "You'll live. Life is full of disappointments. Let's eat as soon as I clean my hands. We can use the Monsignor's office."

By 3:00 a.m., all the latent prints that Mike had recovered were prepared for submission along with a voucher for the rope and pry bar. Mike and Sully then went looking for a room to rest in and found one that appeared to be a waiting area of sorts. After settling into two high back upholstered wing chairs, they tried to get some sleep before daybreak.

Neither man was able to fall into a deep sleep. Soon, it was 6:00 a.m. and Mike phoned the Monsignor at the rectory, "Good morning Father. I hope it's not too early."

When he heard Michael's voice, Scala sounded like a kid at Christmas as he asked, "No, no my son, I'm up every day at 5:00 a.m. Michael, did you get him? Did the burglar come last night? How many do you have?"

Mike heard the breath leave the old cleric as he answered, "No Monsignor, we didn't get them but all is not lost , there's still some good news regarding this incident. Your money is safe and I was face to face with one of the two men. I'll get him when I see him out on the street, I'm sure of it. As to the second man, I'm not too sure."

"Did you recognize him?" the priest asked in anticipation.

Mike hesitated for what he thought was several minutes before answering. He was not comfortable lying to a priest and rationalized it by thinking, *I can't tell the Monsignor that I know it was Michael Guggalarie and the kid's father is a church volunteer, so here goes,* "No Monsignor, I didn't know who it was but as I told you, I'll see him again and get him then and whoever he's with, if it even looks only a little like the guy who ran with him."

"You're telling me that you two guys chased the bad guys. Are you inside the church? Don't go anywhere, I'm coming right over."

Mike said to Sully, "The pastor's coming over now, let's unlock the door," and turned to exit the room. By the time they got to the church entrance, Scala was inserting his own key into the lock. His face was red and he was obviously out of breath as he shouted, "Tell me everything," as he rushed into the church. Mike told him everything but never mentioned the gunfire.

***

Romano and Sully returned to their command by the end of the tour. While still processing the paperwork, they had discussed the prospect of teaming up on their next set of tours so Michael would not have to be alone if and when he saw the man behind the door. Because Michael didn't work the rotating shift chart, he would have to get reassigned to serve as Sully's partner and follow his five day work chart. That adjustment would require seeing a boss higher in rank then a patrol supervisor. Not wanting to bother his captain too soon since his last request, he sought out a friendly ear, Lieutenant Cassidy, who, as Executive Officer was second in command.

After listening to a full accounting of the church incident, Cassidy smiled and asked, "So Michael, you don't know who the man behind the door was and exchanged oh shits with him, but if you see him again, you'll easily recognize him after only a few seconds encounter in a dark church corridor?"

Mike knew that Cassidy liked him and realized that his cop was holding something back, yet trusted him and would allow him to make the arrest if possible. He quickly answered, "I sure can Loo, and my flashlight was in the guy's face."

"Ok Romano, submit your prints and hope you can get an ID. You may never see the guy again."

"Yeah Loo, but I'm betting that it's the same guy that did all the other break-ins and his prints are not on file, so it's up to me and Sully to get him and put his prints into the system."

Cassidy was smiling broadly as he said, "I love a man that has confidence in himself. OK Michael, I'll notify roll call that until further notice you are to be teamed up with Sullivan on my orders. You come back Tuesday morning, is that correct Sully?"

"Yes Loo." He turned to Mike and continued, "Bet we get 'em before the next set of tours is over. Right, Mike?"

Mike could hear a chorus of angels singing "Alleluia, Alleluia," inside his head as he almost shouted, "Oh yeah. They're ours."

***

Romano spent the balance of Monday hanging around his apartment, and then met his kids as soon as they got out of school and then treated them to an early dinner in a restaurant. He must have told them the story of almost catching the church burglar every time they asked which was four times. Mike got them to their house before Betty returned home from work and was grateful that he didn't have to see her. For the last twenty four hours he temporally forgot about the black Bronco and his desire to find it, along with his visits to Arlo Road, his current thoughts were only about Michael Guggalarie and if he would be able to control his temper should the kid resist. Mike hoped that Tommy

Perino was with him, he too would be arrested; let the courts decide what to do if he was underage.

Tuesday morning roll call finally arrived and he was paired with Sully and assigned to Sector John that included the Annadale Train Station, a favorite haunt of Guggalarie.

When they sat down in their patrol car, Romano at the wheel, Sully in a childlike manner asked, "Michael, please before we hunt for anyone, can we please visit Russo's for a short breakfast?"

"Maybe in a little while, first I want to make a sweep of our sector and maybe get lucky enough to see the kid from the church."

Sully replied, "You just spoiled my day but you can fix it if you tell me who you saw in the storeroom doorway. I know you're not sharing all you know with me because I watched your eyes when you lied to the priest. Next, when you asked Cassidy for re-assignment, you two were communicating something in secret code. It's fine, I'm with you, but since we're gonna be out here together, I think I'm entitled to know. What do you say?"

"I can't hide something from a good cop can I? You're right. If you promise not to spend our free time chasing Margie, I'll tell you who it was. Is it a deal?"

"It's a deal. Spit it out."

Romano's face showed a devilish and sardonic smile as he answered, "Michael Guggalarie, one of my favorite people. That's not all; he recently just had his 16th birthday. His prints will be in the system once we get him and whatever prints we recovered Sunday morning are now admissible as evidence to corroborate my personal observation. No defense council can play with that. The kid is going to lockup."

Sully got caught up in Mike's enthusiasm and asked, "So you lied to the priest, why?"

"Because, some time ago, I asked him for a list of church employees and volunteer workers. Guess who's on the list? The kid's father, James Guggalarie that's who. Maybe the old man is in on it."

Sully, eyes expressed surprise as he seriously asked, "Do you really think the kid's father left the window open for his son? It's hard to believe. How do you want to do this? Do we go to the kid's house or what?"

Mike remained silent for a few seconds, then answered, "Well, if we go to his house, we'll only get him. I'd like to find him on the street with Tommy. Do you think you might be able to identify Tommy as the first guy you saw drop out of the window? You chased him and were closer to him then I was."

Sully hesitated before answering, "I don't know Mike. It was kind of dark, maybe, but I'm not sure."

Mike answered his friend with a hint of disappointment in his voice, "Well, let's wait until we see them both on the street. If Michael runs, then we give chase and if we lose him, we'll go to the house and unless he sings like a bird and gives up the second man, we'll never get number two. If we come up empty after visiting his house, we have to give it over to the detectives but I don't want to give anything up; I want the pleasure of collaring him if possible."

Sully answered with, "Then let's get moving. You did all the work, so as far as I'm concerned, it's your collar and you call the shots. So put the car in gear and let's go to work."

Their first tour was uneventful. The team handled a sick call and a neighbor dispute over who's parking too close to their neighbor's driveway, typical residential Staten Island stuff. Both men were disappointed as they signed out that day.

The next three days were more of the same for the team. Adding to Romano's frustration was a message left on his answering machine by his attorney. Arthur wanted him in the office at 4:00 p.m. on Friday of that week to go over final divorce papers for the upcoming court date of May 3rd. Mike called him Thursday morning and pushed the appointment back half an hour.

***

Arthur stood to greet Romano as he walked in exactly on time, “Mike, I’ll say this for you, you’re certainly punctual. If you say 4:30, 4:30 it is.”

They shook hands while Mike remained almost silent, all he said was, “Sir.”

Slotnick, being a generally kind man and seeing the look of worry on Michael’s face tried to make a joke, “Relax my boy, I’m your lawyer, not your executioner. It’s going to be alright.”

Mike replied, “Sorry sir, but I’ve had a rather stressful week. I’m looking for a church burglar and have been unable to find him.”

Arthur was intrigued, “A church burglar. What kind of man would rob a church? Where was God, on vacation?”

Arthur’s little joke and his interest in Guggalarie worked its magic on Mike. His apprehension concerning his up and coming divorce disappeared like a puff of smoke on a windy day. His answer began with, “Well sir, he’s a young dirt bag who likes to snatch old women’s purses and break into churches. I haven’t been able to nail him because he was always too young. His prints are not in the system, so any latent prints that I recovered at two different churches have not been matched to him, but we know they’re all from the same man.”

Arthur was hooked, “Then how do you know that you’re going after the right man?”

Mike related the Saturday night/Sunday morning encounter to his attorney who listened without saying a word. When he was finished, Mike asked, “Mr. Slotnick, do you think that I’m being selfish by wanting to keep the arrest and not turning all of my information over to detectives?”

Arthur, being a fairly religious man answered, “Michael Romano, God knows why He does what He does and allows what He allows. If that boy was not to be arrested by you, He would not have allowed you see the kid’s face and look him in the eye. Having a longer relationship with the Almighty than you, I feel comfortable enough to say, don’t worry, you’ll get him and the other guy too. Now let's discuss what Betty's attorney had to say and what I have to say in response. Ready?"

Mike smiled as he answered, "Thanks for making me feel good. Now please tell me what's been going on."

Arthur began with, "No need to concern you with the legal mumbo jumbo, that's why I get the big bucks." The old barrister laughed at his own joke and continued, "Here's the bottom line, they asked for half your pension when you start collecting it, and she wants too much child support. Now, before I make a final counter offer, let me ask you again if you're willing to give up your share of the house in order to keep your pension?"

Mike was shaken. He asked, "If I'm paying child support like the law requires, why do I have to give up half the house? At least, when the kids are grown and I'm not responsible to support them anymore, the house can be sold and the money split. It doesn't seem fair that I pay for years and get nothing back. She makes more money than I do and doesn't even need my child support. Let her boyfriend give her money!"

Slotnick changed the subject in an effort to calm Mike down. The old man wanted Michael to understand everything he was going to say, "Mike, are you hungry? I can call and have two corned beef sandwiches delivered." He patted himself on his ample belly and continued, "I sure could eat something. How about it?"

Realizing what Arthur was trying to do, Mike responded with, I'm alright now. Thanks again for getting my mind off that witch.. I'm here to speak with you and to listen to you. Why does she get my pension?"

"No Mike, she can't get it all. According to law, because you're married over ten years, she can get half of your pension. If you retire after twenty years, and live at least to seventy years old, your pension is worth more than half the house. Why give away at least $300,000 to someone who doesn't really need it. Your house is worth about $80,000 and if the house even doubles in value, you still don't break even. My advice is to give her the house along with the mortgage payment book and keep your full pension. If you advance in rank, your pension goes up and you keep it all. You have a long promising career ahead of you; you're entitled to keep everything that you will have worked for."

Arthur could almost see the gears turning in Mike's head as Mike asked, "That makes sense, what about child support? How much do I have to give?"

"They asked for three hundred weekly to cover both children," was Arthur's response.

He was about to continue when Michael broke in with, "Holy crap. That's $1200 a month after taxes. That doesn't leave me with anything to live on. Does she think I'm going to live in my car and eat snack foods the rest of my life?"

Arthur gestured with his head and said, "Easy Michael, I won't let that happen. Please have some faith in me."

"I do, that's why I'm here, was Michael's response. He continued, "What do you think, can you get it lowered?"

Slotnick smiled as he answered, "When we're in the courtroom, I'll already know how much the judge will sign off on. Don't you worry about anything. Just go get that bad guy and have fun doing it. Leave Betty and her lawyer to me. Her attorney is only practicing a few years, she's a young chicken and I'm an old fox and foxes eat chickens."

Arthur obviously liked Michael and enjoyed his work because he was smiling like a fox in a children's story. Mike felt better after the assurance from Arthur, but still wanted to get away from thinking about his divorce. Even though Betty was an adulteress and he was the wronged party, he felt like a failure. Without any further comment, he stood, shook Arthur's hand, thanked him and almost ran out of the office.

To make himself feel better, he took the short drive to the Two Oh to drop in on Lieutenant Stonner and Sergeant. Flynn, first visiting Stonner, "Hey Lieutenant," he began as he neared the man's desk, "Any results on the last church prints?"

Stonner answered, "Nice to see you Michael and yes there are some results. Your latest set matches all the other church burglaries in your command but no hit on any identification, sorry. What brings you here?"

"Just in the neighborhood and thought I would stop in to see you. Maybe you haven't heard, but Sunday night at the last break in, there were two guys and I was face to face with one of them, but they got away from us. When I finally see him on the street, we'll get his prints for you to match, then he can be charged with all the burglaries and we'll all be happy."

The lieutenant responded with, "Yeah, I heard, the story of your little foot race filtered down this way. Good luck."

Mike said his goodbyes and walked to the Squad Office. He was immediately greeted by Joe Johnson, "Mike Romano, how's it going. Any luck on finding that Bronco. Listen to me; if you see that truck, you'll probably call out the militia, after you call us of course. Sergeant Flynn says nice things about you from time to time and I'm only goofing about the militia." With a big grin and a friendly handshake he continued, "You really wouldn't call them. Would you?"

Mike's response was a jovial, "Nice to see you too Detective."

Johnson responded with a quick, "It's Joe, Mike, between us, only Joe."

As usual, from in the far corner, Detective James muttered something unintelligible. Mike heard it and shouted, "Jim Jim, nice to see you too."

Flynn heard the exchanges and joined in, "Mike Romano, the man I would most likely choose to replace one of my squad members." In an effort to remain politically neutral, he added, "Should I be asked of course and that never happens. Come on in Mike and tell me what's shaking."

Because of the way Flynn always treated him, Mike felt a swell of obligation. He felt the need to hint around about Michael Guggalarie, after all, if he doesn't see him on the street or the kid runs, Flynn's men might get the case referred to them even though it should go to the Property Squad. Even if he, himself, does make the actual arrest, the DA's office might insist that the case be handled by Detectives and only list him as the apprehending officer. Mike began with, "Well Sarge, I don't know if you get copies of burglary reports from the Two Three, but there's been a rash of church burglaries. You may or may not know that I'm the uniformed print man in the command. Anyway, Lieutenant Stonner's men linked burglaries from three church break-ins to the same man, but the guy's hands are not on file."

Flynn commented, "Nice job, go on."

Mike continued, "Last Sunday, Easter Sunday, into Monday morning, Holy Child of God Church was broken into again. They have at least four burglaries without an arrest."

Mike drew a breath and continued, "This time two of us were there and ready for them. Unfortunately, we failed to grab them, there were two, and they got away, but before that happened, I got a good look at one of them and I'm waiting to see him again. My plan is to arrest him based on my own personal observation. If I get him and he's linked to all the 61's, I'd like to keep the case even if the DA wants the squad to handle it. Can I say that we conferred and I can keep the case, even if the ADA insists?"

"Sure you can Michael and if the ADA doesn't cooperate, just give them my number and I'll speak to them myself. You've earned the right to the case. It'll look good in your jacket. Now if you want something really good in your jacket, find that Bronco for me and that will make everybody's day."

"I'm always looking Sarge, even on my own time sometimes." Remembering that his divorce would soon hit a courtroom, Mike added, "In a few weeks some personal issues will be rectified and my head will be clearer, then I can spend more time on the Bronco case. I probably want him as much as you guys do."

Flynn's telephone rang and Mike used that as an opportunity to take his leave. He got what he wanted, permission to keep the Guggalarie case through the arrest and subsequent court procedures and left the building reasonably content.

***

Saturday morning's eight to four tour was the last day of their set that allowed Mike and Sully to look for Michael Guggalarie before they'd swing out. If they didn't get him then, they would have to double their efforts when they returned back on four to twelve set. Mike Romano silently prayed, *please Saint Michael, send me Michael Guggalarie today. Arthur's right, God wants me to get him and He is never wrong.*

It was almost the end of tour with an hour to go, Mike was driving, when in his head he again heard the beat of what he thought were wings. His mind raced, *maybe I'm going nuts. I'm not under any stress today or in a potentially bad situation, yet I hear wings. I have to take some time off after my divorce.*

He snapped back to normal when he heard, "Mike, watch out for that dog!" Sully continued, "Boy partner, where were you? You looked like a zombie. Are you ok?"

Embarrassed, Mike said, "Just thinking about Guggalarie. It's almost a week and there's been no sign of him." Looking at his partner he asked, "Maybe I should call the squad and give them the ID on Michael or should we go to his house and try to grab him?"

Sully thought for a second, before answering, "Look Mike, I know you're frustrated, but I think you should give it the rest of this tour and at least two days in the next set before you give up on what you want so much. Someone will probably ask, 'why did you wait so long?' and then there's lying about not knowing the kid's face. I don't know if you ever want to admit to that, you could end up with charges and specs for holding back information."

As Sully finished talking, Mike drove past Leona's luncheonette and gasped so hard that he almost swallowed his tongue, "Sully, check out who we just passed. Look in your mirror. Guggalarie and Perino just walked out of Leona's place. Keep your eye on them in case they run. I'm gonna turn around slowly, like we're going to get coffee."

The two burglars acted as if they didn't have a care in the world as Mike and Sully pulled up to the curb near them and stopped. Before he pulled up, Mike had quickly told his partner, "Sully just act as if we're getting out and going into the restaurant.

I'll stop and talk to Michael, you slide around behind Tommy. When you nod your head that you're ready, we'll each grab our guy. I don't think Michael will run because he would have fled already as we turned. He's such a smart ass, that he'll stand still to find out what I have to say. Ready? Don't move too quickly, and act excited. We want to surprise them with a collar. Let's do it."

The team exited the car as Mike spoke to his partner, "Yeah Sully, even though we had lunch, I could use something else."

Sully responded with, "Yeah, me too Mike."

As the team approached the two teenagers, Mike, acting surprised at noticing Guggalarie, looked directly at the kid and said, "Michael, what brings you here, "Preying on old ladies again?"

The kid's response was as expected, "Why are you always picking on me? Don't have anything else to do?"

Romano smiled and said, "Remember Michael, when some time ago I told you that I would someday arrest you once you turned sixteen?"

The kid quickly snapped, "So what. You got nothing on me."

Perino watched intently and never paid Sully any mind as Romano was interacting with Guggalarie. Sully got so close to Tommy that he was almost sharing the kid's shoes with him and gave a slight nod to his partner. With that, Mike quickly advanced toward Guggalarie and hissed, "Well dirt bag, the time has come," as he grabbed the kid's neck with one hand and pulled his handcuffs from his belt with the other. In one smooth motion, Mike let go of the shocked teenager's neck, grabbed his arms and spun him around, snapping on the handcuffs.

Romano knew that Sully had cuffed his man too because Perino shouted, "Ouch. It was all his idea," even before the boys were told why they were arrested.

Guggalarie shouted, Shut up Tommy. They got nothing."

Romano countered, "Sure we do Michael. Do you remember the night in the church when you opened the storeroom door, and had a flashlight shining in your face then shouted, 'Shit?'

Well, the guy holding the flashlight was me! You're under arrest for burglarizing Holy Child Church, and your little friend too."

"You got nothing, you big dumb cop. I'm gonna get my father to sue you. He's got lots of connections."

Romano just smiled and said, "Sure kid. You do that but now you're going to jail. I'll give the courts all they need to put you away for a while." He turned towards Sully and saw a weeping Tommy Perino. "Ok partner, let's pat them down and hook 'em together, then stuff the little shits into the car."

After finding no contraband on either youth, the two agents of the law got the boys ready for transport. Freeing Tommy's left arm, Mike threaded that arm thru Guggalarie's right arm and re-cuffed Perino. The two teenagers were now uncomfortably linked together and roughly stuffed into the rear seat of their patrol car as they whined and complained that their arms hurt. During the ride, Sully read them their Miranda Warnings. The boys didn't respond except to continue complaining about how uncomfortable they were. Their complaints fell on deaf ears.

Mike and Sully marched their two charges before the desk officer, Lieutenant Cassidy, who smiled when he saw them. "Well Romano, let me guess, are these fine young people being arrested for breaking into a church last week?"

Sully just smiled back while nodding his head. Mike beamed and said, "It took some time but no bad guy makes me run without getting arrested sooner or later, because I don't like to run. Yeah, it's the two guys who are trying to guarantee their seats in Hell."

The lieutenant asked, "And do we know their names?" Pointing to Guggalarie he asked, "You, Blondie, what might your name and age be? Don't lie either, because I'll just have Officer Romano add another charge." Of course it was an idle threat designed by Cassidy as a form of entertainment. He had very little tolerance for bad guys, especially someone as low as a church burglar and thought that he would have some fun.

"This cop is crazy. He's made all this up. I didn't rob any church. Hell, I even help my father out with the baseball team, he works at the church." Guggalarie just answered some questions for Romano without knowing it and after his Miranda warnings too.

Cassidy stood up, leaned over the desk and said, "Young man, I didn't ask for your opinion, just your name so I can make a blotter entry. Are you going to answer or should I book you as a John Doe and that way you're guaranteed to spend the entire week end in jail without seeing a judge? Sometimes it's even longer because usually the court system processes John Does last."

The threat of spending several days in jail worked. Guggalarie could not answer fast enough and started giving his name. Perino didn't even wait for Guggalarie to finish when he blurted out, "My name is Tommy Perino and I live at 320 Sinclair Ave and I'm fifteen years old. It was all Michael's idea. He said that robbing churches was easy. Please don't send me to jail." He then hung his head and started sobbing.

As Perino spoke, Guggalarie stopped addressing Cassidy and turned his attention to Perino, "Shut up Tommy. You're a kid and will go to Family Court; your big mouth will send me to Rikers Island. That big cop can't prove a thing."

It was almost comical to listen to the verbal exchanges. The best result was after Mike Romano stated, "You know Michael, the night that I saw you inside the church, I took finger prints that were left behind by the burglars. I'll bet they match your finger prints, but you already know that they will. All the other church break-ins will match too." He then turned to the sobbing Tommy, "Hey Tommy, did you go with Michael to the other churches too or only the last one?"

It happened when Tommy answered Romano's question, as he began to speak, his partner in crime tried to kick him. Sully pulled Tommy back and away from Michael who lost his balance and fell. He was still on the floor when, Tommy said, "No Officer, I only went inside at the big church. I was inside the smaller churches but never touched anything, honest. Does that count? Does it help me?"

Mike didn't answer at once because he was enjoying the exchange. After helping Michael G. stand, he said, "That is up to the District Attorney's Office. I just do the locking up. The DA and the courts make all decisions like that."

Logan and Fitz walked in as the show before the desk was in full swing. They added to the act. Logan slapped Romano on the back and shouted, "Well done, print man."

Fitz asked, "Who's this, the church burglars? Let me transport them, we'll take the long way, thru the swamps in Blue Heron Park, maybe they'll try to get away."

Cassidy was no longer amused by the circus in front of him and as officially as possible ordered, "Romano, Sullivan, you know the drill. Take your prisoners in the back, notify their parents because they're less than nineteen years old and then transport them to the Two Oh for processing and arraignment and for God's sake, don't question them without their parents or a lawyer present. You don't want the charges dropped."

The two boys were taken into the old holding pen in the rear of the station. Inside the area were a small desk and a telephone. Reluctantly, Guggalarie gave his home phone number to Romano, who promptly dialed it. There was no answer. The call to Tommy Perino's home was answered by his mother. It was explained to her that, "Tommy was arrested along with his friend Michael Guggalarie for burglarizing Holy Child of God Church late Easter Sunday and that both boys were going to the 120 Pct." Mike Romano further explained that the boys would be processed and held for arraignment as soon as possible.

Mrs. Perino asked to speak to her son. On the police end of the conversation, the two cops heard, "Yes Mom. Two cops grabbed me and Michael in Annadale. They arrested us for breaking into Holy Child Church."

Perino was silent for a minute as he held the receiver to his ear, then spoke again, "Yeah, I know Mom, but I snuck out of the house and met Michael a couple of times. I only went along because it was fun. It was all his idea."

At that point Romano took the phone from Tommy and spoke to his mother. "Mrs. Perino, the boys were given their Miranda Warnings when we arrested them. So everything we hear

Tommy say can be used in the courts. I recommend that you try to get an attorney and meet us at the Saint George station house in approximately an hour. I'll put Tommy back on so you can tell him to remain quiet until he sees you and his attorney. My partner and I are truly sorry that you have to go thru this. Here's Tommy." Mike handed the phone to the kid.

All Perino could be heard saying, "Yes Mommy, I will." Between sobs, he mumbled, "Daddy's gonna kill me. Bye." Perino put the phone down.

Mike turned to Sully, "Ok partner, let's hook them up again and transport them to booking in the Two Oh." To Guggalarie he said, "Michael, we can make more calls to your home in the Two Oh. You'll also be given the opportunity to phone anyone else you may want to."

The two cops with their prisoners in tow, stopped to notify the desk officer that they were leaving. It was change of tour and Cassidy was turning the desk over to Sergeant Walowski. Cassidy said, "Great job Romano. I knew you would find him." For the benefit of Sullivan he added, "Sully, I'm sure Mike appreciates your help in bringing this thing to a fruitful closure. You guys did a great job."

Sergeant Walowski added, "Don't forget to put yourselves over the air and don't forget to come back when you're finished. Don't milk the overtime. Now get going."

At first, Mike was annoyed at the remarks of Walowski but as they walked away from the desk, Walowski could be seen with an impish smile on his face as he was slapped on the shoulder by Cassidy. Mike saw the slap and felt better knowing that he was teasing.

When they arrived, the team walked their two men into the Two Oh, first stopping to log in with the Desk Officer before bringing their arrestees up to the booking room.

As Sully began the formal arrest process for Perino, Mike began the paperwork for Guggalarie. Michael G., growing inpatient, reverted back to his wise ass attitude with, "Hey, you Mr. super cop, Romano, you never gave me my phone call."

Mike was quick to respond with, "Sure Michael; as soon as you're fingerprinted you can speak to your family. The sad thing is, I can't question you without your parents or your attorney present." That statement was not true, it applied only to Perino, but Mike wanted to play with the kids. He was counting on Perino shooting his mouth off again.

After all the paper work was completed and both youths were printed, Mike taking three sets of Guggalarie's hands and was about to give Guggalarie another phone call or two, when the booking phone rang. Romano picked it up and before he could even say his own name, an obviously annoyed voice announced, "Romano or Sullivan please, this is Officer Gerhardt downstairs, please tell them the parents of their collars are here and demanding to see their kids."

"Romano here, tell them one of us will be right down to escort them upstairs. Thanks."

Before Mike went down, he stopped in the Latent Unit to find Lieutenant Stonner and carried in his hand one of Michael Guggalarie's print cards. The lieutenant usually worked a 10x6 tour and was still present. Holding the card out in front of himself like a jousting lance, Mike went directly to Stonner's desk. "Loo, here's the church burglar's hands, at least the older one of two. Can you try for a quick match against my church latents?"

Stonner smiled broadly as he responded, "Well, well, Mike Romano comes thru. Are you sure you have the right guy?"

Mike could hardly control the joy in his voice, "Sure as sure can be Loo. The little side kick even made statements admitting the Easter Sunday break in." He drew a breath and continued, "And a positive ID will lock at least one of those dummies to all of the church cases."

"You got it Romano but please wait for the formal submission of the cards so we can do a written report for the courts." Twisting his face as if in deep thought, Stonner added, "Never mind the wait. I'll do an unusual occurrence report about the identification referring to your personal eye to eye observation during the night in question, and give you copies for arraignment.

Andy Flynn filled me in. Give me about an hour to generate everything." Stonner then walked over to one of his men and ordered, "Put a rush on these prints against the church burglaries in the Two Three and do it ten minutes ago."

Romano thanked the Lieutenant and went to meet the parents of his two miscreants. In his head Romano heard a soft thumping, maybe it was only the cadence of his own footfalls on the stairs as he walked. When Mike stepped onto the flat lobby floor, he was accosted by a burly, balding man in his early 40's. The guy was irate, pointing his finger, he asked, "You, are you the guy that arrested my son Michael? He's a good boy and helps me at our church where I volunteer."

Before he answered, Mike let his mind wander a bit, *that explains a lot. Do you open the window for the kid or does he con his way inside the storeroom and do it himself?* The senior Guggalarie stared at the name plate on Mike's chest and snapped, "You, Romano, I asked you a question. Are you the guy who arrested my son?"

Mike gathered all his calm before answering, "You must be James Guggalarie, that little devils father." Guggalarie's face looked surprised at the comeback, as Romano put his right hand forward to shake the man's hand. Guggalarie was dumb enough to accept the gesture. Mike gripped the hand like a housewife squeezing water from a sponge, quickly leaned forward and whispered, "I don't give a shit about your connections, your kid is guilty and if you're in on it, you'll be next." On the off chance Guggalarie complained about the crushing grip on his hand, Mike, loud enough to be over heard, quickly continued, "Wow, Mr. Guggalarie, please to meet you. That's some grip you have there. Ouch. I understand there is another parent or parents here to see my partner and me. Do you know who it is?"

The senior Guggalarie was taken aback by the quick exchange, never having met anyone like the cop who stood before him and could only respond with, "She's right over here. The mother of my son's friend and her lawyer, he's my lawyer too," while turning to point to a couple standing behind him.

Mike gently brushed Guggalarie aside and extended his hand to Mrs. Perino saying, “Mrs. Perino, sorry to meet under these circumstances.” Without waiting for her response, he turned to the attorney, again extended his hand and said, Mike Romano, arresting officer and you are?”

“Walter Schmidt here Officer, pleased to meet you. I’m here for both parties. Are you aware that Mrs. Perino’s son, Thomas is only fifteen years old?”

Mike smiled and responded, “Not until this moment, but will you all please follow me upstairs to your respective children.”

Mike led them to the Squad’s office, stopping them at the door with, “Please wait here. I have to secure a room for the meeting. Department regulations, you know. We can’t bring you into the arrest processing area. I’m sure your attorney knows that because of Thomas’ age, he must be interviewed in a non-aggressive area.”

Covering for Flynn was Sergeant Schwartz. Mike walked in and explained that he had a juvenile and one other under arrest. He made sure to tell Schwartz that besides the kids’ parents, their lawyer was present, and that he was requesting to use the squad’s interview room because one kid was under sixteen years old, and regulations dictate that kids be questioned in a non-intimidating area. Schwartz naturally said, “Yes.”

After escorting the trio to the room, Mike excused himself with, “You folks get comfortable if possible and I’ll bring the boys in right away.”

Mike and Sully each brought one of the kids into the room, Guggalarie was with Mike. Both kids were front cuffed. As soon as he saw his mother, Tommy P. broke out in tears and advanced towards her. Sully allowed it. Mrs. Perino looked at her son, then down at the handcuffs and sobbed. She turned to Schmidt and asked, “Can you make them take those handcuffs off please, they’re only children?”

Schmidt looked at the two cops and asked. “How about it Officers?”

Sully turned to Mike as if to say, it’s your show Mike.

Mike, not wanting to give Guggalarie a break answered, “I’m sorry counselor but its Department Regulations when not in arrest processing they must remain cuffed. Making sure that all regulations were adhered to Romano made it a point to once again recite their Miranda Warnings to the boys, then looked at Sully and nodded towards the door. When the two cops were outside they remained at the doorway where they were able to observe all occupants of the room.

From their post at the doorway, the cops could only hear individual words of the conversations between the youths, their parents and their attorney.

Some of the words that floated across the room were “sue”, heard twice from both Guggalaries, also “didn’t do anything,” and “they got nothing.” From Perino, all they heard clearly was, “Mommy, I’m a kid, they’ll hurt me in jail,” accompanied by sobs.

Only Schmidt spoke loud, obviously only when he wanted the cops to hear his words, like, “It’s ok Tommy, and you’ll be treated as a kid under sixteen in Family Court. Michael, keep your mouth shut until after arraignment, we’ll discuss strategies at that time after I know what evidence is against you kids.”

Schmidt then turned and smiled directly at Mike adding, “If any”, before turning back to his client, when he calmly and professionally added, “Don’t worry, I’ll ask for release to your family.” After several minutes with his clients, he again spoke loud enough for all to hear, “Mr. Guggalarie, I suggest that you be present at the court house by 9:00 a.m. That’s when Michael will see the judge. Mrs. Perino, please wait for me downstairs, Tommy will be seen in Family Court. I must speak to the officers first. Thank you.”

Schmidt waited for the parents to say their goodbyes and followed the cops back to the arrest processing room, stopping at the door and waiting until they secured their prisoners.

Once the two boys were secured, Michael in the cage and Perino in a chair near a window, Mike and Sully stepped into the hallway to speak with Schmidt.

Schmidt spoke first, “Gentlemen, just what caused you to arrest my clients? They continue to profess their innocence?”

Romano answered first, Counselor, Mr. Schmidt is it? Please allow me to explain that Officer Sullivan and I are not in the habit of arresting people unjustly. The New York Penal Code requires that we have ‘reasonable cause to believe’ and in this case we absolutely do. I personally saw Michael Guggalarie standing inside the church storeroom doorway and holding a tool that was used to break into a cabinet located inside that room. My flashlight was in his face, so maybe he didn’t know it was me as he slammed the door shut after acknowledging that he was caught by first saying and I quote, “Oh shit.” That is why he was arrested.”

Schmidt responded with, “And why was Thomas Perino arrested too?”

Mike gave the ball to Sully by answering, “After the boys ran from us at the scene, my partner discussed the possibility of the second perp being Thomas.” Pointing to Sully, Mike said, “Sully, if you can please explain to Mr. Schmidt why Perino has been arrested with Guggalarie.”

Sully knew what Mike wanted and responded, “Sir when the door was slammed, I had just run around to the other side of the building in an attempt to prevent the boys from fleeing thru the window that they used to enter the church. I almost got to the window as the first one dropped to the ground and took off running and he looked like your client, Tommy. I took off after him but was unable to catch him. When we saw them on the street today, Tommy still looked like the guy I chased that night.” As he finished speaking, Sully then causally waved his hand in Romano’s direction.

Catching the signal, Mike took up the second part of the answer. “When we apprehended the boys on the street today, Tommy made spontaneous statements concerning the crime and again after Miranda Warnings.” The cautious voice within Mike’s head spoke to him and warned against telling the lawyer about the fingerprints and the other church. Romano concluded with, “There you have it.”

The attorney smiled at them and replied, "Well, I've been doing this for many years and this is the first time that arresting officers have been so relaxed and polite, almost like you're apologizing for arresting them."

Mike quickly responded, Mr. Schmidt, Michael is guilty as hell, I saw him from a distance of not three feet in front of me. Tommy is a kid under sixteen and led astray by Michael. We know Tommy will be taken to Family Court and Michael to Criminal Court. Personally, I think your client Michael, should plead guilty at arraignment. If he goes to trial, he'll end up getting some real time." Mike anxiously wanted to go back to Lieutenant Stonner and dismissed Schmidt with, "Anyway, we have to go to the DA's Office and write up the complaints. See you in court."

Schmidt thanked the cops for their time, turned and left.

As Schmidt walk away, Mike turned and said, "Come on Sully, let's go see if there's any confirmation of the prints." Of course, Romano already knew the answer.

***

After signing in at the District Attorney's Office, three blocks south of the station house, Romano and Sullivan sat down to wait, there were two officers ahead of them. Less than an hour later they were called in to be interviewed by the Assistant District Attorney on duty.

After listening to the account of the Easter Sunday burglary and subsequent arrest, ADA Fanino asked, "Officer Romano, I see by the report issued by the Staten Island Latent Print Identification Unit, that your defendants, Guggalarie and Perino, have been identified through their fingerprints to several other burglaries going back some time, although, defendant Perino has not been identified as often as Guggalarie. When I speak of Perino, I speak about him because of his statements, not from fingerprint identification because he's too young. We can only assume that the unidentified prints are Perino's.

"Yes, I expected that. I'm the recovering officer at every site. It should be there in the report somewhere."

"It is," was the quick response. Fanino continued with, "However, your defendants were both underage at the time of all the burglaries except the last one. I see that Guggalarie turned sixteen last month. That will prevent me from indicting him on those charges. But, I can keep those charges for arraignment because he's over sixteen, later his attorney will probably get all but the last one dismissed. The court will deem that the prints found at the earlier scenes belonged to a juvenile and not charge Guggalarie as an adult regarding those incidents. They will however, be in the court jacket and give the judge some information in determining the length of sentencing if Michael enters a plea, or we get a guilty verdict, should the case go all the way to trial. Perino's write-up and affidavit is referred to Family Court anyway. "

Later that evening, Tommy Perino was released to his mother for an appearance in Family Court on Monday and Michael Guggalarie was lodged in the basement of the Criminal Court House on Targee Street until he could see the judge in the morning. Mike and Sully returned to the Two Three, filled out overtime slips and signed out.

Mike drove directly home and never saw the black Bronco when it once again drove out of the woods and on to Arthur Kill Road before heading for the Outer Bridge to New Jersey. Baggs was going to conduct business.

Late that same night, Mike was in the arms of Morpheus, the Greek god of dreams, when Baggs stopped at Bryan's house and deposited his weekly graft package under the right fender of the blue Buick that was parked in the driveway and quickly left.

***

Saturday morning, Mike, pleased with himself over the previous day's arrests, left his house by 6:30 a.m. and went out for breakfast. After a hardy celebratory meal, he arrived at the Police

Sign in Room inside the Targee Street court house by 8:15 a.m., putting him officially on duty and it was all overtime. Mike went to the appropriate courtroom, sat down to wait and thought, *this money will certainly come in handy. I don't know what will happen in divorce court. Crap, it's only six days away.* To refocus his verves, he went over all the paperwork that he had concerning Guggalarie and Perino while waiting for the judge to enter.

It was 9:15 a.m., when Schmidt walked in and approached Mike in an attempt to engage him in conversation by saying, "Good morning Officer Romano. I see according to the defense copy of the DA's papers that you have alleged fingerprints from the crime scene. Is that correct?"

Politely as he could, Mike looked up from his seat and said, "Mr. Schmidt, you represent the accused, it would be improper for me to have any conversation with you unless the prosecuting attorney is present. So, I will not answer that or any question from you without being officially before the court. Please understand my position."

Schmidt smiled as he answered, "Of course Officer. You're sharper than most cops, usually I can engage them in saying something that I can use to help my client."

Mike responded with, "Thanks for the compliment, but I stand by our conversation of yesterday." The attorney got the hint and walked over to sit with the other lawyers waiting for their cases. As usual they occupied empty seats reserved for a jury when the room was used for a trail. The first rows of public seats in most courtrooms were set aside only for attorneys and cops, but the defense lawyers liked to distance themselves from the police and whenever possible use the jury chairs. Most police officers liked it that way.

At precisely 10:00 a.m. the judge arrived at the bench and court was officially called to order. It was 11:00 a.m. before Mike heard the bailiff announce, "Case Number SI-CC3314-84, State of New York verses Michael Guggalarie."

As the case was announced, Schmidt stood before the judge on the defense side, on the left facing the judge and waited as Guggalarie was produced from the rear holding cell. The defendant was brought in, without handcuffs, to a position beside his attorney by two correction officers who remained standing behind him. Romano took his place next to the ADA and turned around to see James Guggalarie and a woman, probably Michael's mother, standing at the rail behind the defendant.

The charges against Guggalarie were formally read and Mike was happy to hear that all the church burglaries were included and was not surprised to hear a "not guilty" entered from the defendant's attorney.

The judge quickly responded, "Based on what I see here before me Mr. Schmidt, I find that hard to believe, but that is your clients right, so very well, next court date is for Thursday, May 3rd. Bail is set at $10,000 cash or bond. Next case please."

When he heard the next court date, Mike was stunned; he was to be in court with Arthur Slotnick for his divorce. His divorce would be in the Supreme Court building on Richmond Terrace and usually all per trial hearings were held in the Criminal Court Building on Targee Street. Mentally he made a note to work that problem out as soon as he could but first wanted to see if Arthur could help; maybe Arthur had a magic wand. Mike was rattled by the prospect of being in two places a couple of miles apart, possibly at the exact same time.

By noon Romano had signed off duty, filled out an overtime slip, and inserted the slip into the sign in room's time clock for a matching time and date stamp. Needing to do something besides dwell on his court appearance problems, Mike decided to make an attempt to see his children. He found a pay phone and called them. Just as he was about to hang up, someone answered and all he heard was breathing as he asked, "Annie?"

The person on the other end responded with a cold, "Yes?"

Recognizing the voice, he asked, "Can I speak to one of the kids please?"

The icy voice on the other end of the line replied, "Oh, it's you. I'm afraid not, because they are not home. They were depressed when you didn't see them last week, so yesterday, to cheer them up, I sent them to visit with Kelly and the family. Oh, by the way, my attorney suggests that we have no further conversations until next Thursday in Court."

Mike was about to respond when Betty continued in an even more frigid manner, like a wind blowing across the frozen arctic tundra, "Sorry and do not telephone again. Bye." The line went dead.

Once again Betty had twisted Mike's shorts into a knot. Now he had the rest of the day and all day Sunday to himself before returning to work. His emotions flip-flopped from joy about Guggalarie, to anger about Betty and his pending court date, where he would finally get some relief from the pain her adulterous behavior had caused him. By the time Romano returned to his car, he had decided how he would spend his week end. First he would go back to his apartment, maybe pour himself some scotch, and attempt to take a map. With nothing else to do, later that night, he planned to drive to the vicinity of Clay Pit Pond Park on Arthur Kill Road, stealthily park his Chevy and sit there in the dark, waiting to see if the black Bronco showed up.

Romano didn't know that Baggs had already visited half of his collections on Friday before he delivered Bryan's money and again left for New Jersey by 6:30 a.m. on Saturday. Baggs returned to the Quonset hut and switched cars by midafternoon that day. Subsequently, the time Mike spent parked just off Arthur Kill Road that night was fruitless.

On Sunday, Romano busied himself with mindless tasks like grocery shopping and visiting the coin operated laundry mat. He spent the balance of the day sitting in front of his television set watching any program that caught his interest. His next set of tours would be 4x12's, beginning Monday afternoon and spent that morning sitting mindlessly in front of his television.

Arriving at the station by 3:00 p.m., Mike was informed by Lieutenant Cassidy that he had received official notification through Appearance Control, for Mike to respond to the Supreme Court Building, on Thursday, May 3rd regarding the Guggalarie arrest. Mike was also informed that the Captain was waiting for him in his office. Mike thanked his Lieutenant and moved to an alcove to spend a few seconds thinking about the logistics of running between court rooms on May 3rd, decided it wasn't too bad because they were in the same building and walked to the captain's office. Finding the door closed, Romano knocked twice. From within came a cheery, "Enter, please come in."

Even though he was in civilian clothes, Mike loosely saluted his Captain as he said, "Captain, you wanted to see me?"

"Lars responded with, "Sit, Michael, please," indicating a chair opposite his desk. "You have done real well my boy. In twenty two years, I can't remember a uniformed officer with more dedication and tenacity than you have. Well done. Lieutenant Cassidy tells me that he approved your tour change on Easter Sunday. It seems that your instincts were correct, however, if you ever plan something like that again, please run it past me first. I am in charge here."

Mike could see that Lars was pleased with his work and that the minor lecture he had received was only to remind him that, even though it all worked out, he, Lars Anderson, was the Commanding Officer and should be given the option of approving anything like a stake out. So he smiled back and answered, "Yes Sir, Captain, will do and thank you for the opportunity. I know you could have disapproved the change when Lieutenant Cassidy informed you, but at the time there was kind of a rush because I had to get back to Monsignor Scala. Thank you again."

Lars stood up, smiled and dismissed Romano with, "Nice work. Now go out there and find some more burglars."

Anxious to get to work and try to forget his personal problems, Mike quickly acknowledged with a snappy, "Sir!" and walked out, closing the door and went upstairs to suit up.

Once on patrol Mike slowly took a tour of the entire command so that he could be alone with his thoughts. While he drove, Mike thought about his last conversation with Betty and what she might do to keep him from visiting his children whenever he called to do so. Arthur Slotnick told him not to be concerned, but that was easy for him to say, he wasn't getting divorced. To cheer himself up, Mike drove to the Annadale Luncheonette and Leona.

When Mike arrived in front of Leona's diner, the first thing he noticed was that the open sign was not lit, and he slumped in his seat. Almost at the same time, his mood rose, as did his posture, when he noticed some lights were still on and Leona was at the rear of the lunch counter cleaning up. He stopped the car and hit the siren for a quick chirp. She looked up and slowly began to walk towards the window. Seeing Mike as he exited his vehicle, she quickly scooted around and unlocked the door. With a big smile on her face, she greeted him with, "Michael, I heard about the arrests you made. You finally got that Michael boy and his friend Tommy." She gave him a hug and continued, "I'm happy for you. Please sit down, I haven't emptied the coffee urn yet, it may be strong but would you like some and something to eat?"

Mike felt a little tingle at the intimate contact and cautiously and gently put his own arms around her, "Thank you, he answered in a slightly embarrassed tone.

"It's no bother," Leona continued as she loosened her embrace. Feeling Mike's arms release, she guided him to a stool. "Tell me all about it while I get us some coffee."

Mike removed the portable radio from his equipment belt, lowered the volume and began with, "Well, last Sunday night, I and an old friend, Jerry Sullivan planned to sit in the church all night and wait for the burglars. I had set it up with the pastor, Monsignor Scala, about a week before, figuring that the thieves would break in for the Easter collection."

At that point in the story, Leona placed two coffee cups down on the counter near Mike, pushing one towards him. She touched his hand as he reached for it, pulling away as he picked it up and asked, Michael, are you alright? Your hand is shaking; you're going to get burnt with that hot coffee."

Mike knew perfectly well why his hand shook; his whole body was still tingling from Leona's embrace. His mind raced, *I've always had a mild attraction to her. She's good looking, pleasant and divorced, with kids, and we have that in common. Now I know why I subconsciously jumped on Sully when he asked about her. The woman revs my engine. I like being near her because she makes me feel good, but no thanks; I'm too scared to go into any new relationship now. After my divorce is final and things normalize for me, maybe then and she would be the one, but not now. I'm not quite ready.*

Leona, being an intuitive woman, who was attracted to the man in front of her, sensed what was happening and helped him out of his dilemma when she coyly said, "Well, Officer Romano, thank you for the unspoken compliment but we're friends, that's all. You have too much going on right now to think like that." She liked him too and back in the secret place where she kept special thoughts, she promised herself that one day she would explore the possibility that they could be more then friends.

Mike responded with a chuckle to cover his embarrassment and continued, "Anyway here's what happened next………"

An hour passed before they knew it and reluctantly Leona announced that she wanted to go home. She leaned forward, gave a little peck on Mike's cheek, said, "Michael Romano, you're a nice man", handed him his radio and guided him to the door.

Mike, not knowing exactly what emotion he was feeling at the moment could only say, "Thanks", as the door closed behind him.

There was nothing else that was noteworthy for the remainder of the first half of his tour. After taking his meal hour in the rear dining room of Russo's, Mike returned to his car at 9:00p.m. Just as he started the engine, the radio crackled, "In the Two Three, we have reports of people in the water south of Hylan Blvd at the end of Allen Place. Unit's needed to respond, Emergency Service and Aviation has been notified."

Romano heard two teams answer that they were responding and wasn't sure if he should go, even though he was so close. Instead he just sat in Russo's parking lot and thought about the coming Thursday and his divorce court appearance. After seeing Paramedics, Emergency Service cops and two RMP's head towards Allen Place, Mike put his car in gear and slowly started driving to the location without putting himself over the air. They didn't need him, but it was something to do, and drove to Allen Place and down to the water. It seemed that every police unit on the Island was already there, so he parked alongside a corral type fence near some houses. It was obvious to him that the people kept horses. What he didn't notice was that they also had a rather large cow. As he walked closer to the activity, he could see that a sailboat had capsized with its stern slowly going down. Mike estimated that it was about 200 feet off shore.

Two Emergency Service officers were loading equipment into a small skiff while its outboard engine was idling. Along with police there were at least twenty civilians watching the activity. He could see the aviation helicopter getting closer and even though he was in full uniform, nobody paid any attention to him as he leaned against an emergency truck and watched the activity. The helicopter hovered over two people in the water while keeping a large searchlight trained on them. When the two cops in the boat reached the two people and began hauling them into the boat, the searchlight on the chopper moved about looking for others who might still be in the water. Someone inside the chopper unit asked dispatch if he knew how many persons were involved. One of the E Cops responded, "We have two people from the boat and they inform us there were no others on board. Thanks for your help, K"

Aviation responded with, "Ten Four Emergency, we'll light you way."

Mike, feeling low and having seen many rescues during his time on the job, decided to go back to his car. As he walked past the corral, the pet cow stuck her head over the top rail and said, "Mooo," then winked her big eyes, stopping Mike in his tracks. As a child he always had liked cows and their gentle manner, the one that stood before him now was no exception. He gently stroked her neck and was rewarded with another "Moooo." As he began forming a silly idea in his head, he repeated the neck stroke two more times with the same result. Mike withdrew his portable radio from its belt holder and waited and it didn't take long before the boat carrying the two unfortunate boaters and the E Cops reached shore. As the EMT personnel attended to the victims, an E Cop radioed, “Staten Island Emergency Two to Central.”

The dispatcher said, “Go Emergency Unit Two.”

“The boaters are safe. Please thank Aviation for a job well done.”

The dispatcher responded in kind, “We thank all units for your assistance. Please resume your duties. Please respond.”

Mike timed it perfectly, He stroked the cow’s neck and keyed his radio, “Moooo” she said.

The radio crackled with, “What was that Central? What unit was that?”

Before anyone could answer, Mike again held his portable near the cow, “Mooo”, was the response. The helicopter unit rotated in place with the searchlight burning brightly. Anonymously, over the air could be heard, giggles and “Can’t find which unit that was Central.” At least two of the vehicles in the area gave a toot on their sirens. Mike was beginning to feel better thanks to the silliness of his fellow officers. He gave the cow another stroke and keyed his radio, the “Mooo,” was followed by a disguised, “Good night and I thank you all.” Mike returned to his patrol car and completed his tour in good spirits.

The next two night’s tours went well for Mike. There were no unusual occurrences, nothing out of the ordinary. Wednesday, when he arrived at work, Mike put in for Friday as a vacation day. He wanted the day after his divorce to either celebrate or sulk, depending on how good a job Arthur Slotnick did. If, for some reason, he was needed back in court over the Guggalarie case, he could always withdraw the vacation day request. After a short conversation with Lieutenant Cassidy, he was given permission to go directly to court in civilian clothes the next day regarding the church case. Mike never mentioned his impending divorce appearance. On Thursday morning Michael telephoned his desk officer from the police sign in room and signed in, ‘present at court’ at 8:00 a.m. and then went to the District Attorney’s Office and met with the prosecuting attorney, ADA Frank Fanino. The ADA informed him that Guggalarie’s attorney was challenging his eye to eye identification of the defendant and subsequently disallowing the recovered fingerprints and that his court appearance was for an evidentiary hearing. They went over some possible questions that might be raised by Schmidt. Romano excused himself at 9:30 a.m. after explaining that he was to meet with his divorce attorney in the same building that very day. Fanino wished him luck and said not to worry; he would do whatever was necessary to send for him if he wasn't present when needed.

Mike found Arthur in the corridor outside the courtroom marked 'Civil Part 2.' Arthur greeted him with, "Michael, when you called and told my assistant that you had a pre-trial hearing on the same date as your divorce, I became anxious for you. I'm happy to see that you could be here. I assume that the hearing is in this building?"

"Yes Arthur it is down on the first floor," was Mike's quick response. He continued, "I must have a Fairy Godfather. The ADA is aware of where I am if I'm not sitting in the courtroom and that I can respond within minutes when called. Are we ready? Please let me run downstairs and tell ADA Fanino that I'll be down soon?"

Arthur smiled and answered, "Sure my boy but be quick about it. This should be over in ten to fifteen minutes."

Mike was surprised and answered, "I don't know how you can say that, but I'm happy to hear it. Be right back."

Three minutes later Mike and Arthur were standing in a small courtroom next to Betty and her young female attorney. The judge was waiting for them. Arthur leaned close to Michael's ear and whispered, "Say as little as possible, he knows that you have a case downstairs and will move quickly." The room was small with only six chairs where a jury usually would sit. There were no tables before the bench as Mike was used to seeing. What surprised Michael the most was that only one uniformed court officer and a court clerk were present and the officer stood in a corner behind the judge's bench. Mike assumed it was the door to judge's chambers.

The gray haired old man leaned forward and looked down at the two adversaries who stood before him with their attorneys. After shuffling some papers that nobody was able to see for a few seconds, he announced, “I am Supreme Court Judge Walter Rubins and court is officially in session. We are here to finalize a divorce petition between Betty Romano and Michael Romano. Are both parties present and understand the purpose of this appearance?” Each attorney, in turn, answered yes on behalf of their client.

Judge Rubins continued, “For the convenience of all parties, I’d like to dispense with much of the unnecessary dribble and keep things rather informal. “Does each party agree to the settlement as written and have copies of said statement in their possession giving them enough time to consult with their respective attorney prior to this hearing? Mrs. Romano?”

He waited for her to acknowledge. Betty looked at her attorney before replying. The woman nodded yes and Betty replied, “Yes Judge.”

Rubins then looked at Mike, “And you Mr. Romano?” he asked. Arthur whispered in Mike’s ear again, “Say Yes, you’ll be pleasantly surprised.”

Mike answered, Yes, Your Honor. I do.”

Rubins spoke a little firmly as he continued, “Fine, then for the record, Betty Romano is to get full ownership of the marital residence and will assume the mortgage. Mr. Romano will no longer have anything whatsoever to do with that property. Betty Romano, for sole ownership of the property is waiving her claims to any pension rights that Mr. Romano may be entitled to in the future. Next, Mr. Romano will pay fifty dollars weekly towards the support of his children until each child reaches their twenty first birthday or is emancipated. The sum is to cover both children. Mr. Romano will also continue medical coverage for both children until that time. There is no alimony or spousal support awarded in this case. Does everyone understand and agree with what has just been explained?”

Arthur was correct, Mike was pleasantly surprised. He almost got away from Betty without paying a dime. It didn’t bother him to pay child support, after all they were his children and it was his duty.

After all parties nodded, the judge slammed his gavel down and sternly said, "So ordered, Divorce granted. This court is adjourned."

Betty blurted out, "But I thought he had to pay at least fifty dollars for each of my children, not both of them combined! What if I lose my job?"

The judge got agitated and stood up. He looked like he was going to walk around the bench and confront Betty eye to eye as he bellowed, "Young lady, you had months to confer with your attorney. You agreed to everything I asked you and your attorney was present before me. If you lose your job, that's your problem and that's that. It is also my duty to inform you that Mr. Romano is paying for the privilege of seeing his children, if you stand in the way, I urge him to contact this court and I will deal with you. Now please leave this courtroom I have other duties."

Betty began an animated discussion with her lawyer. The judge bellowed again, Betty Romano, leave this courtroom or I'll hold you in contempt."

She almost ran from the room. Arthur smiled and gave a friendly nod to the judge as he ushered Michael into the corridor.

Mike was smiling and couldn't say anything as he hugged his attorney. Arthur patted him on the back as he broke free and said, "I told you Michael, that faith would take care of everything. I took the liberty of seeing what kind of case you have. Now go administer justice, and help punish a man who steals from God. I'll call you when you can pick up a copy of the signed papers and we'll have some pastry and coffee and chat." As he nudged Michael away, Arthur added, "I'm glad that I could help. Go." Arthur turned and walked down the corridor. Mike shouted, "You're a wizard," and almost danced down the stairs to the hearing. As Mike hurried into the courtroom, it was 10:13 a.m. and the bailiff was calling the next case.

By 11:00 a.m. Michael Guggalarie's case was called. The judge asked Schmidt if he was ready. Schmidt stood next to his client and said that he was. Fanino was also formally asked if he was also ready and answered that he was.

***

Once court was called to order and the formalities over with, testimony began. Mike was on the stand and was first questioned by Schmidt. Before specific questions regarding Mike's identification of his client on the night in question, Schmidt cited past interaction between Mike Romano and Michael Guggalarie. He sought to paint Romano as harassing his client. The ADA didn't object, because it was one of the things that he had gone over with Mike Romano during the preparation for the hearing. Fanino was elated that Schmidt himself showed that the arresting officer knew the perpetrator's face very well.

Schmidt asked, "Officer Romano, how dark was the church corridor you and your partner were standing in?"

Mike answered, "Dark, but not too dark. There was enough light that was reflecting from various sources to read a church bulletin if you concentrated."

Schmidt grunted and continued, "And please inform the court, Officer Romano, just what happened when the storeroom door opened."

"After we entered the church with the keys that the pastor gave us, and heard the banging noise inside the storeroom, my partner and I took position outside the storeroom doors. When we were ready, I took the key that the pastor had given to me and unlocked the door and when I opened the door, I was face to face with your client. He was holding a pry bar."

"How were you able to see the face of the person in the doorway?"

"It was easy because, I had my flashlight illuminating his face."

Schmidt then asked, "Officer, if you were concentrating on the offenders face, and needed a flashlight to see it, how could you see if he was holding anything?"

"Because he was holding it above his head as if he was getting ready to strike someone."

Schmidt continued, "Officer, can you tell the court how long, in your estimation, did you actually observe the man in the doorway?"

Mike smiled, anticipating where the question was leading. He knew he would have fun when he answered it, "For two or three seconds at the most counselor."

Schmidt attempted to rattle Romano as he raised his voice and asked, "Then how can you say for certain that the face you saw for less then two or three seconds was the face of my client?"

Mike answered with a hint of challenge in his voice, "Because as you already established, I know your client well and it was his face that I saw in the doorway, the same one that he has in this court today."

Schmidt blurted, "Your Honor, this witness is being argumentative with his answers and I wish to note that he is a hostile witness."

The judge smiled and shook his head before responding, "Mr. Schmidt, the officer is not hostile at all, perhaps, just a little too aggressive." He then turned towards Mike and said, "Officer, the court appreciates your zeal, but please temper the tone of your answers." He turned back to Schmidt, "You may continue."

Seeing that Romano was enjoying the exchange, Schmidt responded with, "No further questions Your Honor."

The judge then gave the prosecution a chance. ADA Fanino began with, "Good morning Officer Romano. Were you present inside Holy Child of God Church in Annadale, Staten Island on and about midnight Easter Sunday?"

"Mike's response was a simple, "Yes."

Fanino gave Mike the floor with, "Please tell us what happened at that time."

Mike began with, "My partner for the evening, Officer Jerry Sullivan and I had just entered the church building when we heard banging inside a locked storeroom used by the pastor to hold Sunday collection money for a bank deposit the following day as was his practice. However, on several occasions the locked cabinet was broken into and money taken."

Schmidt rose to object, the Judge waved him down. Mike continued, "That's why we were there, to prevent that from happening again. Anyway, we heard pounding noises coming from the storeroom, we opened the door and found that the defendant and another person had been attempting to steal money from the cabinet."

Schmidt objected, "Your Honor, the witness is assuming, the court has not yet ruled on the identification."

The judge said, "Denied. Please sit."

Fanino spoke to Mike, "Officer, please continue."

Mike responded with, "Sir. The man inside slammed the door in our faces and after a foot race outside, got away from us. We saw him several days later on the street and based on my personal observation, arrested him and another person who was with him at that time, for the crime of breaking into Holy Child of God Church."

Fanino now wanted to get the fingerprints into testimony. "Officer did you do anything else after the men got away?"

"Yes I did. I recovered several fingerprints from the entry window and the cabinet that contained the cash box."

Fanino held back a smile as he asked, "Did there come a time when you learned the identification of the person that those fingerprints belonged to?"

"Yes, they matched all the other church burglaries in my command, and belonged to Michael Guggalarie and another person." There was an instant sound of whispering among the people sitting in the courtroom, especially between Guggalarie's parents.

The judge slammed his gavel down and called for order.

Fanino addressed the court, "Your Honor, the prosecution has no further questions."

Looking down at Schmidt, the judge asked, "Does the defense wish to re-question this witness?"

Schmidt knew that he was lost and decided to cut his losses. He answered, “No, Your Honor.”

“This court has determined that the identification of the defendant by the arresting officer is relevant and proper. This case is next scheduled for trial. All parties will be notified as to a date. Bail is continued. Court is adjourned.”

Mike telephone his command from the police sign out room after he punched out and asked for lost time. After the recent stress in his life, things were finally going his way. He wanted the rest of the day off to wallow in his double victory.

CHAPTER SIXTEEN

After the success at the evidentiary hearing and the relatively terrific results finalizing his divorce, Mike relaxed after getting back to his apartment. His mind wandered through several topics, from his future relationship with his children, the low child support that he got away with, and picking up his copy of the finalized divorce papers that would give him a chance to ask Arthur Slotnick how he did it. He even thought about Leona. After several hours of switching between those subjects and getting nowhere, he shut them down and his next thoughts centered on unfinished police work like, what will happen to Michael Guggalarie, where does Dennis Bryan live and where is the black Bronco?

After watching television, it was fairly late when he decided to drive around Grymes Hill and look for Bryan's blue Buick. He had confirmed that the graft taking pig still had the car because he saw it parked in the Lamplight Restaurant the day he and Capelli took their meal there. Mike left his apartment after midnight and leisurely headed to Arlo Road in hopes of finding The Great Pumpkin's car. As he turned into Arlo from Howard Avenue, Mike saw Hank Capelli's shiny blue Lincoln Town Car pass him from the opposite direction and looked at his wristwatch; it was 1:05 a.m.

Mike knew that Capelli lived on the north shore of the Island, but thought it was somewhere near South Beach, not on The Hill. He ignored the gentle pounding in his head and kept going. About 1500 feet later, he saw it, Bryan's Buick, parked in a driveway at 329 Arlo Road. His heart almost skipped out of his chest, *but, can I watch this dirty cop and maybe get something on Bryan and what was Capelli doing here at this time of night. I'll have to ask Rocco. It's been too long since I spoke with him anyway. I don't think Hank even knew it was me. Too many Chevys on the road.* Being satisfied with his plan, Romano drove straight home.

Romano's alarm rang at 9:00 a.m. Friday morning. He rose quickly and telephoned Rocco Banducci, his now former sister-in-laws boyfriend. The phone was answered by a female, whose tone indicated that she was possibly suffering from the effects of a hangover, she asked, "Hello, who is this?"

Hearing her voice, Mike remembered an old private conversation with Rocco when the mobster had shared thoughts about his alcoholic wife. Mike quietly answered, "This is a friend of Rocco's, can I please speak to him?"

She yelled, "Rocco, some guy on the phone for you."

Seconds later, Rocco said, "Hello, who is this and what's the purpose of your call?"

Romano answered, "Rocco, it's me Mike; you know Kelly's used to be brother-in-law. Do you have time for me today?"

Recognizing, the voice, Rocco asked, "How about 1:00 p.m. at our usual spot? Can you make it?"

Mike smiled, Rocco was always careful, "Sure I can. See you then, Bye." Mike was excited. He had two days off to formulate what he would do with any information that Rocco felt comfortable enough to give him.

Romano pulled into the parking lot of the Privateer Diner by noon. He went straight into the rear dining room where Rocco usually sat. Not seeing his friend, Mike took a booth and asked the waitress for a double scotch and then leaned back to wait. Halfway thru his drink, Mike looked up to see Rocco approaching the booth. The man was looking as if he walked out of GQ magazine; tall, lean and casually dressed in what was obviously expensive clothing. Mike stood up and shook Rocco's hand as he slid into the booth.

Rocco smiled and said, "Mike Romano, the new dirty word," obviously referring to Betty's family. "I'm so happy to see that you're doing fine and haven't forgotten who your friends are. To what do I owe this visit to?"

Mike cautiously answered, "Look Rocco, I know that we're friends and you consider me family, some day you have to explain that one, especially now that I'm divorced, but I need some information. I finally found Bryan's house, at 329 Arlo Road on The Hill. There was a guy that I know from work, a cop, Henry Capelli that passed me in the opposite direction just before I found the house. It was way after midnight. I don't think the cop lives there. Is this Capelli guy involved with Bryan? Is it possible for you to find out?" Mike drew a breath and continued, "Or am I just too obsessed with Bryan and seeing a bad guy everywhere?"

The waitress arrived and Rocco said, "What are you drinking Mike? Order another one will you? And get some food," then he turned to the girl and ordered a roast beef sandwich on rye and ice tea. Rocco smiled at Mike and said, "Listen kid, I'm not comfortable eating alone, get something."

Mike replied, "Make that two and please bring a plate of fries with it. We can share them. Thanks."

When the waitress left, Rocco spoke, "Well Michael, this time you have made it difficult for me. Yes, I know what Bryan is into and who he's beholding to but while I trust you not to jeopardize our relationship, I must always be careful not to jeopardize myself. I'm sure you understand."

Mike tried to put his friend's fears to rest. "Listen Rocco, I understand your position. You take a chance every time you meet me. You know that I would never harm you in any way or use your name, even in conversation, let alone admitting that I know you. You know that. Then there's my career to protect and there's always the possibility that you or your people would get pissed off at me and that could put me in a bad spot or worse. I know all that, but you said that I could always come to you for help and I hate Bryan. If Capelli is hooked to him, that's his problem. I only want information that I can use against Bryan."

The 'made man' looked at his friend with furrows on his brow and replied, "Michael, I'm sure you remember Brian Wilkey, the man you shot and killed."

Excitedly, Mike answered, "Sure I do, and he used to pay off the fat pig. I have no beef with you guys as long as I don't witness something; I just want a chance to hurt that fat lump of crap. I don't want to involve anyone, you or your friends, I just need information that I may be able to use against him someday. Hell, you even once offered to make him go away for me."

The conversation stopped as the waitress returned with their order. After she was out of earshot, Rocco continued, "Well Capelli is the cousin of a Jersey under boss and took Wilkey's replacement in dealing with Bryan. The boys laughingly refer to him as Dirty Bags because he's a cop and delivers money bags to a dirty cop like Bryan. Only the inner circle knows his real name and when they talk to him though, they call him Bags. He likes the name and calls himself, 'Baggs with two g's."

Rocco laughed at the two g's comment and continued, "He's just sort of being a bad cop, all he does is pay Bryan and sometimes picks up money, that's all he does and he's not a child molester. You should be smart enough to leave him alone. He's not hurting you and as you said, you don't want to piss anyone off. If he ever creates a problem for you, talk to me first before you decide to do anything. You're a straight guy and I'd like you to stay that way. I've told you before; you're the only cop that I ever respected. Leave Capelli alone, he's only a delivery boy. Do I have your word?"

Mike had no way of knowing that Rocco was holding back and he thought that he was being told everything about Capelli and answered based on what he was told, "Sure Rocco, if he never bothers me, I'll never bother him. Listen, I know that some cops aren't the most honest; I'm a grown man and Italian. I've heard about that stuff my whole life and chose to stay away from it. Capelli can do his thing and I'll just have to wait to get fat bigot another way. It's alright and I know the chance you're taking. Thanks for your trust." In his mind, Mike thought, *another dirty cop. Someday, Hank will get what's coming to him, with or without my help, sooner if he screws with me.*

Rocco smiled and said, “Good, now let’s hear about your day in divorce court. The women are bitching about it.” Mike explained what happened and how little he’ll be paying in child support. Rocco’s only comments were, “Always take care of your kids, it’s part of being a man.” He toasted his friend and added “You kept your pension. Good thing there’s no appeal process; Betty would try to get it back.”

Half an hour later, after some small talk, the meeting ended. Rocco picked up the check, stood up, patted Mike on the shoulder and left. Not wanting to walk out with Rocco, Mike ordered another drink to waste time before leaving.

***

His swing was over and Michael Romano returned to his command on Monday for a set of four to twelve tours and went back to working alone. On the morning of his second tour, Arthur called and informed Mike that he could stop in at the office whenever it was convenient and pick up his own copy of the signed divorce decree. Arthur made it a point to add, “Call me a day before and come early so we can have some cake and coffee.” Mike set the appointment for the following day.

The morning of his third work day found Michael sitting in Slotnick’s office having apple pie and coffee while Arthur explained that he knew the judge that had handled Mike’s divorce, in fact they went to law school together and remained friends throughout the years. Arthur explained that it was Betty’s attorney’s first divorce case and subsequently, Arthur was able to, as he put it, “Razzle Dazzle her.” An hour later, after some small talk and too much coffee and cake, Mike thanked Arthur again and left.

The remaining work days in his set were quiet and not extraordinary except for the fact that he learned Michael Guggalarie had pled guilty to one count of burglary and received two years in jail and that Tommy was sent to a youth detention facility.

Two weeks had passed with business as usual, when on a Friday afternoon; Michael was patrolling on a scooter when he came upon Hank Capelli, and he was driving a black Ford Bronco. Instantly Michael went into his archangel mode. Capelli was stopped at a traffic light near Bloomingdale Road. Mike was unaware that Capelli was returning from a quick unscheduled trip to New Jersey. Unable to resist the temptation that was placed before him, slowly, as casually as he could, Mike pulled alongside of the truck and engaged Capelli in conversation. "Hank, this is some nice truck." Referring to the Lincoln, Mike asked, "Where's your boat? That's the kind of car I'm gonna get when I don't have to pay child support anymore."

Having been caught in the Bronco, in his own command, by another cop, Hank relied on an answer he had formulated back when he first started his extra-curricular activities. "My Lincoln is down and this beautiful thing belongs to my brother Pat. It's his and I'm using it for a day or two until I get mine back. Maybe I'll get my own car back today. This thing is nice but rides too hard for me." During the conversation, Mike looked closely at the inspection and registration tags and they were current. After a few short minutes, he said goodbye and drove off, but not without looking at the plate number thru the scooter's side view mirrors. It was hard to memorize the tag because the image was reversed but he repeated it in his mind several times, "*NY plate RI 435Y*". Mike was too excited to look back and see where Hank went as he left the encounter. Once away from the area, he stopped and wrote down the plate number in his memo book then, held it in front of the mirror and viewed it's reflection to be sure it matched what he saw. After several looks, Mike felt comfortable that it did.

Twenty minutes later after running the plate himself, Mike had the information on it. The printout included all the vehicle information and the fact that it was registered to a Pasquale Capelli. Mike knew Pasquale was Patrick in Italian. He could deal with the information that Rocco gave him about Hank being a bag man, but if that cop or his brother was the highway shooter, that was inexcusable and he had to get him. Mike now mistrusted his friend Rocco and his head pounded. Mike hoped that he was wrong.

Two weeks went by and Mike was unable to tie Hank into anything. Caught up in his new quest, he even stopped visiting Bryan's residence on Arlo Road. Mike strongly believed that someday, Bryan would get what he deserved.

Providence again stepped in and while working a day tour and riding a scooter, Mike had a slow day and spent some time forcing the machine in and out of the woods along Arthur Kill Road where he thought the Bronco might be hidden. Capelli was working that day and assigned to a Sector Henry that covered the far border of the command. Mike felt secure in the fact that the bag man cop was several miles away and that his portable radio would alert him if Sector Henry was on the air and what they were doing.

Mike decided to take the chance and continued to explore several dirt roads and trails. An hour later he wandered into the area where the Quonset building was. Slowly riding onto the very "dirt road" that Baggs used, Romano slowly rode into each and every smaller road or path that broke off from the larger one. The main "road" was almost hidden by winding thru a jumble of scrub oaks, vines and brambles and the like, yet it was wide enough to allow an auto to use it. Riding the small paths until he could advance no further he doubled back and then advanced to the next one.

Mike's impulse was to rush in to the end of the larger "road" as it was clear to him that a vehicle or vehicles used it from time to time. Always the disciplined investigator, he methodically worked his way deeper into the depths of the tangled woods. After riding for what seemed like an hour, Mike came upon an area that could be considered a clearing, even though it was heavily weeded. Almost in the center, was what appeared to be two deserted old Quonset hut buildings reminiscent of World War Two GI living quarters. Island history tells of fledgling businesses repairing and using them as far back as the 1950's. The Island was littered with them but Mike knew of only one such business, it was a machine shop and still going strong.

The smaller building had the remnants of a sign that, back in its day, identified the name of a business. Whatever defunct enterprise that once existed, the wood was so weathered that the lettering on it was no longer legible. The larger building was as dingy as the other, yet it appeared to be solid but had no markings.

Mike parked his scooter behind a bush at the rear of the building and slowly advanced on foot. The first thing he noticed was flattened weeds and vegetation that was the width of tire tracks as if a vehicle or vehicles had been parked there. Mike smiled as he thought of lovers using the spot for a tryst. It was a logical assumption. Still smiling, he slowly walked around the building, stopping at what was obviously the front. Mike found himself standing in front of two large doors that were designed to swing open. There were no visible hinges to examine but in the center, he saw a stained, discolored flat piece of rubber hanging. It was hardly noticeable and if he had not been examining the doors as closely as he was, he would have missed it. Reaching for a pocket knife and using the blade, Mike gingerly lifted one corner of the flap. He was surprised to see a large industrial sized brass padlock and hasp. His heart skipped a beat. Mike's thought process went into overdrive; *it can't be. Is this where the Bronco disappears to? It's too good to be true, therefore it can't be true...I can't be that lucky. Should I try to get inside? The windows are covered on the inside. I can't break in. What if it's private property and not abandoned. But what if there's contraband inside? I'm a cop and I have to report it.*

As he was mentally arguing with himself, Mike's portable crackled, "Two Three print unit. Are you available? K." *Funny how a cop can be concentrating on something and never hear the radio until it's for him.*

Mike cleared his thoughts and answered, "Print Unit, go Central."

The dispatcher answered, "Two Three Print. We have a past burglary at 439 Bennit Place, south of Hylan, MOS (member of the service) residence. Your presence is requested by the Patrol Supervisor. What's your ETA?"

Mike instantly answered, "Please be advised that this unit is about two miles away and will respond within five minutes. K"

The dispatcher answered, "Ten-four, Print Unit." The patrol sergeant had heard Mike's transmission and chimed in, "Heard you loud and clear Michael. We need you boy." It was Sergeant Hogan and after Lieutenant Cassidy; Hogan was Mike's favorite boss. After he muttered aloud, "Now I have to come back and figure this out, damn it." He fired up his scooter and took off bouncing and weaving to Arthur Kill Road where he gunned it to Huguenot and almost flipped over making a right turn, a few minutes later he bounced into the subject driveway, shut the engine and keyed his portable announcing, "Two Three Print is ten- ninety eight (on the scene). Please put this unit ten-sixty two, out of service, until notified, K." Sector Henry, with Hank Capelli at the wheel, was just pulling away as he got off the scooter, leaving only Sergeant Hogan's RMP in the driveway.

After grabbing his print kit, Mike strode up to the front door opened it, announcing, "Romano here Sarge. Where are you?"

Lenny, Hogan's driver, answered from the top of the stairs opposite the entrance, "Up here Romano. Come on up, everyone's waiting."

Sensing urgency, Mike took the steps two at a time and quickly arrived at the top. Lenny then led the way to where Hogan and the residents were. Hogan was standing next to a seated man, who had the look of disbelief on his face. Sergeant. Hogan had one hand on the guys shoulder and could be heard saying, "I'll tell you again, not to worry about IAD. You did nothing wrong. There isn't a man alive who would think that a burglar would get in a second story window without a ladder."

They were all in a large sitting room type of alcove that was separate from the rest of the obvious master suite. Next to the alcove was a large bathroom.

Mike, wasn't sure he heard correctly and asked, "Sarge what did you just say?"

"Yeah, you heard correctly, Officer Barkley, Lenny and I think the perp climbed the wall outside to get in. There's evidence that he came in thru this window and the bottom floor is alarmed. Both Mr. and Mrs. Barkley agreed that the alarm was still set when they got home. They have no kids and nobody has a key to the house and alarm except them. Anyway, that's just our theory. You're the expert, you tell us."

After the sergeant finished speaking, Mike slowly did a 360 degree turn and looked around the room. He saw debris strewn everywhere, the place was in shambles. Whoever had been in the room was looking for something real hard. He then asked, "Mr. Barkley, you're on the job?"

Barkley nodded and Mike continued, "Can you tell if anything is missing?"

"Listen, I'm real upset, so I would be more comfortable if everyone used first names. Okay? My first name is Paul as the Sarge knows. My wife is Julie. I see your name is Romano. First name?"

"Mike, you got it, Julie and Paul it is. The Sarge doesn't have a first name, he's just Sarge. That other guy is Lenny"

Officer Paul Barkley smiled at Romano's little joke and said, "Thanks, that helped."

Mike got back to business, "Ok Paul, once again, can you tell if anything is missing?"

Hesitantly, Paul answered, "No not yet. I knew not to touch anything and once Sarge arrived, he asked me the same question. The only thing I'm worried about is an extra firearm that I store in the eaves of the house. Our walk-in closet has a panel that was moved and I didn't want to touch it before you got here. Except for the bedroom phone we didn't touch anything else."

Mike shifted his feet and picked up his equipment case to indicate that he wanted to begin as he said, "Okay Paul, let's start at the closet. Lead on."

Julie fell in line behind her husband and the cops as Mike followed Paul across the large bedroom to the closet. The door was ajar and Paul backed away to allow Mike to enter first. The closet light was already lit. On the far left, Mike saw clothing pushed aside exposing the panel Paul had described. It was slid to the right as if in a track. There was no handle or finger holes, so the perp had to place his palms against the panel and push sideways. Mike turned to whoever was behind him and said, "Please forgive me for the mess I'm about to make. If somebody can get me some newspaper, it should help to prevent the powder from spreading."

Julie answered, "Be right back," and took off.

The men used the time to go over the possibilities of what to do if Paul's firearm was missing. Hogan tried to keep Paul calm by again explaining that the break-in was way out of the ordinary and he doubted there would be any departmental problems.

Paul was still worried, "Sarge, maybe I shouldn't tell you this but I'd rather it come out now, you see the firearm that might be stolen was my father's. He was a State Trooper in Warwick New York and kept his service revolver. When he died two years ago, Mom gave me his gun. I put it a small cash box and stuck it under some insulation in the eaves of the house. What I'm worried about is the fact that I never recorded it on my force record card and IAD is gonna hang me."

Julie returned with two old copies of the Staten Island Advance just as Paul finished his last sentence. Mike thanked her and began his work.

After handing some of the hanging clothing off to those behind him to clear his work area, Mike spread the newspaper out on the closet floor. Because the access panel was painted to match the walls and they were painted in some off-white color, Mike would have to use the black powder and apologized to the Barkleys before he began without removing the panel from its track.

On the panel, after Mike removed the excess powder, he was able to see a partial palm print on the upper portion of it. The lower half produced nothing but smudges. He spoke aloud to nobody in particular, "We have a palm print, if he's in the system this will help," and picked up his lifting tape. Carefully applying two lengths of tape across the print with a slight overlap to assure a tear free lift, Mike removed a large sheet of glossy white paper and placed it flat on the closet floor. He then anchored the corners of the paper with some tape to avoid any movement. Next he gently removed the print and applied it to the backing paper, loudly stating, in triumph, "Got it."

Paul excitedly asked, "Is it a good one? Can I look inside for my gun box now?"

As he moved away from the opening, Mike pulled the panel from the track and placed it against the wall then slowly folded up the newspaper. When finished, he stood up, turned to Paul and cheerily said, "Have at it and good luck to you."

Paul almost dove into the opening, crawling in and leaving only his feet outside. Seconds later he shouted, "Thank God, it's still here." He backed out carrying a standard grey cash box. As he stood up, Julie wrapped her arms around his neck and gave him a gentle kiss on the cheek.

Hogan then spoke, "After we finish here, I suggest you record that piece on your force record card back in your command." In an effort to help Paul, he continued, "It's nice that your Mom gave it to you on your swing when you visited her."

Paul, still enjoying his miracle moment, quickly responded with a short, "Yeah, it sure is."

Sergeant. Hogan commented, "Lenny, we can go. Romano can handle this without us." He then addressed Paul Barkley, "Paul, don't forget to list the handgun on your force record card."

Mike continued his quest for latent prints and after an hour, collected five that were, in his opinion, usable and worthy of transferring to cards for submission, along with elimination prints of both homeowners. After doing a walk-through of the rest of the home, it was agreed by all that the burglar never left the master bedroom. Mike then asked the couple, "Did either of you two or the Sergeant do any walking around out back, particularly under your window?"

Julie answered first, "No Michael, I didn't. My husband and the sergeant went outside while I cried. I don't know where they went."

Paul chimed in with, “I went outside with Hogan before you got here. He called for you while we were outside and couldn’t figure how the guy got up to the window. We didn’t stomp all over if that’s what you mean.”

Mike answered the comment with, “Good, let’s go outside. I’d like to look around and need both of you in case I have any questions.” He knew that Paul would say yes, so he looked right at Julie and asked, “Can you handle this Julie? I never know what I might find and what question needs answering.”

She had gathered better control by that time and said, “I sure can, especially if it can help to get the bastard that violated our home.”

Paul led the way to the rear yard and stopped walking once there. He pointed and said, “That’s our bedroom window, the open one above the picnic table.”

Mike walked over to the table. It was of sturdy wooden construction and sat perpendicular to the house, but not quite touching it. The four legs sat on old granite blocks, commonly called cobble stones when used on roadways and was tilted on a slight angle leading away from the house. After carefully looking at the legs, Mike turned and asked if the table had always been tilted. Both of the complainants answered in the negative. Mike kneeled down about four to five feet from the table and slowly ran his hand, palm down, over the lawn. After a few seconds, he found what he was looking for, stood up and spoke to the puzzled couple.

“What I was looking for was indentations in the ground. The table being tilted downward on one side tells me that our friend probably had someone help him reach the window. I’m guessing that the second person probably waited outside after boosting our man up to your window and maybe, just maybe, number two heard you guys pull up and somehow alerted the man inside. Assuming I’m right, the inside man then dropped down on the table causing it to dig into the dirt under the force of the drop. He then jumped off the table causing another depression in the earth. It’s probably only my overactive imagination, but I think that’s what happened since it appears that the burglar never left the bedroom. He must have known that you're on the job and was looking for a gun, in addition to whatever he could grab, and you'll find out later what's missing. My guess is that you guys came home and stopped his search, lucky."

Julie began to smile and sob happy tears. Paul only replied, "Guess we were lucky."

Mike turned to Paul and tried to include him in his theory and not make him feel helpless by asking, "Paul, you're a cop with a cop's mind. What do you think? Am I all wet or what?"

Paul put his arm around his wife and answered, "You know crazy or lucky or whatever as it sounds, I think you're right. Do you think we'll ever get him or them?"

Mike smiled as he answered, "I've been real lucky with my work lately. Maybe the luck will cover your burglary, there are some good prints and the latent unit is top drawer. Listen my friend, you're a cop, one of the family, the guys are gonna pull all the stops out and work their asses off."

"How do I know if they get someone?" Paul asked.

"As soon as I get notified, and they always notify me, I'll tell you guys about it." Mike saw a puzzled look on Paul's face and added, "After identification is made, the detectives are notified and they go out, find the guy and lock him up. Sometimes the only call you get is from the ADA to sign a complaint, but in this case, I'll personally call you right away when we have an ID. Try not to worry, will you? Don't forget to list the gun in your command. As to the 61, you're on the job, so I would go to the Two Three in person to add what was taken. Bring your gun and tell our desk officer, that you just got it on your swing and want to make a log entry before you transport it to your own command."

Paul nodded and Romano decided to make a joke by adding, "That way, if the guy comes back and you shoot him with that gun, its true justice and you're covered. How about that?" he asked with a chuckle.

It was almost end of tour when Mike left the Barkley residence and having work product to process and forward, he went directly back to command without revisiting the Quonset buildings. Tomorrow was another day and if Capelli was working and again busy on the far side of the command, Mike knew he could return to the Quonset and look around with relative safety against being discovered. Just before he signed out, Mike checked the following day's roll call. Capelli was working the next day and was once again assigned to Sector Henry. In his mind Romano said, *Saint Michael, I know you spoke to God himself to get me thru my divorce, now please help me again tomorrow.*

***

The next work day, Romano returned to the Quonset building and continued to look around, debating with himself whether or not to break in or report his findings to Sergeant. Flynn. Unable to find anything outside that he thought would help, he once again didn't report the hut to anyone, justifying it his mind; *I'll come back again tomorrow if I can and if I come up with nothing, I'll tell Flynn about the place anyway.*

The following day, Mike was the first one out of the station house after roll call and walked directly to the rear of the building where the scooters were kept. He had already taken the key to the one assigned to him and signed out a portable radio before roll call. He checked the gas tank and jumped on. As he rode down the driveway, Mike saw Capelli and his partner chatting with another team. He drove in the opposite direction of his intended destination and on the off chance of being followed, weaved in and out of several small streets before hitting Arthur Kill Road.

As he parked his scooter behind a bush at his destination and dismounted, Mike stumbled and found himself staring at what appeared to be a brown paper bag impaled on a low shrub, surely blown there by the wind. When he stood to walk over to it, he couldn't see it because it was so low.

He thought, *Saint Michael, I sure hope it was you who knocked me down.* Mike felt the bag was important because he heard the now familiar sound of wing beats in his head and bent to retrieve it. He kneeled low and seeing it was definitely a brown paper bag, he carefully used two hands to slide it off the twig that held it. It was discolored from exposure but not torn and without any holes except the one that imprisoned it.

With great expectation, Mike peered inside and was rewarded with another envelope. It was a water stained, business sized, empty white envelope with a return address that read, Fucini Meat Packing Co. 1434 Duncan Avenue, Jersey City 07304. Mike almost jumped for joy, *but what does it prove? That some guy took his girlfriend into the woods for a good time and somehow they lost an empty paper bag. There's no way to connect it to the Bronco. There may not even be anything inside the building. Now I have to see Sergeant. Flynn.* He made a memo entry about the bag, calling it 'recovered lost property' to protect himself in case Flynn told him to voucher it. To explain his presence in the woods, he made a false entry stating that he believed he heard a girl yell and rode in to investigate the sound. Mike then carefully flattened the bag and placed it inside his print kit, and rode back to the station house.

Romano went upstairs to the now empty roll call office and quietly used the telephone to call the One Two Oh Squad. Joe Johnson answered, "Good evening. One Two Oh Persons Squad, Detective Johnson speaking. How may I help you?"

Mike almost jumped into the phone, "Joe, Mike Romano here. Is the boss in? I need to speak to him right away."

"Mike, to what do we owe this call? I heard that your latent prints got the church burglar. Good work. By the tone of your voice, I'm guessing you want Flynn about the Bronco case?"

"Well not quite. I want to see him and run some stuff by him before taking any action. Will he be back soon or be in tomorrow? I'm doing four bys, so I can come in the morning. Will he be there?"

Johnson was hooked and asked, "Mike is it real hot, something that can't wait? I'll reach out to him at home. Maybe he'll come in or meet you somewhere. Do you want to explain it to me and I'll make the call?"

Mike thought for a few seconds before answering, *maybe there's nothing to this paper bag and it was dropped by two lovers. Flynn listened to me about the tire castings when this case started. I owe it to him to tell him about chasing the Bronco into Clay Pit Pond Park,* and then answered, "No Joe, it's only a theory and I'd like to sit with the boss alone." To avoid any insult to Johnson, Mike joked, "I want to tell Flynn because he never laughs at my wild ideas. He must take pity on me for being Italian."

Johnson chuckled and responded, "Ok Michael, he's scheduled to do a day tour tomorrow. I'll leave a note on his desk that you're coming in to see him. You can call first if you want, but when he finds the note, I'm sure he'll stay put." In the background, another phone rang. "Two of the guys are out and I'm here alone. The other line is ringing, see you soon."

Before he left the room, Mike went to a supply cabinet and took a large envelope that's used for Department Mail and placed the bag and envelope into it. Next stop was his locker, where he placed his prize on the top shelf before returning to the streets of Tottenville and completing his tour.

CHAPTER SEVENTEEN

Romano was up early the day after his discovery. By 6:45 a.m. he was on his way to the Two Oh squad office and Sergeant. Flynn, arriving at 7:15 a.m. Holding up his shield for identification, he strode past the desk officer and up to the squad office. Sergeant Flynn was in his office and spotted Mike as he walked in, "Mike Romano, I got your message. Come in young man and let's talk."

Mike walked in carrying the Department envelope in his right hand. He changed hands and reached out to greet the sergeant with a handshake. Flynn's eyes followed the envelope. Before Mike could speak, Flynn asked, "What do you have for me? Joe Johnson called last night and reported that you were all excited and would only speak to me. Ok, you have my undivided attention. Close the door, sit down and talk to me."

"Well Sarge, I haven't been totally forthcoming with what has been going on since the murder. You see, one night I chased a black Bronco along Arthur Kill and into Clay Pit Pond Park and lost him. I've been back several times to look for a hiding place and even prowl around on my own time. Until a couple of weeks ago there was nothing new, then a weird thing happened. While on patrol, on a scooter, I came across a black Bronco that looked like the one that I saw at the homicide and it was driven by a cop in my command!! He said that his personal car was in the shop and the truck was his brothers. I ran the plate, and it was registered to a guy whose first name is Pasquale with the same last name as the cop. The registration, NY plate number RI 435Y is good and current."

Flynn interrupted with, "You know of course that if this is anything that I can work with, we have to get IAD involved? Who is this cop?"

Romano cringed, remembering what he promised Rocco before answering, “Sarge, I have trouble saying it. The cop’s name is Henry Capelli. It’s probably just a look alike truck. No cop would do that, right?”

Andy Flynn agreed, “You’re probably right. Ok, please continue.”

Mike began again. “After seeing the cop in the Bronco, I decided to really get into searching for a hiding place for our truck by riding my scooter deep into the woods and brush around Arthur Kill. Anyway, I came across two old Quonset hut buildings in a clearing. One is small and another is very big, like a large garage or warehouse. It looks like one of those old business locations. The big building has windows that are covered from the inside so I couldn’t see in. And here’s the biggie, there’s a big brass padlock hidden under something to hide it from view and the doors look like they fold back like barn doors. I think something is hidden inside.”

Flynn stated, “Mike, I love your enthusiasm but that doesn’t mean the truck is inside. People do all sorts of strange things. It does not necessarily mean they’re criminals. And as to the working cop, he just might be driving a similar truck. I’m just cautioning you to keep you grounded but I know there’s more, so go on.”

“Yeah, on the third time I went back there, I tripped and found this stuck to the bottom of a bush.” As he spoke, Mike held up his prize, and continued, “I couldn’t see it when I was standing up because it was so low.” With that statement, Mike opened the envelope and slid it towards Flynn. “Inside is an envelope from a meat packing company in Jersey City. You said bodies were found in Jersey and that ballistics tied them to the same gun used in our case. There has to be some connection.”

The sergeant gently picked up the envelope and removed the bag. He gently turned the bag over and dropped the smaller item on his desk, picking it up by the corner. “Michael did you handle this envelope much?”

"No Sarge, I did just what you did, the bag I did handle, but the envelope, I held by the corners and edges like an old phonograph record. In the back of my mind, I thought that maybe someday it would wind up in the lab downtown." Excitedly he asked, "Sarge, is it time for me to be excited?"

"Yes Michael, it's time. First I have to make some calls. Please try to relax."

Mike was wound up like a clock spring at the sergeant's announcement. He excused himself with, "Be right back, I need some coffee."

When Romano returned with two coffees, there were three detectives in the main room, Johnson, Pallack and of course Jim James, Mike's friendly enemy, Jim Jim. Mike waved a general hello and went directly into Flynn's office. Setting the coffee down on Flynn's desk he told the sergeant, "Sarge, sorry but I forgot how you take your coffee so I have cream and sugar in the bag along with two pieces of pound cake. What's next?"

"Please close the door, will you?"

Mike complied and nervously sat down and asked, "What's going on Sarge?"

"Michael, first let me say that I'm sure glad that you're on our side. You have one active mind and work ethic. Second, I spoke to the Boro Commander and asked him to temporally re-assign you to our office until this case is resolved. He agreed and notified your Captain Anderson. Needless to say Anderson was surprised and complained about losing you but he had no choice."

Romano grinned like a little kid and said, "Thank you."

Flynn held up his hand and continued, "All your command will know is that you have been transferred to the Two Oh. Anderson will follow orders and not say anything else, mainly because he doesn't know why the request was made."

Mike was now leaning forward and sitting on the edge of his chair as Flynn continued, "As of start of tour today, you're on the clock under my command. Next, before I notify the rest of my squad about what's going on, you and I will go next door to the Family Court Building and meet with Internal Affairs and TARU to map out a plan of action, I telephoned them and they're on their way. Now, please leave the bag and envelope with me and go prepare a voucher and an evidence bag for this material and bring them directly to me, we'll put the evidence inside seal it together and I'll sign off on it in here. I'll also add the case number to the voucher when you bring it back. Do it now."

Mike went down to the desk officer and asked, "Sarge, I need a voucher and an evidence envelope for some material Sergeant Flynn wants me to voucher."

The desk officer looked down and asked, "Are you Romano from the Two Three, we just got a telephone message saying that you have been assigned to The Squad until further notice? I just finished the blotter entry."

Mike was impressed how fast everything was moving. He tried not to show his excitement as he answered, "Yes Sarge, Mike Romano, and the voucher please. Sergeant Flynn wants it right away."

He was handed a large numbered plastic evidence envelope and a numbered voucher. Mike thanked the desk officer and took off back upstairs. Finding an empty desk he sat down and prepared the voucher. All eyes were on him as he pecked away at the typewriter.

When he finished as much of it as he could without Flynn's input, Mike returned to his office and handed it to him. "Sarge, sorry I couldn't complete it but if I can use your typewriter and you give me what's missing, I'll finish it."

Flynn responded, "Finish your coffee my boy. I'm not crippled."

After the voucher was prepared, Flynn engaged Romano in small talk while he waited for a phone call. Mike was uneasy and felt like he was being too secretive by not telling the other guys what was going on, but he was a good soldier and waited for Flynn's next order. The phone on Flynn's desk rang by 8:45 a.m., he picked it up and said, "Thank you, we'll be right over." Stood up and said, "Duty calls Michael, let's go."

Flynn locked the vouchered material in his desk and they left the office without a word to anyone with Flynn leading the way, first he grabbed a portable radio form the rack outside his office door. As they walked, Flynn explained, “Mike, we are meeting a Captain Saber from IAD’s Manhattan headquarters, the job wants an out of Boro man to avoid face recognition. TARU will be present also. You know who they are?”

Mike answered with a question, “Aren’t they the guys that put in bugs and cameras for the job?”

Flynn answered by explaining the acronym, Technical Assistance Research Unit, yes that’s exactly what they do. Staten Island Boro Commander will be there also and I don’t know who else. It looks like you opened up something as tangled up as my grandmother’s yarn.

Once inside the building, a court officer directed them to a conference room. As they entered, all Mike saw was suits and the uniform of the Staten Island Commander, Assistant Chief Robert Stranire. Mike stopped and saluted even though he himself was not in uniform. The Chief smiled and said, “That’s not necessary Romano, not in here.”

The IAD man started the meeting. “Gentleman, I am Deputy Inspector Rothwell from Internal Affairs. We are here because Officer Romano witnessed a homicide some time ago on the West Shore Expressway. While he didn’t see the actual shooting, he saw the shooter’s truck speed away. It was a black Ford Bronco. Officer Romano has since chased and lost what he believes was that truck in the area of Clay Pit Pond Park here on the Island. Since that time, he looked for that vehicle or its possible hiding place. He has also recently spoken to a member of his own command who was driving a similar truck. Romano thought it looked enough like the vehicle in question that he wrote the plate down and ran it. It’s registered to a Pasquale Capelli. There is a cop in the command with the same last name, Henry Capelli. That cop told Romano that the truck was his brother’s and that he was driving it while his car was in the shop. Tell me if I miss anything Romano.”

"No sir, you're exactly right," was all Mike said.

Rothwell continued, "Thank you officer. Now, here's where it gets interesting, both our cop and the owner share the same address and birthdates. We pulled Capelli's complete jacket and he recorded a twin brother, Pasquale, on his job application when he joined The Force. Capelli has been a model officer since he joined the force and we have nothing on his brother except a driver's license and vehicle registration. Now there's more, Romano found a discarded paper bag near two old Quonset huts in the woods near Clay Pit Pond Park and that bag contained an envelope with the name of a meat packing company in New Jersey. The Major Case Unit informs us that the same meat packer might be tied to the Sanducci crime family out of Bayonne. Romano reports that one building is large enough to accept a truck and he believes that someone uses the building for storage. The building has windows along the sides that are blocked from the inside. Are there any questions up to now?"

One of the men around the table spoke, "Sergeant Gilbert Sawn, TARU, I'm guessing that you want some kind of surveillance set up near that building, correct sir?"

That's correct. Officer Romano will show you where the building is and you guys do your thing. Be advised that we have to go there when Capelli is working. We can't take the chance that he is a bad guy and might go there while we're there too. This has to be a totally clandestine operation. For the sake of the job, I hope Capelli isn't involved. My office will try to get a photo of the brother, if he even exists. We raised a Social Security number for Pasquale and haven't run everything yet. Everyone will report directly to Sergeant Flynn, copying my office and Chief Stranire daily and sooner if something is breaking. Chief, sorry to hog the meeting, if there's anything you want to add?"

Stranire cleared his throat gently for effect before speaking, "Gentlemen, needless to say this is a sensitive operation that will reflect directly on the Job once it's completed, especially if there are any embarrassing arrests. As the highest ranking officer here, I personally would like to keep it out of the media so let me say, if it leaks and I find out the source of the leak, that person will have disobeyed a direct order and I will add the crime of Obstructing Governmental Administration to any other charges that I can think of. Do I make myself clear?"

Everyone except Rothwell mumbled, "Yes sir!"

Stranire turned to Rothwell and announced, "If Inspector Rothwell has nothing further to add, this meeting is over. Get to work gentlemen." There was silence followed by the sound of the Chief's chair being moved as he stood up to leave. Everyone followed his lead.

Once outside, Flynn motioned to Rothwell, "Inspector, can you have someone fax my office a copy of every roll call in the Two Three, for every tour assignment until this is over?"

"Sure can Flynn. Roll calls will begin coming to you in the morning. Meanwhile, have someone call the Two Three and find out what tour Capelli is working today. I want Romano to take Sergeant Sawn and his people out to the subject area for a look around and determine what equipment they might need and where they're going to put it."

The expected response was forthcoming from Sergeant. Flynn, "It will get done as soon as I return to my office. Let's go Michael.

Sawn said, "Sarge, we'll be near the outer bridge in an hour with an unmarked truck on tactical channel 3. Call us when you're ready and we'll meet."

Mike followed Sergeant. Flynn back to the office. Flynn spoke as they walked, "Michael, I saw the guilty look in your eyes when the men watched us go. Rest assured that they will be brought up to speed as soon as TARU is set up and everything about the Capelli brothers is known. It should be sometime tomorrow."

Mike smiled and said, "Thank you. You're right of course, the guys treated me well the last time I was in the office on the day of the shooting, and I feel like they looked at me with disdain. After all I'm only a uniform cop."

"Don't sell yourself short Romano, from what I see; you're as good as any man in the unit. Maybe even better then some."

Within half an hour, Flynn and Mike were in Flynn's personal car and heading for the outer bridge. Flynn had insisted on using his own vehicle, a Volvo, because it didn't look like a department car. As they approached, Flynn radioed TARU that they were in a maroon Volvo. As he released the key, a weathered, crappy looking step van pulled off a side road and stopped. It was Sawn and his team.

Wanting to show off his toys, Sawn invited Flynn and Romano into the rear of the truck. The truck's exterior hid an electronic wonderland. Video monitors, cameras and a rotating periscope hidden inside a dome on the roof were what Romano noticed first. Sawn explained that they could also record what was around them. Detective Warren, sitting at one of the monitors, played back a video of Flynn's approaching Volvo, he was impressed and asked, "Sawn, can you set up something like this anywhere?"

"Almost anywhere, and if the subject site has no electricity available, we'll need lots of cover to hide our batteries and converters. Let's go look. Lead the way but park on the paved road. We'll walk in."

Mike directed his new sergeant to the unpaved road where he found the Quonset huts. Flynn parked and locked his car about one hundred feet away in a small clear area alongside the paved roadway. The van stopped just behind him. Sawn handed Flynn a white rag and asked him to tie it to his car as the universal signal that the car was in trouble and told Flynn that would explain why it was on the side of the road. He then went back and brought his men out, each carrying a 35 mm camera. After securing the truck, Sawn turned to Mike, pointed to his van and said, "It always looks like a breakdown, Ok Romano. Let's do it. Lead on."

Everyone followed Mike into the woods, Flynn walked beside him as much as possible, with the TARU team following close behind. Once in awhile, Mike heard the click of a camera. As the men walked into the clearing, Flynn turned to Mike and commented, “Holy crap Mike, these buildings are well hidden from the main road and that big hut can certainly hold a truck. Show us the lock please. Mike showed his boss the padlock under the rubber shield. The cameras clicked like mad. Mike then showed Flynn around the building and the bush where he found the paper bag. Sawn and his team walked around in the brush and woods trying to determine where they would place their equipment. The men made sketches and took many photos. Half an hour later, Sawn announced, “Ok Sergeant Flynn, we have enough and know what’s necessary for tomorrow. We’ll be operational two hours after we arrive. You guys can hang back and make sure we’re not disturbed.”

Once back on the paved roadway, Flynn threw the white rag into his back seat and both men returned to the Two Oh. Sergeant. Sawn, his men and their toys went back to wherever they had their office. Mike never did learn where it was.

Back in the Squad office Flynn commented, “Too bad we couldn’t see any good tire tracks for castings. That would have been beautiful.”

The rest of the tour was spent with Joe Johnson and the case officer, Bill Stattler, going over previous evidence regarding the Bronco homicide. The men in the squad were curious, to say the least, when their boss announced that Romano was temporally assigned to the squad. Flynn promised his team that they would be told everything before noon the following day. They seemed satisfied, all except Jim Jim and he mumbled the rest of the tour.

Mike was ordered to report in for a day tour the following morning, not wanting to feel out of place he arrived at 7:30 a.m. dressed in a sport jacket, white shirt and tie. As the men filtered in, each one welcomed him and in essence, asked, “What’s going on Romano, why are you here?”

Mike only answered; “Sergeant Flynn will explain it today. Sorry.” Jim Jim totally ignored Mike and he was happy with that.

Flynn walked in a few minutes before 8:00 a.m., and went directly to his office. He quickly opened a Department Mail envelope and reviewed its contents. He then walked into the main room looked around and asked, “Is everyone here?” Answering his own question he said, “Good, Jim please close the office door.” Det. Jim James winced because he thought the lowly Romano should have been given the order to close the door, but he complied.

Flynn continued, “First, let me say, everything I’m about to tell you remains in this room and only in this room. Got it?” He waited for effect, then continued, “Gentlemen, you all remember Mike Romano, I’m sure. He has found, buried in the woods of Tottenville, a building where we now believe the black Ford Bronco used in the Paul Capria homicide may be stashed. As of today, TARU has the subject area under electronic surveillance. Mike here has seen a truck that looks very much like the subject vehicle within the confines of the Two Three. The plate comes back to the brother of a working member of our Department. This whole case could get messy. Any detective doing work on this case after today will not discuss it outside this room and be exact and I mean exact with his written reports. Any DD-5’s will be completed, in full, at once and before you go home for the day. The 5’s will immediately be placed on my desk for my review. There are no exceptions. Oh yes, Officer Romano is here at my request with the approval of the Boro Commander and will be treated as a regular member of this squad, are there any questions.”

Det. Bill Stattler, the actual case officer asked, “Sarge do we know who the shooter might be? And can you tell us the name of the cop?”

“That is on a need to know basis,” was Flynn’s answer. “Ok guys; go back to whatever you were working on. Romano is under my direct supervision for this case. If he asks for anything, it’s because I told him to ask, so don’t refuse him.”

Mike Romano was embarrassed by the attention given to him, yet he was proud that Flynn thought that much of him.

“Flynn turned to him and ordered, “Romano, in my office, now.”

Inside his office, Flynn explained, “Mike, Inspector Rothwell sent me some info. It seems that even though Hank

Capelli's brother Pasquale has a SS Number, he has no credit history or work history. There's nothing on him except a driver's license and vehicle registration."

Mike blurted out, "Did you get a picture of both brothers."

"Yes Michael, it gets better. Here are several photos of Henry Capelli, including the picture on first Department ID card. Here are several photos of Pasquale from DMV records. Tell me what do you see?"

"Mike haltingly responded, "Either these guys are identical twins, really identical, including the same haircut in all the pictures or all the photos are of the same guy, only the shirts are different. It's weird."

Flynn stated, "Mike, now you know why this has to be kept between as little of us as possible until an arrest is eminent. Only the cops in that meeting yesterday can know everything, including you and me naturally. I'm trusting you Michael, don't let me down."

Mike could not tell Flynn why he would never say a word or what information he was holding back. He had given his word to Rocco. He was friends with a mobster and if the job ever found out it would mean the end of his career, never mind what Rocco and "the boys" might do to him. Nothing was worth that.

Mike answered, "Sarge, believe me, there's no way anything we talk about goes beyond you and me and the guys from yesterday. I love my job and myself too much to screw up."

Flynn answered, "I don't know what makes you so adamant about what you just said, but I'm happy to hear it. Now let's ride out and see what TARU is doing and make sure Capelli doesn't interrupt them."

After calling Deputy Inspector Rothwell to thank him for the package, Flynn had Romano sign out two portables and left for the confines of the Two Three, again using his own private car.

Flynn and Romano stopped at the target site for a quick look to see if TARU had been there. They weren't and it was now lunchtime and Flynn asked, "Michael, we have lots of time to waste before the four to twelve tour arrives. What do you say that we go for lunch? How does the Lamplight Restaurant sound, its real class joint and close by. It's my treat."

Mike was taken aback by the request; he had been there with Capelli and saw Bryan there. "Sarge, that's very nice but there are plenty of places we can eat and for a lot less."

"Not to worry Mike, it's part of the investigation and I can put in for reimbursement. I didn't tell you but, Major Case tells us that it's a mob joint and if you're correct about Capelli, maybe we can get lucky."

Mike was flabbergasted and thought, *this guy Flynn is the best boss ever. When this is over, I have to find a way to work for him,* clearing his head, Mike responded, "Sure lets go. I got the tip."

Before heading to the restaurant, Flynn drove to the Two Three. Stopping some distance away, he ordered Romano to remain in the car while he went in to check the roll call. Lieutenant Cassidy was on the desk as he walked in, "Sergeant Flynn, is that you?" he asked. "It's been some time since our last meeting. How are things? What can we do for you? Help you catch a bad guy?"

"No, just stopped by to look for one of your men. Can I have a look at the roll call sheets for all of today's tours? If my guy is working, I might have him meet me somewhere. I'll put it over the air."

As Flynn finished speaking, Cassidy handed him the desk copies of all three assignment sheets for the day. "Here you are my friend. Can I help?"

Now that he had the sheets in his hand, Flynn decided to be less than truthful and answered, "Maybe, is Romano, your print man working?"

Cassidy responded with some surprise in his voice, "Didn't you know, he's been transferred to the Two Oh a couple of days ago? Weirdest thing I ever saw, by telephone message ordered by the Boro Commander. I wonder who he pissed off or who he owes something to."

Andy Flynn continued to play the game, "No, I had no idea but that makes it easy, I can see him later, right in the command."

He spoke as he continued looking at the sheets, pretending that he was, "Looking for other guys he might know."

Once he confirmed that Capelli was due in at 4:00 p.m., he returned the sheets with, "Nobody I know, thanks. I might as well go back to the office now. It's been nice seeing you."

Back at the car Flynn announced, "He's working later. Let's eat," and drove to the Lamplight.

When the waitress came for their orders, Flynn saw that Mike looked uneasy and thought it was because of the prices. He tapped Michael's menu and laughingly spoke like a salesman ripping off his boss, "Don't be concerned, but don't go overboard either, the company is paying for this, it's all for business."

Knowing that Flynn didn't want to announce their presence, he continued the charade, "OK, if the boss is paying I'll order something that I like," he looked Flynn in the eye and quietly added, "But not too expensive."

During the meal, both men exchanged quips about the job and the guys in the squad room. Flynn had asked Mike how he got the print assignment at the Two Three because they never had one on the Island. Mike gave a long discourse about how he managed to convince the CO and even recounted the night of the church burglary. On the off chance that they could be overheard, nothing was mentioned about the case they were working on. All in all they both enjoyed their time together and somehow, the two men managed to linger at their table for two hours.

With some time to waste before the men usually began to arrive at the station for their tour, Flynn decided to find a vantage point on Main Street. The street was one way, and with the train station on the dead end to their backs, they took a position just before the intersection of Arthur Kill that allowed them a good view of the station house area as the cops arrived for their tour. Flynn was obviously prepared and ready for the job because once they parked; he reached into his rear seat and came up with a pair of 20x50 binoculars and settled in. Later as the men began arriving, Mike shouted, "There's Capelli's blue Lincoln," as it passed the corner and turned into Main Street.

"I see it too Mike, we know the plate and the kind of car his wife drives too. Remember, we did an entire 'round robin' (everything that could be found) on him. Now we wait ten minutes, then go and see if TARU is setting up."

They arrived at the access road to the subject location and parked the Volvo directly across it. Flynn remembered the white distress rag in his back seat and tied it to the car's antenna. He then locked his car and walked in to the hut area with Mike.

When they got to the site, Sawn was there with two men and an old jeep. "Hey Sarge, so far it looks good. We parked our truck about 1000 yards down the road in case we need anything we couldn't bring in with the jeep. This should take less then two hours to set up. The biggest problem is to run electric from our batteries. We're gonna put them down well back from this area near the shoreline and do our best to hide the power cables. It looks like whoever uses this place never goes back there anyway. We'll be using two systems, electronic transmission for when we have our truck within 1000 yards of the place, and video recording that we have to come back and check every two days."

Flynn asked, "When you come to check your film or tape or whatever, do you change it too?"

Sawn answered with a chuckle, Yes and we also check our batteries and change them if necessary." He chuckled before adding, "Don't worry we'll come in from the shoreline. We don't mind walking through the woods. If the bad guy is here, we'll see him before he sees us. Don't forget, we have electronic video transmission too."

Flynn was satisfied and said; "Please notify me when it's operational. Let's go Mike they have it covered."

Sawn gave a parting remark, "Hey, Sergeant Flynn, I personally want to thank you for this one. It's different and is sure to be lots of fun. Thanks."

***

The first few days of the surveillance at the Quonset hut produced nothing. It was hard to say who was more upset, Romano or Flynn. Romano's jumpiness first centered on wanting some kind of action to prove that his crazy theory was correct. The second reason was so Flynn could let the entire squad in on all the particulars of the case. They began to look at Mike as an interloper, even his friend Joe Johnson. It bothered Mike.

Flynn was upset because he stuck his head out to get Romano and he too wanted to let his men in on everything that was happening but could not. As a result he felt that his squad members were beginning to distrust him a little.

Relief came by mid-afternoon on Friday from TARU. Sawn alerted Flynn by radio over the secure band that Capelli's blue Lincoln just drove past their operations van and was heading south towards the subject site and that he was not scheduled to work that day. Flynn was alone in his office when the call came in. After he checked his copy of the roll call, he yelled, "Way to go, we got action."

The men in the squad room all looked up when they heard him and the men buzzed with muffled conversations at the uncharacteristic behavior of their boss. Their wonder at his behavior increased when they saw him joyfully dial his telephone and engage in two animated conversations as he notified both Rothwell and Stranire. When he put the phone down, Flynn then opened his door and shouted for Romano.

Detective James gleefully answered, "He's not here Boss, maybe he's in the head or whatever."

Flynn, always aware of the friction between the two men, countered with, "I'm giving you a direct order, "Get off your ass and go find him. I need everybody. Now!"

James, unaccustomed to Flynn speaking in that tone, almost fell over as he jumped out of his chair and shot out of the office.

Less than a minute later, Romano walked into the main office and said, "Jim Jim told me that you wanted me forthwith Sarge. What's up?"

Flynn answered with, "Where's James? I want everyone here now." Without waiting for an answer he continued, "Please somebody go find him and get him here quickly. The whole squad's probably going out." Det. James walked in just as Johnson began moving towards the door. Flynn ordered, "James, close the door and sit." When he was satisfied that everyone had stopped talking he began with, "I'm sure you have all been curious why Mike Romano has been here this past week. Well now you're going to know why."

He paused for effect before continuing. "As you know, Mike was here on the night Bill caught the Capria case. That was because Mike witnessed what was probably the shooter's truck flee the scene. You all know that there is good forensic evidence in the form of tire castings taken from the scene and we even know what kind of tires they belong to. We have established that the weapon that was used in that shooting has been tied to several homicides, both here and New Jersey. What we do not have is the truck and the weapon."

To lighten the mood, Stattler asked, "Sarge, is Mike the shooter, and we can close the case?" There was laughter all around, even Romano chuckled.

Flynn chuckled and continued, "Nice try Billy, but no, he didn't do it. What he did do though was refuse to give up finding the truck. As a result he may have found the location of where the truck has been stashed and maybe even the shooter. TARU has had the location rigged and under surveillance for the last week. Now here's the tricky part." He took a breath and explained, "You all know the reason for all the secrecy has been because the perp may be the brother of a cop or Heaven helps us, the cop himself. Because of Romano's effort, we have been working with the dreaded IAD and the wizards of TARU."

Det. James commented, loud enough for all to hear, "Guess you're not such a dummy after all Romano."

Mike answered, "Coming from you Jim Jim, I think that's a heavy compliment, thanks."

When the Ohhhs and Ahhhs quieted down, Flynn continued, I just received notification from TARU that one of the subjects, the cop, is headed for the subject location in his private car. If we get confirmation that the subject is entering the location, then we all better be ready to go to Tottenville. Grab fresh radios and get ready to roll out of here. Get cracking and just in case, bring your vests. Romano's riding with me."

He turned to Mike and said, "I'm calling the desk, go get the keys to whatever unmarked auto is available and do not say anything except thank you." Flynn picked up the closest phone and spoke to the desk officer. All Mike heard was, "I'm sending a man down……….." before he was out of earshot. The squad room was a buzz of activity as Mike walked out the door.

By the time he turned to go back upstairs, the men were scurrying down with Flynn behind them. As he hit the last step he said, "You drive kid and don't worry I got two," indicating the bullet resistant vest he held under his arm.

As the men began driving away from the station house, Flynn ordered over the radio, "This is Flynn, no sirens, just move it and meet at the service area of the Outer Bridge."

As Romano drove, Flynn was in contact with Sawn on the secure channel. "Sawn here Flynn, it's confirmed that a black Bronco is leaving the subject building. Do you want us to try to stop it?"

Flynn spoke rapidly, "Negative, We're on our way. Where ever he's going I don't want a chase. When we get there, we'll make plans to arrest the driver when he returns. If we need more men, we'll have some time to get them. Listen do you have a vehicle that can follow him and keep us informed?" Negative, we weren't prepared for this, Sorry."

To mask his anger and ease the tension of the situation, Flynn answered, "I'm greatly disappointed. Please meet us at the service building of the Outer Bridge in fifteen minutes or less, we're almost halfway there."

"Sawn on the way," was the only response. Flynn called his men, "Alright guys, switch to Tac channel three for the rest of this operation and acknowledge on that channel." He wasn't happy to put such an order over the division radio for all to hear, but things were happening fast and Capelli was in the subject truck so he took the chance.

Fifteen minutes later everyone was in the parking lot of the bridge service area. Flynn asked all units to stay put and went into the service building to use their telephone. After informing Rothwell of the situation, he phoned the Boro Commander's Office in the One Two Two. Stranire was not in but the lieutenant who answered asked for the phone number that Flynn was using and assured him the Chief would call back within minutes.

Andy Flynn thought it was the longest two minutes he spent on the job when the phone finally rang. It was the Chief, "Stranire here, what's going on Sergeant?"

As calmly as he could, Flynn updated the Chief, "It's confirmed Chief, Capelli drove his Lincoln to the hut and pulled out in a black Ford Bronco. His car is parked and locked behind the subject building. We didn't have the manpower for a forced stop, so I authorized Sergeant Sawn to let him leave the area. I'm now here with my entire squad including Romano and three men from TARU. If we position ourselves properly, we should be able to arrest him without incident when he returns, whenever that is. Can we have your approval sir?"

The answer was twofold, "Yes you have my approval, but that's only if the subject returns before I arrive with an Emergency Service Unit. I want to be there if possible and just in case the idiot returns with friends or fights, I want ESU there also. What channel are you people using?"

"Tac 3 Sir, was Flynn's only response.

Stranire responded with, "Good, I'll see you soon. Try to wait for me.

Flynn went back outside to inform the teams of the latest developments. After updating them that the Boro Commander, Chief Stranire, was coming with an E Unit, he formulated a plan. Not knowing when Capelli would return to his lair, Flynn decided that the E Truck with a driver would be hidden close by, possibly in Clay Pit Pond Park Pond out of sight from the paved roadway. He then asked Sawn if he and his men would sit back in the woods behind the building and be able to rush to the front of it quickly. Sawn said that he was not pleased to be sitting in the woods with bugs and snakes and other things, but would do it. Flynn then told his men that they would be paired up with an E-Man for firepower. Two of Flynn's men would sit on the road as if broken down and notify the others when the truck returned and assuming that he did not race in, it would take a full minute for the subject to reach the building. The idea was to catch him as he got out of his vehicle to unlock the building door, and overwhelm the subject with an obvious display of firepower in an effort to take him without a firefight.

Flynn turned to Sawn and said, "Sergeant, please go back to a position where you can monitor our target location, while we wait for the Chief and the Emergency unit. If the subject shows up, call us as he turns off the main road so we have time to get there. I think we can get back in less than two minutes. It'll be close but I think it should be ok. By the time he switches vehicles, we should be able to take him." He ordered Stattler and Pallack to go immediately and take the phony breakdown position on the roadway.

Sawn moved towards his van and motioned for his men as he said, "Sure thing. We're on it. See you later."

Stranire, five E-Men and the Island's Battle Wagon arrived half an hour later. After a briefing by Sergeant. Flynn the plan was approved with minor changes. The E-Men would be secreted in a large perimeter around the front of the building and they, with their shields would rush the subject. All parties agreed it to be the best move and that having the E-Truck nearby was necessary should they need nighttime equipment, though it would be hard to hide during daylight, it would be easier to do if the subject returned after dark.

Mike stayed with Flynn and the Chief in one of the hidden side roads leading to the huts as did Johnson and James.

***

It was dusk, just before the sun dropped out of sight, when a TARU voice whispered, “The Bronco is on the way in. Everybody get set. He has his headlights on and we think he’s alone.”

As the Bronco turned off Arthur Kill, Pallack keyed his radio and whispered, “He’s turning in, be alert.”

The glow of headlights bouncing off the vegetation allowed the units to actually monitor when the Bronco passed their respective locations. As the truck passed each team, they started their engines and slid, without lights, some 100 feet, behind the Bronco. Capelli pulled within twenty feet of the building doors and hit his high beams before exiting his truck. As he lifted the rubber flap and concentrated on the lock, he was struck from behind and held against the building by the battle shield of the largest cop in the world. As Capelli grunted and tried to move his trapped hands, two more cops handcuffed him before he could even speak and one of them removed his Colt Diamondback from his shoulder holster.

Over Tac3 came the call, “Mission accomplished we got him. He’s secure.”

Sergeant Flynn and his passengers pulled up just as the radios crackled. The woods were alive with cops converging into the area from every direction. Still some distance away, the loud air horn of the War Wagon sounded in celebration.

As he was pulled to his feet, Capelli spotted Mike Romano and had the nerve to ask, “Mike, you know me, what the hell is going on.” Mike remained silent and turned away. One of the E-men pushed him back down on the ground and into a sitting position, then leaned him against one of their cars and stood guard.

As things settled down and the Bronco was searched, it was established that Henry Capelli was indeed a bag man for the mob. The truck contained Capelli’s satchel and it contained several envelopes and paper sacks stuffed with money. One even had an envelope with a return address, Fucini Meat Packing Co. 1434 Duncan Avenue, Jersey City 07304. Mike Romano silently said, *thank you Saint Michael*, when he saw the envelope. The Chief himself read Capelli his Miranda warnings. The keys to the Lincoln were taken from Hank, but no one even opened the door of the vehicle because Flynn reminded them that it would be best to obtain a search warrant first.

Because TARU recorded the Bronco drive out of the hut with Capelli at the wheel, and then when he returned and was attempting to open the lock, the hut was fair game. It was searched thoroughly by Emergency Service and Romano under the supervision of Sergeant Flynn with Stranire as an observer. Nothing incriminating was found except some oil stains where the truck was always parked.

Flynn ordered, “Bill, it’s your case so please transport this piece of garbage to the Two Three and take Jones and Pallack with you for safety. Johnson and Romano safeguard that Lincoln. Nobody goes near it until I get back. I’m gonna try for a warrant. This bum carried his brothers ID and his own too, he even had his shield and Department ID Card. No telling what’s in the car.” He turned to the Emergency unit and thanked them for their assistance, adding, “If it’s alright with the Chief, you boys can go home. Thanks again for a job well done.”

Stranire just smiled and said, “Yes of course.”

Once in the Two Three, the Chief commandeered the Captain’s Office as a temporary command post. He notified Rothwell and said that he was responding. Flynn used a telephone in an empty office to contact the District Attorney’s Office and requested a telephone approved search warrant. The ADA on the other end balked, saying that he never did it before. Flynn assured him that it could be done and if he explained everything to a supervisor, after hearing the circumstances, a warrant would be written and a judge would be located to sign it. Flynn then proceeded to explain the “twenty five words or less version” of the last two days. Forty Five minutes later Flynn recorded the warrant number in the station house blotter. He was assured that the signed original would be in the Three Two by the time he returned from searching scene. After thanking the man on the other end, Flynn phoned for a Department Tow for both the Lincoln and the Bronco to be brought to the Two Three. He gave the dispatcher the approximate location of the cars and told him to have the drivers call on the radio for an escort to the site when they were close.

When he returned to the scene, Flynn gave Mike Romano the honor of unlocking the Lincoln and searching it with Johnson as the recorder. The first place Mike looked was under the front seat and that's where he found a .38 Smith and Wesson snub nosed revolver. Excited at his find, he held it by the wooden grips and announced to Sergeant Flynn and Johnson, "Bet this is his service revolver. Didn't the ballistics report state that the rounds from the shooting were from a Colt?" Realizing what he just said, Mike exclaimed, "Holy shit, he's the shooter, a dirty cop, caught with his dirty bags of money."

Two hours, later the vehicles and all parties were present at the Tottenville station house, including IAD. Crime scene was sending a forensic team to cast copies of the tire treads on the Bronco and to match them against those of the Capria homicide and Inspector Rothwell, along with a Department Attorney from the Legal Division and a PBA delegate, attempted to interview Henry Capelli. He was not cooperative. When he was given a monitored phone call he spoke to his wife and was overheard saying, "Please call my cousin and tell him where I am and that I need a good lawyer. I'll be here for several more hours. Thanks."

Everything was vouchered and recorded in the desk blotter and signed off by Chief Stranire himself. Flynn gave Johnson and Romano the job to "Get these guns to the lab in the Police Academy and have them test fired forthwith. Tell them to compare rounds from both of them to the Capria case. The case number is on the vouchers and don't come back without a ballistics report. Any problems when you get there, call here and the Chief himself will talk to them. That should put a flame under their asses. Don't get hurt, but hurry back." To emphasize the need for speed, Flynn added, "Lights and sirens all the way."

On the way to the Academy, Joe and Mike chatted about the case and the bond that had developed between them. Joe asked

Mike if there was anything that prompted him to suspect a cop was involved.

Mike explained that it was only the chance encounter when he saw Hank Capelli driving the Bronco. Mike further claimed that he had no idea what made him check the plate number that started the whole operation of the last few days. Joe Johnson had apparently accepted the explanation because it was not mentioned again.

Upstairs at the lab's sign-in desk, Joe once again took the lead and asked, no, almost demanded to see the ranking officer on duty before the two guns were even put down on the receiving desk. The cop on duty was young and very nervous, subsequently he phoned a Lieutenant Wiley from somewhere within the bowels of the complex. When Wiley arrived at the front desk, he was quick with, "You Detectives are always in a hurry. If the guy is already dead, what difference does it make if you wait three days for your report?"

Joe was quick, "Our Squad Commander sent us here to get this tested and compared to a fairly recent homicide, both he and Chief Stranire want to know if the cop we arrested is a murderer and so does Inspector Rothwell at IAD."

Wiley almost snapped to attention and asked, "Is there anything else you guys need?"

Mike remembered that there was one potential little bit of evidence that might be needed and said, "Oh yeah, please have someone dust the weapons for prints too and will you please include any findings with your other reports. It's been a long day for us and we're going out to get some food. Will an hour and a half be good for your people?"

Wiley answered, "Please sign these weapons in so we can start right away. I think an hour forty five is better. See you then."

Johnson and Romano giggled like two school girls in the elevator on the way down to find a restaurant. Down the block, on the corner of Second Avenue, was what looked like a decent place, they went in and sat down.

The two men renewed their friendship that began the first afternoon they met and what had transpired since. Joe asked, "Mike, you know that you really solved this case for the squad and because there's a bad cop involved, IAD and a Chief, jumped into the mix. Sometimes one of those big shots get a flash of conscience and wants to reward the man who broke the case, like the Son of Sam cop who wrote the summons in Brooklyn, that finally broke the case wide open. If they ask you, what do you want?"

"That's an easy one Joe, to stay in the Squad with you and the guys. I think Sergeant Flynn is one great boss. Do you think I can pull it off?"

Joe looked at his friend with sad eyes, "I've been here on the Island for six years and as far as I know both the Persons and the Property squad only take Detective rank members. It's not like the big city where a guy can be designated as "White Shield Detective" and work in an investigative capacity and earn his own shield. Even there you would still be a cop and not a detective by rank." Seeing the look of disappointment on Mike's face, Joe tried to cheerfully add, "But, by all means if given the chance, ask away. I know that Flynn likes you better than chocolate ice cream, maybe you can even replace Jim Jim."

Soulfully Mike answered, "Yeah, thanks for being honest with me Joe. I'll have to find another way."

It had been almost two hours when the men returned to the Police Lab. As they walked up to the desk, the kid behind it said, "It's done Detectives. Hold on a minute," and called the shaky lieutenant. Wiley showed up almost immediately and excitedly said, "The Colt is a match to the Capria homicide and we're still checking for others. Both weapons have the same prints on them. We ran the serial numbers through Force Records and the Smith comes back to Henry Capelli, a cop assigned to the One Two Three on Staten Island. As he handed a report folder to the two cops, he continued, "Is that a help? Are the results what you and the bosses expected?"

Johnson answered for both of them, "Yeah Loo, it does and it is. We'll let everyone know how helpful you and your people were. Can we use your phone to call this in?"

Obviously wanting to gain favor with the big wheels involved with the case, Wiley answered, "Please this way, you can use my office."

Johnson broke his bubble by answering, "Thanks, but we thought it was polite to ask before we used this phone right here." He picked it up and dialed the Two Oh.

When Flynn heard the news, he was delighted and turned to Stranire, "Those two are an incredible team Chief, is there any way that I can keep Romano?"

Stranire was silent for a moment and then answered, "I'm afraid not Sarge, here on the island we don't have White Shield cops assigned to our Detective Bureau. If the young man gets a gold shield someday, you can request him and if I'm still in command, I'll get him for you, you have my word. In the meantime, I agree that he should be rewarded. The quickest way to a shield is by spending time in Narcotics."

The Chief put his best counseling grandfather face on and continued, "Ask him if he's willing to go to Manhattan Narcotics, they need good people and we'll give him a push. Meanwhile you can keep him until a trial is over or the cop takes a plea, and then you have to give him up. I'll personally put a good write-up in his jacket."

Flynn answered, "Thanks, for the suggestion. I'll talk with him and at least I have him for a few more days and I don't see a trial here."

***

During the days that followed the arrest of Henry Capelli it was easy for Mike. Besides the pep talk from Sergeant Flynn about going into Narcotics to get on the fast track to a Gold Shield, he had more time in the squad room as a well-respected, although temporary, member of the team. Even Jim James stopped badgering him. Mike was notified by Lieutenant Stonner himself, that there was identification on the Barkley break-in. The burglary victim's nephew had a sheet, was subsequently arrested and gave up his accomplice who boosted him up to his uncle's window. As a result of recent events, Mike never notified the Cassidys about their son's prints being identified on Mrs. Cassidy's jewelry box. Mike felt sorry for them when he found out that Lieutenant Stonner had also notified the Property Squad, and they arrested the kid.

On his time off during those last few days, Romano met with his friend Rocco Banducci at the diner in Queens and explained what had transpired that resulted in the arrest of Hank Capelli. During his account of the story, Mike nervously exerted great effort explaining to Rocco that he never broke the trusting bond they always shared and that he never used any information Rocco had given to him at any time.

Rocco assured Michael, that he and lots of other people knew who he was; an honest person whose word is his bond and happens to be a cop. Rocco told Mike, "My friends know that you had nothing to do about Baggs being caught except that you did your job." Rocco added that, "Capelli got too big for his britches and would have been caught eventually anyway."

During their conversation, Rocco claimed no knowledge of Capelli's other service to his "Family." Rocco also reaffirmed his offer that Mike could call him anytime for help and that he was still considered a friend. To drive the point home, Rocco again stated that he, Michael Romano, is the only cop he, Rocco, ever respected, also adding that some of his people, also respected Mike because he never changes who he is and "doesn't bullshit anyone."

Further investigation results from several Department sources regarding Henry Capelli produced several interesting bits of information. It seems that he was a first cousin of Rocco Lucelli, the right hand man to a reputed Bayonne mobster, John "Johnny Eyes" Sanducci, the son of Victor Sanducci, a Bayonne Crime family.

As the loose ends were being tied regarding the case against Capelli, it was determined that Henry Capelli was actually born at home with a midwife and christened Enrico Capelli, the Italian equivalent of Henry. He had a twin brother Pasquale and when the births were registered and Social Security numbers obtained, the Capelli household, for some unknown reason, listed Enrico as Henry, and his brother, Pasquale, retained the original Italian name. Pasquale later died from unknown causes at the age of two.

The Lucelli side of the family saw the possibility that sometime in the future, a false and untraceable identity might prove beneficial for them and the death of little Pasquale was never reported.

Years later, when Henry spoke about joining the Police Department, his cousin Rocco Lucelli, convinced Henry, who was always a greedy kid that wanted more, what fun he could have working both sides of the fence and Capelli was hooked. It was about that time that Henry obtained a Pasquale Capelli driver's license using the genuine birth certificate in Pasquale's name, supplied by the New York Board of Health and began buying and registering cars in his alternate identity.

The Colt Diamondback did actually belong to Henry Capelli. Federal tracking of the weapon revealed that Capelli bought it using his police ID from a gun shop in Rome, New York and never put it on his force record card, obviously deciding that it would be his moonlighting weapon. On the remote possibility that he was challenged by police while driving the Bronco, he could show Pasquale's registration and driver's license. Henry was never challenged about wearing a gun and if that ever happened, he planned to flash his shield and never show his ID card.

During intense questioning, Henry Capelli never gave up anything about the other members of his crime family. Just about the only thing he said during a pretrial hearing was, "Guilty your Honor," and pled to the shooting of Paul Capria and the others. On the day he was sentenced, Mike Romano, Bill Stattler and Sergeant Flynn made sure that they were present in the court room.

The judge handed Capelli a life sentence without parole and he never said a word. As he was escorted out, Henry turned and looked hard at Mike, who never backed down from a challenge. Romano excused himself from the others and approached Henry, asking the court officers if he could speak to the prisoner for a second. Naturally, they said yes, and backed away giving Mike some privacy. Michael leaned close to Henry and whispered, "You're nothing but a dirty cop, that's you Dirty Baggs, with double g's."

Capelli was stunned and loudly asked, "You're a cop, how could you know my……. ??????

Henry never got to finish his question because the guards pushed him away from Mike.

Mike only smiled and quickly answered, "Because I can Henry, because I can."

The following day, Michael Romano completed his last and final interview before being assigned to a Narcotics unit in Manhattan.

www.ingramcontent.com/pod-product-compliance
Lightning Source LLC
Chambersburg PA
CBHW031148270326
41931CB00006B/193

9780989722728